International Screen Industries

Series Editors:
Michael Curtin, University of California, Santa Barbara, and Paul McDonald, University of Nottingham

The International Screen Industries series offers original and probing analysis of media industries around the world, examining their working practices and the social contexts in which they operate. Each volume provides a concise guide to the key players and trends that are shaping today's film, television and digital media.

Published titles:
The American Television Industry *Michael Curtin and Jane Shattuc*
Arab Television Industries *Marwan M. Kraidy and Joe F. Khalil*
East Asian Screen Industries *Darrell Davis and Emilie Yueh-yu Yeh*
European Film Industries *Anne Jäckel*
European Television Industries *Petros Iosifidis, Jeanette Steemers and Mark Wheeler*
Global Television Marketplace *Timothy Havens*
Hollywood in the New Millennium *Tino Balio*
Video and DVD Industries *Paul McDonald*

Forthcoming:
The Global Videogames Industry *Randy Nichols*
The Indian Film Industry *Nitin Govil and Ranjani Mazumdar*
Latin American Film Industries *Tamara Falicov*

Latin American Television Industries

John Sinclair and Joseph D. Straubhaar

A BFI book published by Palgrave Macmillan

First published in 2013 by
PALGRAVE MACMILLAN

on behalf of the

BRITISH FILM INSTITUTE
21 Stephen Street, London W1T 1LN
www.bfi.org.uk

There's more to discover about film and television through the BFI.
Our world-renowned archive, cinemas, festivals, films, publications and learning resources are here to inspire you.

Palgrave Macmillan in the UK is an imprint of Macmillan Publishers Limited, registered in England, company number 785998, of Houndmills, Basingstoke, Hampshire RG21 6XS. Palgrave Macmillan in the US is a division of St Martin's Press LLC, 175 Fifth Avenue, New York, NY 10010. Palgrave Macmillan is the global academic imprint of the above companies and has companies and representatives throughout the world. Palgrave® and Macmillan® are registered trademarks in the United States, the United Kingdom, Europe and other countries.

Cover images: (front) TV Xuxa (2005–), TV Globo; Aló Presidente (1999–2012), Gobierno Bolivariano de Venezuela

Set by Cambrian Typesetters, Camberley, Surrey
Printed in China

This book is printed on paper suitable for recycling and made from fully managed and sustained forest sources. Logging, pulping and manufacturing processes are expected to conform to the environmental regulations of the country of origin.

British Library Cataloguing-in-Publication Data
A catalogue record for this book is available from the British Library
A catalog record for this book is available from the Library of Congress

ISBN 978-1-84457-388-2 (pb)
ISBN 978-1-84457-389-9 (hb)

Contents

Acknowledgments

Although the authors have known each other and published widely on Latin American television over many years, they have not collaborated before this book. They first met in Brazil in 1992, and were already aware of each other's early publications. Indeed, recalling the explorer Stanley's historic encounter with the missionary Livingstone, Sinclair introduced himself to Straubhaar with 'Dr Globo, I presume? I am Dr Televisa' – Sinclair had completed his PhD on the media conglomerate Televisa in Mexico, and Straubhaar on its counterpart Globo in Brazil. They have been tracking each other's work ever since.

Neither explorers nor missionaries, the authors have nevertheless dedicated much of their academic lives to making the television industries of the Iberoamerican world deservedly better known and comprehensible to English speakers, and demonstrating their unique significance within a global context.

In doing so, however, the authors are 'cultural intermediaries', assimilating the corpus of Iberoamerican communication theory and research, and interpreting it for the Anglosphere. Whatever elevation of perspective they gain in this is because they are standing on the shoulders of at least two generations of Iberoamerican communication researchers, many of whom have personally shared their work and offered their collegiality. The authors wish to gratefully thank them for their generosity and friendship.

Thanks are also due to Michael Curtin and Paul McDonald, both for their considerable contribution to the field of global media studies, and for their initiative in bringing forth the series of which this book forms a part.

Finally, Sinclair would like to acknowledge that most of the twentieth-century historical material in this book draws on his *Latin American Television: A Global View* published by Oxford University Press in 1999, while Straubhaar has drawn on material on Brazilian television history from his 1981 dissertation and from his chapter 'Brazil', in L. Gross, ed. *International World of Electronic Media*. New York: McGraw-Hill, 1994.

Introduction: Latin American Television Industries

The television industries of the Spanish- and Portuguese-speaking Iberoamerican world (that is, Latin America plus Portugal and Spain), with its more than 500 million people in dozens of countries spanning both sides of the Atlantic, have their own particular dynamism and influence, but have been largely overlooked within the academic field of television studies in the English-speaking world. In seeking to redress this neglect, this book demonstrates how Mexico and Brazil dominate the Spanish- and Portuguese-speaking television markets of the world in much the same way as the United States does the English-speaking markets. Although much of this story is about Latin America as an important cultural space and market, by no means are these territories confined to Latin America alone: in particular, the book traces Mexico's influence in the Spanish-speaking US, and Brazil's impact in Portugal and Portuguese-speaking Africa. As well, it examines the emergence of second-tier producers in the region, from nations such as Venezuela, and the globalisation of Latin American television, including its export successes in remote markets such as Russia and China.

Latin America occupies a unique place in the history of the internationalisation of television as an institution. For one thing, it has greater linguistic and cultural cohesion than any other world region. Because of their long distant colonial origins, nearly all Latin American countries are Spanish-speaking, with the very significant exception of the region's largest nation, Brazil, which speaks Portuguese. This linguistic and cultural cohesion has greatly facilitated the development of a regional market for television production and distribution. In the regional ecology, to follow Rafael Roncagliolo's classification from the 1990s, Mexico and Brazil, as the largest and oldest television nations, come first as 'net exporters', followed by Venezuela and Argentina as 'new exporters'. Much further behind are Colombia, Chile, and Peru, while the rest of the nations in the region are 'net importers' (1995, p. 337). This categorisation is by no means fixed, however: we shall see that Colombia has since joined the second tier, while Chile has achieved a measure of self-sufficiency, as have other smaller nations.

Secondly, most Latin American countries adopted the US's commercial model of broadcasting at an early stage, as distinct from the public service model instituted in most European countries and their former colonies in Asia and Africa. It will be shown how the commercial broadcasting model has proven congenial to the development of a distinct pattern of family commercial media empires in Latin America, who have managed their political relationships with successive governments to avoid the regulatory constraints that have limited commercialisation elsewhere.

This has meant that most Latin American nations have had a long familiarity with commercial television, and did not experience the convulsions which most countries in the other world regions went through in the course of the neoliberal wave of privatisation and commercialisation that occurred in the 1980s. Furthermore, Latin America has had more time in which to develop and institutionalise its own television genres, notably the *telenovela*. This complex fusion of commercial imperatives and popular culture has not only become the characteristic mainstay of programming throughout the entire region, but also has emerged as a model for importation and emulation by less-developed markets in unexpected corners of the world.

Indeed, just as the US has long dominated television programming in the English-speaking world, the major production and distribution companies that have a solid base in the largest domestic markets in Latin America have been able to exert influence well outside those markets. In the first instance, this has meant other countries in their own cultural-linguistic world region – Brazilian companies have had a significant role in the programming schedules as well as the form of liberalisation taken by television in Portugal, for example, while Mexican and Venezuelan interests have actively cultivated a nation-wide market for Spanish-speaking television in the US.

Among the specific cultural processes at work in the spread of this influence, we can identify two that link television managers, producers, and audiences. Firstly, the idea of cultural proximity is that, all things considered, audiences will prefer to watch culture on television that is as close to their own as possible. Local or national references in humour, national gossip, knowledge of national stars, historical references, even ethnicity, scenery, and music are all likely to be more interesting and entertaining in something produced locally or nationally. If a show can be produced nationally, then audiences will probably prefer that; if not, they might well prefer a show from a similar country (Straubhaar, 1991). If networks can afford to produce a programme, rather than importing it, research on scripted, game and reality programmes tends to show that local or national production is more attractive to audiences and hence more profitable. Secondly, the converse of cultural proximity is what is called the cultural discount. That argues that if the culture reflected in a television show or film is too different in values, ideas, images, etc. from what an audience is used to, they will tend to reject it or discount it, compared to other options that might seem more familiar or comfortable to them (Hoskins, McFayden, & Finn, 1997).

A cultural discount may apply even within the same national culture. For example, there are elite audiences in Latin America with the cultural capital to find an US television comedy like *Friends* interesting on satellite television, even though it would seldom appear on broadcast channels (at least not in prime time), because it is frankly too culturally distant from the knowledge and interests of the mass audiences based in middle, working and working poor classes in Latin America (Straubhaar, 2003).

Although cultural proximity and discount explain much of what has happened in television flows between the countries of Latin America, clearly the wider success of Latin American programming outside its cultural-linguistic space shows other factors at play. Just as US content penetrates even countries where English is not the national language, so do Latin American *telenovelas* find markets in linguistically and culturally alien territories, building on similarities of themes and genres rather than the commonalities found in their own region. This global reach of Latin American television deserves to be better known and understood. Audiences do find themselves drawn to stories that are from at least somewhat distant cultures, but which have other kinds of proximity or attraction to them. A significant example of this phenomenon was the success of *telenovelas* in countries such as Russia and China that had little or no cultural proximity with Latin America (Vasallo de Lopes, 2004). One fairly common form of proximity or attraction that cuts across cultures is genre proximity (La Pastina & Straubhaar, 2005; Obregon, 1995). In this idea, audiences in diverse countries and cultures can be drawn to stories that are told in familiar ways, as with the melodramatic storytelling of *telenovelas*, which can draw on audience familiarity with the conventions of the genre, even if the specifics of the story relate to a culture that is not familiar to them.

Latin America has played an active role in the technological as well as the commercial reach of television as a medium. In their quest to exert international influence, Latin American producers and distributors have fostered innovation, not only in entrepreneurial production activities off-shore, but also in the development of the technical infrastructure of distribution, their role in the expansion of domestic and international satellite services in the 1980s being a notable example. In more recent decades, they have partnered with US-based direct-to-home subscription television companies in bringing digital global television to the homes of the region's elites, and are currently positioning themselves to ensure that internet television proceeds under their control. A Brazilian interactive digital television standard, building on a Japanese basic digital standard, has now been accepted by most of the rest of Latin America and may prove popular in

Latin American *telenovelas* have found an audience outside their own cultural-linguistic region, such as this one, *Sortilego*, dubbed in Russian

other emerging markets. That Brazilian initiative intends to create technology that can be manufactured and sold in Latin America, a new instance of the long term import substitution strategy used by many Latin American countries in both industry and television contexts. It also intends to create a new form of interactivity via terrestrial television that may reach many poor Latin Americans long before the internet reaches them or is affordable.

In short, this book explains how Latin America has developed its own way of television, with programming and genres which are popular at local, national and regional levels, and which extend into global markets, but it also will be shown how this is a mediascape in which a small number of companies have been able to seize a strategic advantage by capitalising upon linguistic and cultural similarities, and so build themselves hegemonic positions over the development and institutionalisation of the medium, first in their home nations and then across the region, and into global markets.

LINGUISTIC AND CULTURAL REGIONS AS MARKETS

Like the 'Anglosphere', the diverse and vast territories of the world which speak English, the immense and varied Spanish-speaking world reaches across oceans and continents. This is even more true of the Portuguese-speaking world, the history of which in its major aspects is quite similar to that of the Spanish, except that less of it is geographically contiguous, unlike Spanish-speaking Latin America. Also like the English-speaking world, such wide linguistic spread is the legacy of colonial expansion in centuries past. And just as the US has long overtaken Britain as the largest nation in the English-speaking world in terms of both population and the output of cultural goods and services, including television programmes and their means of distribution, so it is in the Spanish-speaking world, where Mexico has eclipsed Spain, and in the Portuguese-speaking world, where Brazil has outstripped Portugal.

A fundamental argument of this book is that language and culture must be taken into account as primary 'market forces' which enable the major producers and distributors of television programmes and services to gain access to markets outside their nations of origin, where those markets have the same language, and/or share cultural similarities. This is a necessary, though not sufficient, insight if we want to understand how the globalisation of television production and distribution has developed and assumed the ever more intensive and complex forms that it has today. For that purpose, rather than think of strictly geographic regions or 'worlds' that share a common language, we will use three concepts: 'geolinguistic region', 'geocultural region', and 'cultural-linguistic space' or market. A 'geolinguistic region' is defined not so much by its geographical contours, but more in a virtual sense, by commonalities of language across global space. We shall see that in the case of television programmes and services, such regions have been the initial basis for the globalisation of the media.

However, we also need to think in terms of 'geocultural regions', in recognition that cultural similarities in themselves, even in the absence of a language in common, also create a basis for programmes made in one country being able to find an audience in another. Thus, the Spanish-speaking nations of Latin America can trade programmes with Portuguese-speaking Brazil, to the extent that they are able to appreciate non-linguistic similarities such as each other's historical context, religious background, manners and mores. While analytically distinct, geocultural and geolinguistic regions tend most often to overlap in practice, as transnational cultural-linguistic spaces which may have no geographical connection. To take a familiar English-language example, although far separated geographically, Australia and Canada form a ready market for US programming because of their historical formation and contemporary cultural similarities, not just their language. In the same way, the Spanish-speaking and Portuguese-speaking world regions are for the most part both geolinguistic and geocultural. Spanish is the 'mother tongue' of some twenty countries in Latin America which, together with Spain, form a geolinguistic whole. Spanish thus has a greater degree of world-regional geocultural reach than Portuguese, in that all the speakers of Portuguese in Latin America are in the one country, Brazil. Yet Brazil is not only the largest country in Latin America, but also in the Portuguese-speaking, or Lusophone world, with nearly twenty times as many the number of speakers as in Portugal (United Nations, 2011). There are several other former Portuguese colonies in the world, but they are in Africa and Asia, where there is no common Latin heritage, Portuguese is not the mother tongue of the majority, and the television markets are small and restricted (Rønning, 1997). Nevertheless, it will be seen that the Lusophone world forms a cultural-linguistic whole so far as the international trade in television programmes is concerned.

Although we still live in a world in which the nation-state is the effective unit of cultural as well as economic and political governance, geolinguistic and geocultural regions should not be thought of as combinations of nation-states. Rather, these regions are virtual, in the sense that they are interconnected by convergent media such as television via satellite or over the internet, and this transnational interconnectedness often now becomes more important for personal and collective identity than actual location within, or citizenship of, a nation-state. As markets, geolinguistic and geocultural regions do not necessarily correspond to the borders of nation-states in this era of the global movement of peoples – migration, displacement, exile, diaspora. On the contrary, linguistic and/or cultural minorities isolated within a large nation-state can be given unity by their connectedness to global television and other media. The most outstanding example in the present context is the 'Hispanic' population of the US. This 'minority' is now over 50 million people, or 16 per cent of the total population, and served by two national television broadcast networks and a host of other television and media services in Spanish (US Census Bureau, 2011). However, this market has certain unique characteristics which have led some commentators to argue that its apparent linguistic and cultural unity is a commercial facade which conceals a wealth of actual diversity (Dávila, 2001; Sinclair, 2006). Indeed, the US Hispanic audience constitutes a special case in cultural proximity. A large fraction of that audience comprises first generation immigrants, predominantly from Mexico. So for them, the first level of attraction in terms of cultural proximity is likely to be for television and other cultural products from back 'home'. For second generation immigrants, who have grown up in the US, the cultural proximity of Mexican television has to compete with cultural proximity based on cultural and linguistic capital, and a new layer of identity acquired in the US. This is even more true for third generation immigrants. In this book we will note how this conflict between cultural-linguistic heritage and national belonging is shaping these audiences' demand for programming.

The economic basis of geolinguistic/geocultural markets was discovered long ago by the US in relation to the English-speaking world: having a competitive position in a large domestic market allows television producers to recoup all or most of their costs in the home market, so that programme exports can earn relatively cost-free profits. Historically, US television programmes have found their initial and maximum penetration in markets which speak English, and are culturally similar, although, as is well known, US programmes can and do successfully enter non-English-speaking territories. In the case of the key Latin American television networks, in addition to the economies of scale and scope similar to those enjoyed by the large producers in the US, they have had the additional advantage of being allowed to integrate production and distribution since their inception. The Latin American networks that have risen to dominance in their domestic markets have always produced their own programming. Successful programmes thus have their costs recovered even before being exported, enabling the networks to maximise their profits.

However, the exploitation of any such comparative advantage within a geolinguistic or geocultural region does not offer a complete explanation for the success of Televisa, Globo, and others like Venevisión in building their export markets, because of the enthusiastic take-up of the *telenovela* in linguistically and culturally remote territories such as Eastern Europe, Russia, China, and elsewhere far beyond the boundaries of the Latin world, in the 1980s and 1990s. Again, as in the case of US television exports, the Latin American companies were able to cross over into alien markets. There are various explanations for this phenomenon, canvassed in Chapter Five. Suffice it to mention here an economic one, namely that these remote export markets have been fairly poor with relatively little production capacity of their own, and Latin American productions, though particularly *telenovelas*, have offered a very affordable option with which to fill expanding schedules.

CURRENT TRENDS

The golden age of television in Latin America has been the era of free-to-air, analogue broadcast television for large, popular audiences, usually on a national scale. This 'mass media' model is now under challenge from new means of distribution, just as elsewhere in the world. Pay-TV was until recently the preserve of the upper and upper middle classes, with the costs of connection and subscription being the major barriers to its growth. However, significant changes in social structure and technologies of distribution, and the regulation of them, are seeing the emergence of a greater middle class, and more affordable access to subscription television. Digital cable and direct-to-home (DTH) satellite services have brought down the costs of pay-TV, relative to traditional cable distribution, and governments have been liberalising the regulation of these new means of delivery, particularly as television converges with telecommunications and the internet. Deregulation has allowed the entry of global and regional conglomerates in the latter fields, which has in general challenged the national incumbents, and made for more competitive and diverse markets for television.

The Latin American Multichannel Advertising Council estimates that, in Latin America as a whole, with its 576 million persons in 163 million TV homes, pay-TV penetration has tripled between 2008 and 2011 (LAMAC, 2012). However, as this book will show, these changes are taking place in quite different ways in the various countries of the region. For example, while Argentina is expected to reach 77 per cent pay-TV penetration by 2016, Brazil will be at 33 per cent

('Digital TV homes to triple in Latin America', 2011). The same industry study calculates that by that same year, there will still be 22 per cent of analogue terrestrial TV households in the region, and although this represents a dramatic drop from the 62 per cent of such households in 2010, the figure should serve as a reminder that, notwithstanding the rapid growth in the new means of distribution, it is too soon to declare the end of the age of television as Latin America has known it.

I

The Development of Broadcasting in Latin America as a Region

The many options that we have today for receiving television make it easy to forget that, historically, television developed as a form of broadcasting, and that the foundations of broadcasting were laid down by radio. That is where we must begin, and to understand the development of radio and then television in Latin America, the same three sets of factors need to be taken into account. Firstly, there is the influence of the United States, both via its government and the organised private interests with a stake in broadcasting development, namely the networks, the equipment manufacturers, and the transnational advertisers and their agencies. This chapter will put this influence in perspective, relative to the other factors. For instance, the fact that Latin American countries chose a commercial rather than a public service model for broadcasting was as much due to pressure from Latin American entrepreneurs as from the US interests. The second set of factors has to do with Latin American governments, and the highly variable relationships which they have assumed with regard to television over time, ranging from zealous hands-on control, notably during dictatorships in countries such as Brazil, Argentina, and Colombia, to apparent laissez-faire disregard, as in the recent era of neoliberalism. The role of the Latin American broadcasting entrepreneurs constitutes the third set of factors: particularly individuals such as Goar Mestre, a Cuban radio entrepreneur who was exiled by Castro's revolution, and was instrumental in introducing television to parts of continental Latin America and organising other entrepreneurs on a regional scale. These included Emilio Azcárraga in Mexico and Roberto Marinho in Brazil, founding fathers of the family empires that have developed into private national media corporations dominating their domestic markets, namely Grupo Televisa in Mexico and Organizações Globo in Brazil. These entrepreneurs not only shaped the organisations, but the powerful emerging genres their organisations created, like the *telenovela*.

As explained in the Introduction, what makes Latin America 'Latin' are the languages of Spanish, the official language in nearly every country of the region, and Portuguese, as spoken in the region's largest nation, Brazil. Along with these languages, Latin American nations have inherited considerable cultural similarities, although they long ago became independent from Spain and Portugal, the countries which created them as colonies in the heyday of imperial expansion after 1492. While these similarities certainly should not be overemphasised, the twenty or so nations which constitute Latin America exhibit much more in common when compared to what neighbouring countries share in most other world regions – think of the difference between France and Germany in Europe, for example. These relative similarities of language and culture have greatly facilitated the growth of a region-wide exchange of television programmes and services, and in that sense, the region is as much geolinguistic and geocultural as it is geographic.

What makes Latin America 'American' is not just the region's continental linkage with North America, but the geopolitical hegemony historically wielded over it by the United States. The Monroe Doctrine of 1823 warned European powers away from what the US saw as its 'natural' sphere of influence over the whole hemisphere, and the US has over many years made several military interventions in the region to protect US interests. While trade and investment from the US has been significant for Latin American economic development, such development has been criticised for its 'dependency' and the political and cultural influence which goes with it. However, this chapter will show that although the nations of Latin America almost universally adopted the commercial model of broadcasting as it had been institutionalised in the US, the development of television in the region was not a mere unproblematic extension of US influence, but had its own 'Latin' dynamic.

Finally, what makes Latin America 'Latin American' is its hybrid blend of cultures and peoples. Indigenous, Afro-descendent, and European peoples and cultures have blended to produce a varied, but regionally recognisable basis for television programming that has its own geocultural logic based in cultural proximity, the preference by audiences for national and regional programming that either reflects one's own culture directly or comes from culturally similar neighbours (Straubhaar, 1991). It has been argued that one of the historical strengths of US media in achieving its global supremacy has been the ability to blend its cultural diversity into narratives of universal appeal, not just in its domestic market, but beyond (Olsen, 1999), and we shall see that this also applies to Latin America. As argued in the Introduction, the historical and cultural similarities between the nations of Latin America, evolved as they are from Spanish and Portuguese colonies, enable us to think of it as a geocultural region.

The 1970s saw a great international debate about 'cultural imperialism', focused on the penetration and apparent influence, in what was then called the 'Third World', of news services, films, television entertainment, and advertising from the West, mainly the US. This debate has cast a long shadow over how

Latin American television has been thought about ever since. Critical academics and activists in the English-speaking countries were influential in fostering a whole discourse of cultural imperialism, about how the US communication corporations were seen to act in concert with the US government and US consumer goods corporations in the supposed imposition of 'consumerism' as a way of life upon defenceless local cultures (Tomlinson, 1991). It was in Latin America itself, where the manifestations of such cultural imperialism were directly observable, that most of the serious theorisation and research was carried out. In Venezuela, for example, theorists such as Ludovico Silva (1971) denounced ideological domination, while researchers like Antonio Pasquali analysed its manifestations on television (1967). One of the works from this period, although about comics rather than television, became widely available in English, and now stands as a classic of the mode of ideological content analysis being carried out at the time: *How to Read Donald Duck* (Dorfman & Mattelart, 1975).

As formulated by Herbert Schiller, Alan Wells and others, the role of local 'élites' in facilitating the incursion of Western communication infrastructure, business models and media contents into the subject nations was acknowledged, but the weight of analysis rested upon the omnipotence of US interests as drivers of the process. In its attempts to explain the development of television in Latin America in particular, the emphasis in the critical literature was placed primarily on the influence of the US, meaning variously its federal government and the several private sectoral interests with a stake in television development, namely the networks, the equipment manufacturers, and the transnational advertisers and their agencies (Schiller, 1969; Wells, 1972). This discourse of cultural imperialism became the dominant critical paradigm in the West until the 1990s. At this stage, it came under challenge as the 'complex connectivity' of cultural globalisation became regarded as a more accurate conception of the multiple and interactive flows of international cultural influence (Tomlinson, 1999). Nevertheless, the assumption of an all-powerful US has never really gone away. Even some quite recent accounts of globalisation tend to equate the process as synonymous with 'Americanisation', though not necessarily in a critical perspective (Fraser, 2005)

Thus, while US influence on Latin American broadcasting development is not in dispute, it becomes important to understand it in context: that is, not to diminish it, but to see it in relation to other prevailing factors. For one thing, US influence needs to be balanced against that of the governments of the Latin American nations themselves, and the quite different positions which they have assumed with regard to television from time to time. This has meant strict hands-on dictatorial control of broadcasters in some instances, while in others, quite laissez-faire environments have been permitted to flourish – what Latin

Americans call *capitalismo salvaje* (savage, or unmoderated capitalism). Another critical set of factors is constituted by the role of the Latin American broadcasting entrepreneurs themselves, and other commercial interests in Latin America, such as national advertisers, and their influence on their national governments. This chapter will show that close attention to the history of broadcasting in certain Latin American countries brings to light the active involvement of internationally-oriented entrepreneurs who, both individually and collectively, ensured that their industry was established on a commercial basis, both by lobbying their national governments and providing mutual support on a regional level. Certainly they were encouraged in this by US broadcasting interests, and during World War II the US government expressly sought to influence broadcasting content, but it was the Latin American entrepreneurs themselves who were instrumental in having broadcasting institutionalised on the US commercial network model, albeit adapting it to their own national and regional circumstances. Notably, the oligarchic form which Latin American media entrepreneurship took had its roots in Spanish and Portuguese colonisation, which left behind a pattern of capitalist enterprise dominated by family groups, on the one hand, and on the other by a Latin tradition of close entrepreneur-state cooperation (Malloy, 1977)

RADIO DAYS

Debates about cultural imperialism on television have tended to overlook the degree to which the establishment of radio in Latin America in the period between the world wars had already cast the mould in which the subsequent development of television came to be shaped. Since radio involved the same assemblage of interests as television – that is, government and private companies, both in the US and Latin America – it is necessary to take account of the continuities found from the one broadcasting medium to the next so as to understand how television assumed the form that it did in Latin America, which is the primary purpose of this chapter.

In the 1920s, corporations such as General Electric, through its broadcasting division RCA, were joining radio stations into networks in the US. Latin American entrepreneurs, wanting to bring the new medium to their own countries, formed partnerships with them. This was in response to the active presence of some of those same US radio equipment manufacturers and broadcasters in the region, as well as to the official encouragement of US agencies in favour of institutionalising radio as a privately-owned, rather than a public, medium (Schwoch, 1990). Given these circumstances, commercial radio went on to become well established in Latin America by the 1930s. With the onset of World War II, it became a priority of the US Government to counteract the influence of the Axis in the region. As one of several initiatives to secure the ideological defence of the hemisphere, the US Government set up the Office of Coordinator of Inter-American Affairs under Nelson Rockefeller. From 1940 until 1946, this agency gave strategic support to the expansion of the US networks into Latin America, and even produced and distributed its own programming in Spanish and Portuguese (Fox, 1997).

Towards the end of the war, in 1945, an intercontinental organisation formalising links between the Latin American entrepreneurs and the two major US networks, NBC and CBS, was established. This was known in Latin America as AIR, the Asociación Interamericana de Radiodifusión, or Interamerican Association of Broadcasters. One of its first objectives was the introduction of the new medium of television to the region, and AIR was committed to ensure that, like radio, television would be introduced on the privately-owned, commercial 'American' model, rather than the alternative, a 'European' state-funded, public service basis. This choice has been one of the most fundamental in broadcasting history. Latin American entrepreneurs positioned themselves so that they could take advantage of the fact that there was US official and corporate interest backing them in their region, and they supported each other in resisting attempts by national governments to impose any regulation which would have restricted the commercialisation of the new medium. It is important to emphasise that there were already powerful family-based media empires in print media that wanted to go straight into broadcasting. Like the US and unlike most of Europe, these entrepreneurs succeeded in moulding radio as an industry that they could enter. At one stage, the US Government was showing interest in setting up its own service to Latin America. Fearing such competition from their own government, NBC and CBS were driven to find common cause with the Latin American entrepreneurs. Thus, the subsequent prevalence of the commercial model of television in Latin America should be seen to be at least as much due to its embrace by Latin entrepreneurs, as to the influence of the US companies that had been lobbying the various national governments over this crucial period (Fernández Christlieb, 1987).

THE LATIN AMERICAN ENTREPRENEURS

Some of the most active entrepreneurs were not only significant figures in their own countries, but played a prominent role elsewhere in the region. The prime example was Goar Mestre, the founding president of AIR, who was involved with radio and television in Cuba at a time when Cuba was a leading nation in commercial broadcasting development (Rivero, 2009). Mestre and his brother Abel were backed in their station CMQ with investment from the US network NBC, at that time the broadcast division of the equipment manufacturer RCA,

Headquarters of Goar
Mestre and his commercial
broadcasting powerhouse
CMQ in downtown Havana,
prior to the Cuban Revolution
of 1959

which, as noted, was in turn a subsidiary of General Electric. Mestre was one of
the first exporters of radio programmes to the region, including the then innovative Latin commercial genre of the *radionovela*. Originally designed to attract
housewives to sponsors such as Colgate-Palmolive, the *radionovela* was an
immediate ancestor to the *telenovela*, the popular cultural form which was to
become the dominant export genre of the incipient television era, first to the
region and then beyond. Once the revolution of 1959 put an end to commercial broadcasting in Cuba, Mestre became an exile in Argentina, where he
formed a company in association with US media interests, namely CBS and
Time-Life. This was Proartel, which enabled Mestre to become active in television production, film distribution and dubbing in the region. With the same
partners, Mestre also invested in a Venezuelan television network, and had a further association with CBS in a Peruvian channel (Luis López, 1998). Mestre was
a leading figure amongst the many entrepreneurs, programmers, writers and
directors who left Cuba and fanned out across both Spanish-speaking and
Portuguese-speaking Latin America, and were influential in creating common
regional administrative and programming styles, not only in the *telenovela*, but
also in distinctive regional versions of genres such as the variety show. However,

these Cuban figures, important as they were, joined entrepreneurs in a variety of nations who were already developing commercial radio and television.

AZCÁRRAGA AND TELEVISA

Mestre was followed as president of AIR by Emilio Azcárraga Vidaurreta, the leading entrepreneur in Mexican radio. Azcárraga had built up a chain of stations affiliated with RCA's broadcasting network, NBC, and then a second one with CBS. NBC was also able to establish affiliates in several other Latin American countries, thanks to Azcárraga's programme distribution connections (Muraro, 1985). However, it had actually been Emilio Azcárraga's brothers, Raúl and Luis, who had opened CYL, the first commercial radio station in Mexico City in 1923. They were all sons of a Spanish immigrant from Navarre (Martínez, 1996). Raúl had a radio sales business, and had received technical training in Texas (Mejía Prieto, 1972), while Emilio had also been educated in Texas (Esparza, 1997). Emilio managed an RCA Victor phonograph and radio dealership in Mexico City, the Mexico Music Company. In 1930, he too opened a commercial radio station in the capital, XEW, which was backed principally through the Mexico Music Company. Although he was married into the wealthy Anglo-Mexican banking and mining Milmo family, his access to capital was through RCA, and hence the connection with NBC (Fernández Christlieb, 1976; Fernández & Paxman, 2000).

From this point, Mexican commercial radio entered an era of rapid expansion. Initially, the revenue model for radio had been based on the selling of radio sets, hence the early interest of RCA. However, with the adoption of the practice of attracting audiences for the sale of advertising time, Emilio Azcárraga set about building XEW into an NBC-affiliated network of stations, concentrating on the populous central and northern provinces. He developed an entertainment format which capitalised on Mexican popular culture genres, both musical and narrative, such that the XEW network soon achieved great success as 'The Voice of Latin America from Mexico' (de Noriega & Leach, 1979, p. 17).

Azcárraga had put himself into a position from which he could also take advantage of CBS, the other major US network wanting to have Latin partners able to attract the large US national advertisers who had become interested in advertising in Latin America by this time. Unflustered by any conflict of interest with his links to RCA and NBC, in 1938 Azcárraga opened another station in Mexico City, XEQ, this time with capital from CBS, and this became the basis for another network (Mejía Prieto, 1972). In doing so, Azcárraga was clearly adopting the US network model of operation for both his 'Tricolor' XEW-NBC and 'Blue' XEQ-CBS chains: basically, that the affiliates were provided with programmes from the network in return for time which the network could then sell to advertisers (Arriaga, 1980).

While there was some Spanish-language programming produced by NBC in the 1930s (Fox, 1997), Azcárraga's networks were successful because of their fostering of Mexico's own popular culture. Azcárraga's company, Radio Programas de México, produced popular music, *radionovelas*, and other entertainment programming. Furthermore, Goar Mestre was developing commercial radio in Cuba along similar lines at this time, so Azcárraga was able to enter into programme exchanges with his productions. Also on the regional front, Radio Programas de México was active in affiliating new stations in Central America, and instrumental in assisting NBC to enter countries further afield, such as Colombia. In brief, both Mestre and Azcárraga had been quick to develop an orientation to their region, not just their own countries, both in the commercialisation of popular culture and in the political furthering of their interests in AIR (Mejía Barquera, 1989).

The transition to television in Mexico begins with the entrance of another media entrepreneur, Rómulo O'Farrill Silva, who opened a radio station, XEX, in Mexico City in 1947. The following year, he took control of a major newspaper, *Novedades*, and integrated it with the station. Both O'Farrill and Azcárraga were lobbying the President of the time, Miguel Alemán Valdés (President 1946–52) to grant them licences for the introduction of television. In response, Alemán appointed a commission in 1947 to visit the US, UK and France, to investigate which kind of system Mexico should adopt for the establishment of television, private or public. There were only two commissioners: one was Guillermo González Camarena, an engineer with a long record of successful experimentation with colour television (not all technical innovation in television was happening in the US). González Camarena had taken out a patent on his colour system in 1940, and was conducting regular trial transmissions by 1946. The other was a distinguished poet and writer, Salvador Novo, at the time director of the national theatre. The commissioners did not agree in their findings: while Salvador Novo wanted the European public model, González Camarena's recommendation in favour of the US commercial model must have been what Alemán wanted to hear. Alemán granted the licence for the first television station, not just in Mexico, but in Latin America, to Rómulo O'Farrill for XHTV Channel 4 in 1949. It began transmitting the following year, during which a second licence was granted to Azcárraga for XEWTV, Channel 2, which went to air in 1951. González Camarena was granted yet a third licence in 1952 for Channel 5 (Sánchez Ruiz, 1991; Hernández Lomeli & Orozco Gómez, 2007).

However, Mexican television could not at first be adapted to the commercial model. Just as radio broadcasting could not take off until a critical mass of radio

Forgotten pioneer of television in Mexico, Guillermo González Camarema, demonstrates his 'chromoscopic' colour-wheel system for television in the 1940s

sets had been sold, so it was with television. Since so few people owned sets in the early 1950s, television was attractive neither to advertisers, nor to sponsors who were willing to buy air time for their own programmes, as the system then still worked in the US. Since Azcárraga had experience in cinema as well as radio, he had the idea of running his production studios like a theatre, charging admission for live productions so as to compensate for his costs in building them (TV in Mexico, 1951). By March 1955, the owners of the three channels decided that the market was too small to sustain them in competition, and that they should merge. Thus, they formed Telesistema Mexicano (TSM), a pooling of the three licensees' operations, but firmly under the control of Azcárraga and O'Farrill: González Camarena was frozen out, without so much as a seat on the board (Fernández Christlieb, 1975).

As with the expansion of radio networks, Azcárraga and O'Farrill set about extending the coverage of TSM's channels, particularly in the north, and to differentiate each channel's programming to appeal to particular audience segments. Apart from such consolidation of the domestic market, TSM launched itself into strategic international activities, initially with a programme export arm, Teleprogramas de México. Azcárraga and O'Farrill positioned themselves to attract the foreign technology and investment which they needed to propel the expansion of TSM, as Azcárraga had done with his radio networks. By the end of the 1950s, television programme production and distribution was about to be transformed by the advent of videotape, which permitted television recording of a quality and durability not previously possible, and hence greater distribution of programmes. In 1958, a TSM station in Monterrey acquired the first of many Ampex videotape machines from the US, which were to enable TSM to extend domestic network programming as well as its nascent export activities. This expansion of production activities was undertaken with a direct 25 per cent investment from the third major television network in the US, ABC, which was becoming actively interested in the region at this time. Thus, in 1962, a new subsidiary was created, Teleprogramas Acapulco. This was under the direction of Miguel Alemán Velasco. He was the son of the President who had granted the original licences and who had become a partner in TSM at the end of his term.

From the first Mexican *telenovela* in 1958, *Senda prohibida, telenovelas* were broadcast live, like most other programming, with the exception of a few which were recorded using the crude technology of the kinescope and sold to stations in the US (TSM's own) and Central America (Paxman, 2003). However, enabled by the far superior videotape technology, Teleprogramas Acapulco could concentrate on the mass production and wider international distribution of this highly commercial genre (de Noriega and Leach, 1979; Peréz Espino, 1979). In another important international initiative around this time, Azcárraga was setting up the first Spanish-language television stations in the US, and supplying them with TSM programming. In fact, the Mexicans were to run Spanish-language television in the US for the next 25 years, having developed the network known today as Univisión. For its part, TSM became the corporate ancestor to today's media conglomerate, Televisa, which has come to dominate the industry in ways which will be outlined in the next chapter.

MARINHO AND GLOBO

As for Brazil, Latin America's other major pioneering broadcasting nation and major market, there is a comparable historical pattern. US corporations and their advertising agencies took an active interest in ensuring that radio developed there on the commercial model, that of providing entertainment programming calculated to deliver audiences to advertisers, and networks were built upon audiences attracted by the exploitation of popular culture genres (Straubhaar, 1996). Quite a few of the national media entrepreneurs who had been successful in the newspaper business wanted to extend their advertising base and political power by moving into radio and then television. Notably, one of the main television networks of the 1950s–70s emerged from the radio arm of a very large, but loosely organised media empire, Diários e Emissoras Associadas, run by Francisco de Assis Chateaubriand Bandeira de Melo. That group already had commercial radio and newspapers in most major Brazilian cities before they added television in 1950.

When television became a possibility in the 1950s, Brazil had only a small number of set owners, and advertisers were not interested, just as in Mexico. In fact, when Chateaubriand opened up Brazil's first television station, TV Tupi Difusora in 1950, he was acting against the explicit advice of US consultants, who had told him that the advertising base was too restricted to support commercial television (Ferraz Sampaio, 1984). However, Chateaubriand's media empire, Diários e Emissoras Associadas was not based solely on advertising revenue, but also the sale of political influence based on control of a variety of media outlets, so television was a very logical expansion of such interests.

However, as advertisers eventually became more attracted to television, their expectation was that it should be run very much on the basis of the 'sponsorship' system which had characterised commercial radio in the US and Latin America alike up to that point. Instead of buying advertising time as 'spots' within programmes which the network was responsible for providing, which is still predominantly the universal commercial practice today, advertisers would actually produce the programming themselves, complete with advertising. Thus, a principal function of advertising agencies over this period was to produce such programmes for their clients. The *telenovela*, like the *radionovela* before it in the 1940s, first came to Brazil thanks to this system. Under the auspices of sponsors such as Lever and their advertising agency, Lintas, the popular narrative form was transplanted to the new medium (Mattelart & Mattelart, 1990). As is well known, the US eventually abandoned the sponsorship system in favour of selling spots to advertisers according to the ratings of independently-produced programmes, especially after the quiz-show scandal of 1959 (Barnouw, 1979), but it persisted in some Latin American countries. In Brazil, the production of variety shows and even news programmes and *telenovelas* by advertising agencies lasted until as late as 1970 (Straubhaar, 1982; Mattos, 1992).

It should be stressed that Chateaubriand and the other few *bandeirantes* (pioneers) of the early years of Brazilian television were not dependent on direct investment by US interests, although several groups did in fact have foreign loans or investments. They were primarily using their own capital, largely derived from existing radio, and sometimes related print, operations. In this respect, TV Globo, the network which subsequently arose in the 1960s, came to overtake TV Tupi, and ultimately dominate Brazilian television right up to the present, was exceptional, because it did have the substantial benefit of a direct investment from a US media corporation, Time-Life. Yet even TV Globo had grown out of a radio network. It began as the television division of the integrated media holdings of the Marinho family, originally based on the Rio de Janeiro daily newspaper *O Globo*, which had opened in 1925. Led by Roberto Marinho, the counterpart of Mexico's Emilio Azcárraga, Globo then spread into other publishing enterprises, as well as commercial broadcasting with a radio network it opened up in 1944, long before making its move into television (Organizações Globo, 1992).

Although it was for a finite period of time, from 1962 until 1970, the Time-Life investment opened up a decisive advantage for Globo over its competitors, one which they have never since been able to close. However, the impetus given by Time-Life's capital only partly explains Globo's subsequent domination of the Brazilian television market. Perhaps the most important impact of that capital was that it enabled TV Globo to hire away quite a bit of the best talent in sales, management, programming, directing and writing from other Brazilian television networks. That concentration of talent was perhaps most crucial in its rapid success. Timing was another significant factor, and the political relationship which Globo developed with the succession of military presidents who ruled Brazil from 1964 until 1985 should not be underestimated. As in Mexico, where Televisa remained closely identified with the ruling party for decades, congenial relations with the government of the day was a necessary if not a sufficient condition for perpetuating its market dominance, at least until the era of neoliberalism. Indeed, throughout Latin America, the major private, commercial television networks have tended to have close relationships with governments. Alisky (1981) characterised the government role as one of censorship or guidance. Compared with other developing or emerging world regions, most Latin American governments have tended to prefer to 'guide' commercial television, rather than seizing and directly controlling the media. There are often tensions, however, particularly between commercial media and governments of the Left, as the case of Chávez in Venezuela demonstrated over the first decade of the 2000s. But the pattern of indirect rather than direct government influence has been consistent across decades in the region.

US INFLUENCE: 1950s AND 1960s

As shown in the case of the Time-Life involvement with Globo, there were various US interests looking for opportunities and developing strategies to gain a foothold in the region during the 1960s. Silvio Waisbord has provided an authoritative analysis of the development of Latin American television in which he discerns three stages, in each of which the relation to US interests is a defining feature (Waisbord, 1998). Firstly, as has been outlined, US interests gave support to Latin entrepreneurs such as Mestre and Azcárraga, and sold equipment, both for transmission in setting up stations and sets for reception by an audience. However, during the early 1950s, when television was still new in the US itself and Latin markets were too small to be profitable, and the US networks were still preoccupied with building up their home market, they had little interest in direct investment in Latin America. As has been seen, the Latin American entrepreneurs were not waiting for that to change before they launched into television: both Mexico and Brazil had their first stations in 1950. Argentina and Venezuela, the nations which came to form a second echelon of television production and distribution, had their first stations in 1951 and 1952 respectively (Roncagliolo, 1995). This was at an early stage of the medium's development, not far behind the US and well ahead of most other world regions. Cuba is worth a special mention in this respect. Given its size, it had the distinction of being the first nation in the world to extend television to its entire national territory (Bunce, 1976). As noted, Cuba established itself as a regional leader in the commercialisation of television during the 1950s, and in the years following the 1959 revolution, not just Goar Mestre but many technical and managerial personnel exiled from the new regime in Cuba found their way into significant roles in the development of the television systems of continental Latin America (Rivero, 2009).

By the end of the 1950s, US corporations had supplied equipment, technical and managerial assistance, and in some countries up to 80 per cent of programming to Latin American stations, but only then began to take an active interest in making strategic direct investments. The largest of the three US television networks, NBC, continued to concentrate more on the sale of management services and equipment, but also exploited the new technology of reliable videotape recording by investing in programme production (Frappier, 1968). The newest but smallest network, ABC, was the most active, setting up affiliates in Latin America and other world regions through an international division, Worldvision. It was noted above how ABC was investing in *telenovela* production in Mexico, while CBS was giving its support to Mestre, by then exiled to continental Latin America. CBS also had an association with Time-Life, independent of Time-Life's decisive investment in Brazil in 1962 which had launched TV Globo, and enabled it to become not only the national but a regional market leader (Marques de Melo, 1992). ABC's intervention in Latin America went the furthest, adapting the same model that all the US networks had used to establish themselves on a national basis in their home market: its most characteristic strategy involved the setting up of international networks of affiliates within sub-regions (Janus & Roncagliolo, 1978). Notably, when the US government and some corporate interests persuaded the Central American countries to form the Central American Free Trade Zone in 1960, ABC signed up affiliates in the five countries involved, creating the Central American Television Network (CATVN) (Bunce, 1976). Similarly, ABC investments in stations from Mexico to the Southern Cone countries of Chile and Argentina were later brought together as its LATINO network (Janus & Roncagliolo, 1978). However, it seems likely that these initiatives were only ever potential networks, and never attracted the advertisers necessary for them to function profitably (Fox, 1979).

It is important to bear in mind that this was the crucial stage at which many US-based corporations were striving to transform themselves from a national scale into what were then known as the 'transnational' (or 'multinational') corporations of the 1960s and 1970s. Television seemed to offer them access to their

prospective markets, just as it had proved to do so well in the US. Thus, attracting such advertisers was the driving force behind the networks' strategic efforts
to internationalise and commercialise the new medium in Latin America.
However, there were competing models as to how the various corporate interests should position themselves in order to develop these potential new markets.
Clearly, ABC's approach was to provide a transnational medium for transnational advertisers, which would enable them to standardise their marketing
campaigns across a sub-region. By contrast, the US-based advertising agencies
that were setting up offices in the region around the same time hoped to attract
transnational clients by providing them with services in each national market.
They were happy to work with nationally owned broadcasters, if those provided
the audience that they needed. These contrasting strategies presaged the subsequent debate in the 1980s between advocates of global advertising campaign
standardisation as against those who favoured tailoring campaigns to specific
markets (Mattelart, 1991). The US trade journal *Television* neatly expressed this
contrast between ABC's transnational networks approach and the market-by-
market strategy of the US advertising agencies at the time:

> ... ABC can sell *Batman* to an advertiser and then place *Batman* along with
> designated commercials in any Worldvision country where the advertiser wants it to
> appear. ... ABC's approach is the reverse of what the agencies are doing. ABC is
> attempting to create a single world-wide medium that an international advertiser
> can buy in a centralized way, while the advertising agencies are attempting to
> spread their services abroad to bring them closer to the variety of media around
> the world. Both, however, are banking on the existence of a sizeable group of
> international companies with marketing plans that cover large portions of the globe
> (Quoted in Frappier, 1968, p. 4).

US INFLUENCE, 1970s AND 1980s

Waisbord's second stage of Latin American television, as defined by its relation
to US interests, was when the networks began to withdraw from the region,
such strategies having proved futile, and direct investments failing to meet their
expectations. As one NBC executive commented, 'We simply overestimated
the market ... For a while everyone thought it was a new frontier. We quickly
found out it wasn't.' (Quoted in Salwen, 1994). Apart from increased competition in the region, the networks were greatly affected by a decision of the US
regulatory body, the FCC (Federal Communications Commission), which in
1971 ruled that they had to separate their distribution from their syndication
activities. Without the advantage which such vertical integration had given
them, and in the light of the disappointing returns, both CBS and NBC sold

off their foreign investments (Read, 1976), while ABC drastically curtailed its activities, retaining only quite minor overseas holdings (Varis, 1978). Time-Life started to pull out of its association with Globo in 1968, in part because of similar lack of profitability, though also because of political pressure against the foreign presence (Straubhaar, 1984). Furthermore, although the networks did continue to supply programmes to the region, this period saw considerable growth in several key domestic markets, a significant maturing of Latin American production companies, and an increase of programme exports on a regional basis.

Thus, it was really the 1960s era of US network intervention during the previous phase that earned it the epithet of 'cultural imperialism' (Schiller, 1969), or, even more specifically, 'picture-tube imperialism' (Wells, 1972). Yet, by the late 1970s, it was apparent that the critics had jumped too soon to the conclusion that dependence upon direct investments, and seemingly high levels of programming imported from the US, were permanent structural features of Latin American television. Rather, as is now known to be a common pattern in the adoption of television in other world regions, what was being observed was a transitional start-up stage in which there was an inevitable reliance on external resources, but this was soon to be followed by development of the medium at the local level as national and regional markets matured (Tunstall, 1977). As Goar Mestre knew well, Latin American audiences '… don't mind the occasional American program, but what they really like are shows with local flavour.' (Quoted in Salwen, 1994, p. 120) In fact, this preference for national or local material became evident in Latin America before it became clear in the rest of the world, one reason that the theories of cultural proximity (Straubhaar, 1991) and cultural-linguistic regions (Wilkinson, 1995) were first developed about Latin America.

Again, this is not to deny the active role of US influence, but to set it in a longer perspective than was provided by the discourse of cultural imperialism. With television, as with radio, US officials encouraged Latin American governments and media entrepreneurs to pursue the US commercial model while, at the same time, US networks sold them the technology and the management services, and even invested directly. The networks also sold US programming, but the fact that programmes like *I Love Lucy* shone everywhere from the region's television screens for a time was only a superficial indicator of a more fundamental transformation. The consequential and enduring significance of US influence was not the presence of foreign capital, nor the high levels of programme imports, neither of which was sustainable, but the institutionalisation of the medium on the commercial model throughout the region (McAnany, 1984).

Cuban exile Desi Arnaz and Lucille Ball in *I Love Lucy*, emblematic of the era of 'picture-tube imperialism'

Indeed, the almost universal adoption of the commercial model made Latin America distinct within the developing world, the rest of which by and large adopted the state-owned alternative. However, while actual state ownership of television may have been rather limited in Latin America, state control is quite a different matter. That is, state policies with respect to television, or the absence of such policies, have been consequential for the development of the medium as an institution, regardless of whether the state has also been involved in the ownership of stations. It is difficult to draw generalisations, because there are complex histories of broadcast regulation distinct to each nation, and integral to their political histories as a whole. Nevertheless, it can be said that the two main phases in which Latin American governments have taken an active role in controlling television were the 1950s, when populist dictators in Argentina, Brazil, and Colombia implemented severe nationalistic policies to assert direction over broadcasting and other media; and the 1970s, when, in the context of the NWICO debate (to be explained below), several governments took up the rhetoric of 'national communication policies'. This meant moves towards reform and the strengthening of public broadcasting in Mexico, Venezuela and Chile in the first half of the decade, and then a more region-wide discourse being generated about the protection of television and other media industries from foreign influence and competition. This included the affirmation of their public service and civic functions, such as the construction and defence of national cultures, but no national communication policies as such were ever implemented (Fox, 1988).

Yet even where Latin nations did have state ownership of their television systems, revenue generation from the sale of advertising time was still the norm. For example, in Colombia, the state maintained ownership of the television channels, but leased broadcasting time to private companies. The lessees commercialised the time by supplying the programming and selling advertising spots and sponsorship (Fox, 1997). In Peru, there was a system of majority state ownership of television during the era of the Left-wing military regime between 1969 and 1981, but, even then, the system ran on a commercial basis. Reflecting the widespread belief in the educational potential of television at the time, Bolivia and Chile made exceptional arrangements in that universities owned the stations, not the state as such, but again, they too were funded from commercial advertising (Roncagliolo, 1995). In Mexico, there was a stage at which state-owned commercial networks provided some weak competition to the dominant private conglomerate, Televisa, as will be explained further in Chapter Two (Sinclair, 1986). The obvious exception to the hegemony of the commercial model is Televisora Nacional, Cuba's state-owned monopoly which was formed in 1960 by Castro's revolutionary government, amalgamating the Mestres' CMQ and the other pre-1959 networks (Lent, 1990). At a later stage, military governments in Argentina and Peru took over television systems for a time, but eventually returned them to the private sector (Salwen, 1994; Fox, 1997). In recent times, Chávez in Venezuela had been forcing out those private broadcasters who had supported his opposition, while building up the state sector in media.

Staying with Waisbord's chronology, it was during the second stage in the development of Latin American television that much international attention was given to patterns of television programming exports and imports, as already noted with regard to the cultural imperialism critique. The 'flows' of television 'traffic' even became one of the central issues around which there was an international movement demanding a 'New World Information and Communication Order' (NWICO) within UNESCO during the 1970s and 1980s. Latin American and other developing countries sought to formulate national communication policies so as to defend themselves against the perceived threat of cultural imperialism, which they saw in the news, entertainment and advertising carried via television. Some benchmark comparative studies of television flows from this era had special significance for Latin America.

Building on previous work by Nordenstreng and Varis (1974), a wide-ranging international study by Tapio Varis confirmed that the flow of programming was a 'one-way street' from the US to the rest of the world, but identified 'a trend toward greater regional exchanges', notable in Latin America (Varis, 1984). In another study, Everett Rogers and Livia Antola not only confirmed this tendency toward regionalisation, but were able to document the very considerable extent to which the *telenovela* had become the preferred commercial genre within the Latin American regional trade (Rogers & Antola, 1985). This trend was very much as Jeremy Tunstall had predicted as early as 1977, when he argued that 'hybrid media forms', such as the *telenovela*, would carve out an intermediate level in world programme trade, between the global and the local (Tunstall, 1977). Coincidentally, in that same year, Ithiel de Sola Pool argued prophetically that audiences would come to prefer programming which was made in their own language, and had cultural familiarity for them (de Sola Pool, 1977).

With the wisdom of hindsight, now that the development of television can be seen in a long-term and comparative perspective, the Latin American experience demonstrates what is now known to be a common pattern of transition, from an initial stage of external dependence to an eventual maturity of the national market, both in terms of growth in audience size, and domestic programme production. The consensus amongst researchers now is that audiences prefer television programming from their own country, and in their own vernacular, or if that is not available, from other countries which are culturally and linguistically similar: 'audiences will tend to prefer that programming which is closest or most proximate to their own culture: national programming if it can be supported by the local economy, regional programming in genres that small countries cannot afford' (Straubhaar, 1992, p. 14). For example, research in smaller Latin American countries, like the Dominican Republic, has noted that much of their programming in key genres like drama (notably *telenovelas*), comedy and music comes from other Latin American countries, not the US any more (Straubhaar, 1991). Latin American *telenovela* producers like Televisa and TV Globo also provide cases in point in a debate on whether such producers are creating an effective counter-flow to US dominance at the global level. Brazil has exported *telenovelas* to over 120 countries. Both Brazilian and Mexican *telenovelas* were hugely popular in a number of emerging markets, even parts of Europe in the 1990s. However, critics of this idea have pointed out that the volume of such counter-flows never seriously challenged US dominance at the global level (Biltereyst & Meers, 2000), as opposed to more specific regional flows in Latin America and elsewhere. An analysis of television flows among 23 countries in six cultural-linguistic markets or geocultural/geolinguistic regions showed an overall dominance of global flows by the US (Straubhaar, 2007). However, within the Arab World, East Asia, and Latin America, intra-regional programme flows have increased, a trend noted in other more recent studies as well (Hyun, 2007; Iwabuchi, 2002; Kraidy, 2002a).

US INFLUENCE: NOT QUITE THE 'POSTBROADCAST' ERA

To round out Waisbord's periodisation, the third stage in which the development of Latin American television must be assessed in relation to US interests brings us up to the present. With the advent of 'post-broadcast' cable and satellite technologies of distribution and hence more opportunities in the multichannel environment, a new generation of service and content providers has entered the field, and US corporations are prominent amongst them. Digital direct-to-home (DTH) satellite delivery in particular has encouraged the major Latin American producers and distributors, notably Televisa and Globo, to enter strategic alliances with US satellite and cable service providers. Rupert Murdoch's Sky Latin America entered into a consortium with Televisa, TV Globo and others, while Galaxy-DirecTV joined with second-string regional powers like the Cisneros Group (Venezuela) and Editora Abril (Brazil). Televisa and Globo have continued to be partners after the subsequent merger of Sky and DirecTV under the Sky name in 2004 ('News Corp sells Sky Latin America stakes', 2004). Nevertheless, although such arrangements bring Latin American television into the mainstream of globalisation, the audience for pay-TV remained extremely limited (outside of Argentina, an exception) until the 2000s, and even beyond the end of that decade, by far the largest audiences continue to be for free-to-air channels. Thus, the contemporary situation is that the US-based corporations have occupied the global level of distribution which digital technologies have opened up, and have also sought to build up audiences of elite subscribers at the regional level, in competition with the Latin American corporations. That may be slowly changing. At least in Brazil, the expansion of the cable and pay-TV audience after 2010 has to do both with rising affluence and even more the increasing provision of national content for segmented cable channels by GloboSat, MTV and other firms. However, by and large, the latter continue to maintain their predominance over domestic competition in broadcast television within the national markets where they have their roots and still earn by far the bulk of their income, and to dominate the regional trade in programmes for broadcast television, which continues to be a relatively mass medium.

The era of national communication policies has been left far behind by the spread of deregulation and privatisation, the whole overarching ideological disposition that Latin Americans call *neoliberalismo*, and the embrace of globalisation. In terms of television as a social and economic institution, the broad trend which became consolidated over the 1980s and 1990s was towards ever more private control, in the form of deregulation as well as ownership. The quite evident triumph of the commercial model is of course also the triumph of the oligarchies who have sought and now benefit from its institutionalisation. Although from time to time there is strong public criticism of private control in those countries where television is the most monopolised, there is also little faith in the state's capacity to act in the public's interest, as distinct from its own. Given the general fragility of democratic traditions in the region, and because state regulation is associated historically with dictatorial control and authoritarian states, such as with Brazil and the other cases mentioned above, the private media have been able to secure much greater legitimacy as an alternative base for the provision of political and cultural leadership than can be imagined in most English-speaking nations (Waisbord, 1995; 1997).

Some Latin American television companies also benefit from this discredited heritage of state control in that they enjoy a lightly regulated environment in which to operate. Whereas even the US, the heartland of neoliberalism, maintains regulatory restraints against monopolisation, in Latin America, manifestly monopolistic practices such as the integration of production and distribution in the television industry, although not universal, are the norm. There is a similar tolerance towards the quite extreme commercialisation of the medium, for example, in the large proportion of airtime given over to advertising, or the inclusion of commercial messages in editorial or entertainment content via product placement (Straubhaar, 1991). In Mexico and Brazil in particular, where in each case a dominant private network has emerged, the consensus of observers is that the mutual accommodation which developed between government and network was a formative factor in establishing this dominance (Rogers & Antola, 1985; Fox, 1997; Waisbord, 1997). This is a point which, while undeniable, is easily oversimplified at the expense of actual contradictions and shifts in the balance of interests between the two parties, and so is better left to the analysis in the following chapters dedicated to these specific countries.

OLIGARCHIC CHARACTER OF MEDIA OWNERSHIP

The ownership of television continues to be largely oligarchic, although expansion of possible television channels through UHF, low power television, cable, satellite, digital television and, now, the internet, opens some spaces for local or regional, community-run, university-based, religious, or educational channels. It is certainly safe to say that the main channels watched by most of the audience remain in the hands of oligarchs, whether they be commercially minded, like most of the family television empires, or politically minded, like commercial channels owned by politicians in many countries, or the smaller number of state channels growing in places like Venezuela or Brazil.

In most countries, television viewing and power continues to be concentrated in a few stations. Most of these are still run by family media empires that have developed over the decades. The common historical pattern has been for one or two of these to dominate television in each nation: Televisa in Mexico, TV Globo in Brazil, Venevisión in Venezuela, Clarín in Argentina, Cadena Radial Colombiana (Caracol TV) and Radio Cadena Nacional (RCN TV) in Colombia, etc. The degree of dominance also varies considerably. While Televisa and TV Globo are widely considered the dominant television companies of Latin America, Televisa retains more dominance of the Mexican market than does TV Globo in Brazil, where competition from other networks has increased since the 1990s. The new entrants in television are sometimes older non-television media empires, like Editora Abril in Brazil, the dominant company in magazine publishing, which finally entered television via cable systems in the 1990s. In some cases, particularly in smaller markets like Chile or Central America, other major players in the region enter as new hegemonic competitors, as Salinas Pliego of Mexico's TV Azteca did by purchasing television stations in several Central American countries (Rockwell & Janus, 2003). Sometimes the new entrants are owned and controlled by governments, like Telesur, the regional satellite network for government television, based in Venezuela, or the new TV Brasil, an effort by the former Lula government to create a national public television network.

In some cases, technology like cable and internet infrastructure offers hegemonic competitors from other industries, particularly telephony, an opportunity to enter cable and/or internet services and compete in television, telephone and internet triple-play service offerings. While such telecom-based owners may not own individual content channels in the traditional sense of 'television', they now decide which channels get carried on their services. There is also a partial return of another hegemonic force, religious institutions, both Catholic and Protestant, to activity in broadcasting. Some Catholic stations had been closed during the era of military governments, when some of them were seen as overly progressive. Some new networks, like a new national Catholic television network in Brazil, have been created to counter the increased presence of US-style Protestant tele-evangelism. Some of those networks are becoming powerful, particularly in Brazil and Central America, where Protestantism is growing rapidly, reflected in media and politics. TV Record in Brazil, operated by the Universal Church of the Reign of God, is now the number two network in ratings and income. Its parent church has also now become a transnational, operating stations in Central America, Mozambique, and the US (Reis, 2006).

PENETRATION OF CABLE AND DTH IN THE REGION, AND DIGITISATION

Cable television, pay-TV and satellite direct-to-home (DTH) began to slowly change the face of television in Latin America, starting in the 1990s. Aside from Argentina, where cable penetration and use has been high since the 1980s, cable, satellite and pay-TV have had much more limited success in penetrating the Latin American market than in comparable developing and emerging markets in other parts of the world. An early study done of home video, one of the first widespread technologies to offer alternative viewing options to broadcast television, compared Latin America to Asia and the Middle East. It showed that penetration and growth of home video in Latin America was lower and slower than the other two regions (Boyd & Straubhaar, 1985; Boyd, Straubhaar, & Lent, 1989). That seemed to be because, more than in Asia or the Middle East, most Latin American countries had by the 1980s already developed commercial television industries that delivered a great deal of popular entertainment and information to their audiences. This can be attributed to the fact that television in Latin America was commercial from the beginning, and free-to-air markets were mature and well-established by then, whereas Asia and the Middle East had had decades of government control over broadcasting. Accordingly, audiences in Latin America were substantially less interested in spending relatively scarce funds on other alternatives for television entertainment and information, since they were relatively satisfied with what was on broadcast television. That same attitude seemed to hold true for cable, satellite and DTH for much of Latin America up through the 1990s and even in some cases, like Brazil, well into the first decade of the 2000s (Reis, 1999). For many countries, satellite, cable and pay-TV were luxury goods primarily consumed by the upper middle class and upper class. The exception, Argentina, was interesting because it represented a case where, unlike other Latin American military regimes, the Argentine military took over the existing commercial television channels, ran them very badly, and created a situation where, like many developing nations outside Latin America, cable television was seen as a welcome alternative to state run, poorly programmed broadcast television. Argentina also presented the unusually favourable situation for cable of a large affluent population heavily concentrated in the capital city.

Elsewhere, cable television was initially restricted to the more affluent core areas of major cities. It required major investments in physical infrastructure. Even a large company such as the Globo Group in Brazil, almost became insolvent over the investments and loans required to lay subterranean cable (Wallach, 2011). So cable grew slowly in most countries, limited initially by relatively low demand. Interest in it accelerated in the 2000s, when physical cable came to be a more valuable infrastructure for offering triple-play packages of telephone, cable or pay-TV, and internet access. When that prospect became more concrete, television or other media companies which had invested in cable infrastructure found themselves competing with deeper-pocketed telecom firms, from within the region, like América Móvil, owned by Carlos Slim of Mexico, or from outside, like Telefónica of Spain. Both companies have market-leading cellular or other telecom operations in most of Latin America.

The use of satellites as a television reception technology includes both satellite dishes designed to pull down national broadcast television channels in areas of poor reception as well as for DTH pay-TV systems. In the early days of broadcast television, reception was extended across rural areas and small towns as television networks, or in some cases local governments, put up terrestrial repeaters to bring television to nearly all parts of most Latin American countries. Areas not covered by such repeater infrastructure in many countries also saw a proliferation of satellite dishes designed to pull down unencrypted national television signals, so that people in rural areas, small towns and even the sprawling peripheries of large cities could get a good quality signal of the national television channels they wanted to watch. An equivalent technology in many cities was satellite master antenna television (SMATV), which put a dish on apartment building roofs and distributed television over cables within the building. That was sometimes done primarily to get a good broadcast signal, but also began to bring in pay-TV signals, depending on how the system was set up.

Pay-TV, delivered via satellite-to-cable or DTH, grew more slowly, but it still attracted investments from large broadcasters like Televisa and TV Globo, as well as investments by other media companies, like Abril Publishing in Brazil, in the 1990s as the services began to attract the interest of at least the more affluent and internationally oriented audiences in Latin America. It also attracted significant outside investment as both the Murdoch group, through its Sky satellite television brand, and DirecTV, originally owned by Hughes of the US, both went into Latin America. First, those companies offered limited options, essentially what they already had available globally, like CNN and HBO. Some global companies began to package channels specifically aimed at Latin America, like the Sony channel, which programmed US sitcoms for those in Latin America who knew enough about US culture to enjoy them (Duarte,

2001). To increase demand, they found that they had to localise their programming more, dubbing first in Mexican Spanish for all of Latin America, then
realising that they also had to dub at least into Portuguese for Brazil and into
Andean or Southern Cone Spanish for the southern part of Latin America
(Straubhaar & Duarte, 2005). The growth of pay-TV varied. It reached over 20
per cent of Mexico, for example, in the early 2000s, while attracting less than 10
per cent of Brazilian households. It has grown more, notably in Brazil, as it has
added more locally produced content to reduce the cultural discount (Hoskins,
McFayden, & Finn, 1997) that international content received from most of the
audience, or conversely, to increase its attraction to audiences via cultural proximity (Straubhaar, 1991) by having more national or regional channels. It has
also grown in several countries, again notably Brazil, as those countries have
grown economically in the 2000s, bringing more of the population into the middle class where they can afford such a relative luxury as pay TV (Folha, 2012).

Digital broadcast or terrestrial television has also finally begun to arrive in
Latin America. Most countries have adopted the Japanese standard ISDB-T
(Integrated Services Digital Broadcasting), with modifications and interactive
middleware (the Ginga standard) created in Brazil in 2006 (Soares & de Souza
Filho, 2007). ISDB-T International was developed by the Brazilian government
and is being widely promoted and adopted in several other Latin American
countries (Anguloa, Calzadab, & Estruch, 2011. There are several goals for the
new system. The most important is to create an interactive digital television standard that allows at least limited interactivity to television viewers who are not
likely to have the internet soon. Another is to create a technological platform
that can be manufactured in the region, particularly in Brazil but also in other
countries, minimising the economic effects of adopting an outside television
standard, which often leads to importation of technology and related manufactured products from other countries. An ultimate goal is to create a common
market in Latin America, for both programming and technology, based on that
standard.

REGIONAL TELEVISION PROGRAMMING INNOVATION IN LATIN AMERICA

Television programming in Latin America has been increasingly innovative
since its beginnings in the 1950s. Even then, a distinctive adaptation of the
global tradition of melodrama had emerged in the Latin American *telenovela*
(Martín-Barbero, 1987). The region has also produced extremely innovative
versions of the variety show (Straubhaar, 1983); television and alternative video
documentaries (Aufderheide, 1993); music video; and some reality television
formats that have been sold abroad. The most innovative form of television

content, the thing that people identify as branded with Latin America in international television trade, is the *telenovela* (Havens, 2006). The *telenovela* emerged as a hybrid genre, out of the interaction between US interests in commercialising television and selling soap, the creative localisation of the genre form of the US soap opera, and already localised forms of melodrama and story telling (Straubhaar, 1982; Paxman, 2003). In that, the genre is an interesting example of the concrete interaction of many of the forces, particularly foreign commercial interests and national entrepreneurship, discussed above.

The story of how the *telenovela* originated in Cuba is an excellent example of that interaction. Colgate-Palmolive had enjoyed great success using radio and then television drama as vehicles to sell soap to audiences, particularly housewives, in the US: hence the term 'soap opera'. In the 1940s and 1950s, when Cuba was one of the most advanced consumer economies in Latin America and also its most advanced commercial media centre (Rivero, 2009), Colgate-Palmolive decided to localise what it knew from the US, and so created a version of the soap opera genre in Cuba, first on radio, then television (Lopez, 1995). 'By adapting the US broadcasting system in terms of production, programming, and advertising practices, and by gathering a workforce that mastered the technical, business, and creative aspects of radio and television, Havana's broadcasting industries became the commercial model for the region' (Rivero, 2009, pp. 276–7). As Rivero and others note (Paxman, 2003), key Cuban professionals, such as Goar Mestre, mentioned above, left in the 1950s and early 1960s to help build or reinforce commercial television operations in Argentina, Brazil, Peru, Puerto Rico, and Venezuela, among others. However, other writers emphasise that there were many other roots for the *telenovela*, besides the soap opera and the marketing desires of Colgate-Palmolive, and those formed a crucial part of the hybrid genre that emerged (Hernandez, 2001). Thus, the telenovela should not be thought of as merely a Latin version of the soap opera. The genre tended to focus on the love stories and family drama typical of all melodrama, but the *telenovela* also takes up contemporary themes such as social mobility (Martín-Barbero, 1987), coping with social change like rapid urbanisation, and, depending on the country, even social issues like land reform (prominent in a Brazilian *telenovela*, *O rei do gado* (*The Cattle King*, 1996–7).

The *telenovela* was spread throughout Latin America in part by the circulation and sale of scripts, an interesting forerunner of the current television format trade (Straubhaar, 2011). Professionals also flowed, not only writers and executives, but also all kinds of producers and technicians. By many accounts, *telenovelas* retained a somewhat Cuban flavor until the 1960s, when local and national variations and adaptations began to firm up in Argentina, Brazil, Mexico, Peru and Venezuela. Later Colombia and others also began to develop

Mexican television personality Veronica Castro, star of the internationally successful *telenovela* from 1979, *Los ricos también lloran* (*The Rich also Cry*)

distinctive national forms of the *telenovela*. Lopez characterises the Mexican ones as more romantic, the Brazilian and Colombian as more realistic and social (1995). Not all countries were wealthy enough to create their own, so Latin America also became one of the first extensively developed geocultural regional markets, in which *telenovelas* were sold extensively within the region (Antola & Rogers, 1984).

The *telenovela* has proven to be more than a regional success in the television trade. When global demand for imported entertainment increased rapidly in many countries, following the wave of liberalised entries of new private networks in the 1980s, *telenovelas* were sufficiently developed as a commercial entertainment product that could be extensively exported around the world. Eventually, even Russians would devotedly watch classic *telenovelas* such as *Los ricos también lloran* (*The Rich also Cry*, 1979) (Baldwin, 1995). Although subsequent research has demonstrated that the export flow of *telenovelas* has been quite limited in quantitative terms, compared to the dominant flows still coming out of the US (Biltereyst & Meers, 2000), the 1980s was the time when the large scale and ever more internationalised character of the Latin American television industry began to appear on the radar of media and communication scholars in the English-speaking world. Observers began to speak of *telenovelas* as part of a counterflow of television programming that went from South to South, or even South to North in the world, challenging common assumptions about television flow (Rogers & Schement, 1984), and demanding a less Anglocentric view of the world.

This book aims to demonstrate the unique character of television in Latin America and to explain its increasing significance in world. Subsequent chapters examine the history and structure of the television industry as it has developed in the major countries of the region, and show how the popular appeal of its programming has enabled it to achieve a global influence far beyond the geographical contours of Latin America.

CONCLUSION

Latin American television grew over time in a fairly distinct regional pattern. Commercial television dominated public and state systems decades earlier than in most other world regions, due to a combination of US corporate pressure, the desire of national media entrepreneurs to expand from already commercial radio empires, national governments that largely preferred to guide commercial media rather than run government media channels themselves, and advertisers, both national and transnational, who wanted to expand growing consumer societies. Substantial intra-regional flows of people, genres, organisational models, and even *telenovela* scripts led to a distinctive regional set of genres and contents, most famously characterised by the dominance of *telenovelas* within prime time across the region. Starting in the 1970s, an active early regional market for programming developed, one of the first true regional spaces and markets, leading to theorisation in the region about cultural proximity, cultural-linguistic markets, geocultural and geolinguistic spaces, that were then applied to other world regions as well (Sinclair, Jacka, & Cunningham, 1996). Innovative satellite and cable technologies in the 1990s, in conjunction with deregulation and liberalisation of national television systems, ushered in a more globalised era. The new century has seen even further convergence of distribution technologies with transnational flows of contents beyond national and regional borders.

2

The Dominant Markets – Mexico

In Mexico, the development of television has been very much formed by the entrepreneurship and political wiles of three generations of Emilio Azcárragas: first, the commercial broadcasting pioneer from the days of radio; then, 'El Tigre' (The Tiger), the founder of Televisa and ruler of its 'golden age'; and the current Emilio Azcárraga, who has brought Televisa through its financial crisis of the late 1990s and into the new, more competitive and technologically transformative era of this century. Televisa is an institution in Mexico: a quasi-monopolistic, cross-media conglomerate which not only has dominated the Mexican television market for decades, but has been actively pursuing its ambitions in most of the rest of the Spanish-speaking world. It has also commanded great influence in the political culture, even if the personal lives of the Azcárraga dynasty have sometimes provided the public with almost as much intrigue and scandal as one of the company's trademark *telenovelas* (Sinclair, 1999; Paxman & Saragoza, 2001). The three Azcárragas are: Emilio Azcárraga Vidaurreta, as seen in the previous chapter, an active agent in first establishing radio and subsequently television in Mexico, presiding from the 1920s until his death in 1972; his son, Emilio Azcárraga Milmo (1930–97), who then formed Televisa and directed it for over two decades of domestic consolidation and international expansion; and subsequently his son, Emilio Azcárraga Jean (1968–).

Because of its domination of what is the largest domestic television market in the Spanish-speaking world, Televisa has been able to use its pre-eminence in its home market as leverage to enter other markets in the region. It is also advantaged by being permitted to maintain a corporate structure which is both vertically and horizontally integrated: that is, it can distribute its own productions, and can capitalise on synergies between the different media under its umbrella. Its international activities have involved participation in network ownership as well as program export and service provision, not only in Latin America, but also Spain and the United States.

However, in the 1990s, the Mexican government's embrace of privatisation ended Televisa's golden age and its relatively unchallenged domination of its

Heart of the empire: Televisa's production studios on Avenida Chapultepec in Mexico City

domestic market. The government had been operating two networks as public service alternatives to Televisa since the 1970s, but they had proved uncompetitive. In 1993, these networks were put out to tender and sold to an electrical goods retailer who relaunched them as a private network, TV Azteca. TV Azteca has since largely developed itself in imitation of Televisa and in full frontal competition, both domestically and internationally, notably in commencing a network in the US, Azteca America. Yet although TV Azteca was able to attract audiences very quickly, it has not been able to push its audience share much beyond a third of the national market (Informe Annual TV Azteca, 2011). Effectively, television in Mexico is now a duopoly, but with Televisa still dominant. Of more immediate concern for Televisa and TV Azteca alike are the competitive challenges opened up by television's convergence with telecommunications, and their capacity to adapt to an era in which television delivery technologies and their audiences are becoming more diverse, fragmented, and internationalised.

THE FORMATION OF TELEVISA

The fact that radio today has become so much a taken-for-granted, unglamorous medium, incapable of rousing the passions associated with debates about television and new media, can make us underestimate the formative influence which it has had in its time in building up the whole institutional structure upon which television was later to base itself. The previous chapter has shown how true this was in Mexico, and how radio technology became available at a time when both foreign capital and Mexican entrepreneurs were looking for new investment opportunities. Yet significantly, the very first radio station in Mexico was not in Mexico City, but in the industrial capital of the Northeast, Monterrey, a city with a reputation both for its spirit of capitalism and for its receptiveness to US influence (Fernández Christlieb, 1976). Similarly, in the television era, while Azcárraga and O'Farrill were consolidating the market position of Telesistema Mexicana (TSM), they found themselves confronted with competition based in Monterrey. In 1968, a licence was granted to a film producer, Barbachano Ponce, to open a station in Monterrey, Channel 12, which he subsequently built into a network, Telecadena Mexicana, in the north and central regions. That same year, the powerful industrial group Alfa, owned by the Garza Sada family of Monterrey, was given a licence to open Channel 8 – but in Mexico City. Their company Televisión Independiente de México (TIM) had been operating in Monterrey since 1960, but the move to Mexico City threw down a direct competitive challenge to TSM. Also in Mexico City, a radio entrepreneur, Francisco Aguirre, had been granted a licence to open Channel 13 (de Noriega & Leach, 1979).

By this time, the political climate had changed from the days when, as was seen in the case of Miguel Alemán, a president could grant a company a television licence in a virtually unregulated environment, and then move on to join it as a partner at the end of his term. The first comprehensive broadcasting regulatory regime was not established until the presidency of Lópes Mateos (President 1958–64), while his successor Díaz Ordaz (President 1964–70) sought to tax all the television licensees, who were enjoying the use of the microwave network and satellite station which the government had built to broadcast the 1968 Olympic Games held in Mexico City (de Noriega & Leach, 1979). However, the licensees united behind TSM in resisting this proposal, and offered a compromise under which they offered to provide broadcasting time to the government for its own use, instead of the tax, to be known as 'fiscal time'. The government accepted this, foregoing the revenue, but never actually taking full advantage of the 12.5 per cent of transmission time thus 'ceded' to them (Granados Chapa, 1976).

The 'Mexican standoff' is a contemporary cliché, but it does give some sense of the fraught relations between the government and the television industry in the 1960s and early 1970s, particularly in the case of Luis Echeverría (President 1970–6), who was determined to secure a place for the state in television broadcasting, and to reform the industry more broadly. This was in the spirit of developing national communication policies in the era of UNESCO's New World Information and Communication Order, referred to in the previous chapter. In 1972, Echeverría's government established its own specially-targeted rural network (de Noriega and Leach, 1979), bought the bankrupted Channel 13 from Aguirre, and began operating it under a state agency (Mahan, 1985). This was profoundly confronting for all of the television networks, faced as they were with the implicit threat of more regulation and the intervention of the state in a hitherto totally private market, one in which they would now have to deal with a public broadcasting competitor. The defensive reaction of TSM and TIM was an historic step: the formation of Televisa, a merger of both networks' operations under the umbrella of a new company. Originally an acronym for Televisión vía Satélite, Televisa thus brought together the initial three licensed companies which had merged in 1955, TSM, plus the former competing network from Monterrey, TIM (de Noriega and Leach, 1979).

The formation of Televisa was not only a consolidation of the main players within the television industry as such, but of the national bourgeoisie as a social class, bringing as it did the Grupo Monterrey into alliance with the other powerful industrial groups that were behind TSM: the Grupo Alemán, and O'Farrill's Grupo Puebla (Bernal Sahagún, 1978). In terms of the politics of television and the state in Mexico, it demonstrates 'the relative autonomy of the industry in the face of state initiatives to control it' (Mahan, 1985, p. 62). It is often assumed by commentators that the Mexican state has always facilitated (Rogers & Antola, 1985; Paxman & Saragoza, 2001) or even lurked behind (Valenzuela, 1986) the monopolistic expansion of private television interests. However, this demonstrably is not the case in this instance, nor even with the previous milder presidential reforms. The industrial groups and the state were each acting in accordance with their own respective logic and interests, and this was a cause of conflict. However, in the creation of Televisa, we see that the intervention of the state had a formative and enduring effect in shaping the structure of the industry, but in an unintended and quite counterproductive manner.

Nevertheless, once Televisa was formed, the more general framework in which relations between the state and the private television owners were conducted was one of mutual support and ideological consensus for decades to follow. Throughout most of the history of commercial broadcasting in Mexico, at least from the 1930s until 2000, Mexico was ruled by the same party, the Partido Revolucionario Institucional (PRI). As self-declared supporters of the PRI, Televisa's owners and managers had no qualms in keeping its news and current affairs programs in the government's favour (Fox, 1997). As noted, Televisa's glory days in the 1970s and 1980s were largely attributable to a horizontally and vertically integrated business model, which went unchallenged by government regulation. Further, from 1972 until 1993, Televisa faced only nominal competition in the domestic market, and this came from the state-owned commercial network, Channel 13. Even though Barbachano Ponce's Telecadena Mexicana, upon its collapse in 1975, was acquired by the state and integrated with its network, Televisa's dominance of audiences and advertising revenues was never under threat. Rather, a kind of implicit division of labour developed between Televisa and the state network, such that the state's efforts seemed to complement and legitimise Televisa's operations, and so shore up its quasi-monopoly.

Miguel Alemán Velasco, one of the triumvirate who directed Televisa in these halcyon years and, not coincidentally, son of the president who had granted the first television licences, praised 'the Mexican formula' in precisely this sense. In other words, attempts at state intervention had tended to reinforce the hegemony of the private interests, rather than break it down (Sinclair, 1986).

TELEVISA'S GOLDEN AGE

With the merging of TSM and TIM, Televisa could look forward to a golden age: perhaps not a *siglo de oro*, but a good twenty years. However, the founding father of the dynasty, Emilio Azcárraga Vidaurreta, never lived to see the formation of Televisa, having died in September 1972. The agreement to form Televisa was made in the following December, with formal operation under that name beginning early in 1973. The older Azcárraga's death had hastened the merger, and created the opportunity for Emilio Azcárraga Milmo to assume the position of the company's first president, ruling in conjunction with the younger Alemán and O'Farrill, sons of the founding fathers of TSM in the 1950s. This entrenched an oligarchic as well as a patriarchal character to its management, although undoubtedly Azcárraga Milmo was the dominant force, particularly after he acquired the 25 per cent share of the Garza Sada family who sold out in 1982 (Mahan, 1985; Sánchez Ruiz, 1991).

Even further than their fathers had done with TSM, Televisa's directors segmented the national market by differentiating programming, territorial coverage, and demographic appeal on its range of channels. Channel 2 was the mass market, national network with family programming, such as variety shows and the latest *telenovelas*; more downmarket films, *telenovelas* and sport ran on Channel 4; Channel 5 offered viewing for young audiences, such as imported series; while relatively more upmarket films and series were found on Channel 8. Significantly, Televisa produced most of its own programming, around 60 per cent at first, rising to more like 80 per cent towards the end of the 1970s, by which time its channels had captured 93 per cent of the audience, and a comparable proportion of advertising revenue, leaving little for the state channels which also needed advertising for their support. From the advertisers' point of view, Televisa had evolved into 'the most attractive package of saturation coverage ever put together in the history of Mexican television' (de Noriega and Leach, 1979, p. 53).

Some of the most popular programming of this era could all be found on the same channel, the national Channel 2, branded as the 'Channel of the Stars', and included *telenovelas* such as *Los ricos también lloran* (*The Rich also Cry*, 1979) and *El derecho de nacer* (*The Right to be Born*, 1981), that indeed helped Televisa to develop its own star system, in both these cases the star being

Televisa's legacy to children's television: the comic anti-superhero *El Chapulin Colorado* (*The Red Grasshopper*)

Veronica Castro. In variety programming, there was *Siempre en Domingo* (*Always on Sunday*) a family fixture which ran from 1969 until 1998, hosted by Raúl Velasco (no relation to Televisa partner Alemán Velasco), while *El Chapulín Colorado* (*The Red Grasshopper*) stands out in the children's category. This super-hero parody, identified with comedian Chespirito, ran initially from 1972 until 1981, but has been successively re-run, not only in Mexico but elsewhere in Latin America, Spain, and in the US. The character's costume is in demand at Halloween both in Mexico and the US, and can be recognised more globally, since Bumblebee Man, one of the recurrent characters in *The Simpsons*, in a nod to the influence of Mexican television, is based on el Chapulín Colorado.

Given the absence of a private commercial competitor, and under a favourable regulatory regime, Televisa was able to consolidate its strength in the national market by the vertical integration of production and distribution. A whole production infrastructure was put in place, not just studio facilities, but auxiliary activities such as talent schools. Televisa also ran a dubbing operation for imported programming, a longtime speciality of TSM. As well as enjoying full national coverage for its broadcast signal, distribution was augmented with cable. There was horizontal as well as vertical integration: in particular, Azcárraga's radio networks and record labels were brought under the Televisa corporate umbrella with the merger, while the O'Farrill family's interests in magazines and their daily newspaper *Novedades* also facilitated cross-promotion and ever more intensive commercialisation of the diverse media interests of the Televisa partners. This form of integration meant ready access to publicity for television celebrities and programmes in the press, cross-promotion of recorded music on television shows, and so on. During the boom years, a film production division, Televicine, was added in 1978, while in 1985, Videovisa commenced, a unit for the production and distribution of video hardware and software (Sánchez Ruiz, 1991). As to the recording of *telenovelas* for export, this had begun long before, under TSM in the 1960s, almost as soon as videotape had been invented, although actual distribution was limited until the satellite era.

True to the initial conception of 'Televisión vía Satélite', Televisa was one of the first media corporations in the world to see the strategic advantages of satellites for the distribution of programmes to distant and dispersed audiences outside its borders, particularly those which shared linguistic and cultural similarities with the nation of origin. Much of the technological development which was undertaken in these years had to do with Televisa's ambitions to extend its distribution to targeted audiences on an international scale. Notably, Televisa's sales division, Protele, used satellite distribution to facilitate its role of selling programme rights and physically distributing programmes on an international basis through its foreign offices. As early as 1976, Televisa commenced a venture it called Univisión, a weekly satellite feed of its domestic programming to a US border station for subsequent relay to stations that it owned in the US. Even Spain was not too far by satellite: in 1977, Televisa established an office in Madrid, and began occasional satellite transmissions there (de Noriega and Leach, 1979; Sánchez Ruiz, 1991).

Thus, the use of satellite transmission played a strategic part in the development of Televisa's operations in the US and other international initiatives, including Spain. Yet an even more ambitious and consequential step made by Televisa into satellite broadcasting was taken on the domestic front, in response to a further instance of confrontation with the state in Mexico. This was in 1982, when the new President, Miguel de la Madrid (President 1982–8), promulgated a constitutional change which reserved all powers over satellite development to the state, so pre-empting any move which Televisa might have wanted to make into domestic satellite development in Mexico. The Mexican government forged ahead, engaging the US satellite corporation Hughes International Communications to build and subsequently launch its domestic satellite system, known as Sistema Morelos, but in 1984 Televisa went beyond the government's jurisdiction. Acting through its associates within the US, Televisa applied to establish an international satellite system to be based there, and capable of reaching not only North and South America, but also Europe (Fernández Christlieb, 1985; Valenzuela, 1986; Sánchez Ruiz, 1991). Within a few years this was successfully established as PanAmSat.

Once again, the notion that Televisa has always enjoyed favourable treatment from government is not borne out by close attention to its actual history. Furthermore, just as Televisa's loyalty to the PRI was not able to protect it from de la Madrid's albeit unsuccessful attempt to bring all satellite development under government control, on another front the state was continuing to develop its own national television network, however weak that might have been in competition with Televisa. Notably, the reach of the state's network was augmented in 1985 by converting most of the former state rural service into a second network, Channel 7, combined under a new entity, Imevisión (Sánchez Ruiz, 1991). Indeed, the two Imevisión networks, Channels 13 and 7, were to last until the 1990s, when, in accordance with the global ideology of privatisation prevailing at the time, the regime of Carlos Salinas de Gortari (President 1988–94), put the Imevisión channels up for sale to private owners (Mejía Barquera, 1995). As noted, this opened up a totally new competitive situation, to be examined further below.

As its manoeuvres around satellite development would indicate, Televisa was looking to shore up and integrate its international activities around this time. These developments were closely linked to Televisa's strategic moves in the US over 1986 and 1987, led by Azcárraga himself, which are discussed further in Chapter Five. In terms of providing programming for external markets, Televisa mobilised its US satellite-to-cable subsidiary, Galavisión, as the base for the transmission of an international service of the same name. The programming mainly came from Televisa's popular Channel 2 schedule in Mexico, though this was combined with an international news service that Televisa had established, ECO (Empresa de Comunicaciones Orbitales), also based in the US. However, in the US market, Televisa was seen to lack credibility in the area of news, precisely because of the close relationship that it had to the ruling party in Mexico. The political benefits of the relationship had served Televisa well in the domestic market, and so had been more important to Televisa than its legitimacy as a news source, but it started to become a problem in the second half of the 1980s, not only in its international aspirations, but even within Mexico itself. This was because popular support was beginning to grow for the major opposition party, the conservative PAN (Partido Acción Nacional), but Televisa's partisanship for the PRI was without restraint. Televisa assisted the PRI in a notorious cover-up of an electoral fraud in 1986 in a state election in Chihuahua, by ignoring the story entirely. Similarly, Televisa was shameless in its support for the PRI candidate, Carlos Salinas de Gortari, in its coverage of the 1988 presidential election campaign. Azcárraga even declared himself publicly to be a 'soldier of the PRI' while Alemán later departed to become a PRI Senator (Zellner, 1989). The national news and current affairs programme nightly on Canal 2 was *24 Horas*. Running from 1971 until 1998, its agenda was tightly controlled over these decades by another PRI loyalist, the anchorman Jacobo Zabludovsky. So, although ECO was officially launched in 1988, with transmission to Europe (notably Spain) and parts of Africa as well as North and South America, the contradiction of mounting an international news service which compromised its credibility by allegiance to its home government was never resolved. ECO was eventually closed down in 2001 without ever having turned a profit.

The beginning of the end of Televisa's golden age, as characterised by a virtual monopoly of its domestic market, and presided over by the patriarchs of three oligarchic families, was becoming apparent as the 1980s drew to a close. The costs of international expansion were taking a toll on Televisa, giving it a large debt to service, and substantial losses to bear in both 1988 and 1989. However, there had been a crisis developing within the management group at least since 1986, when Televisa had been obliged to divest itself of its national network of stations in the US. This had meant a significant change in corporate fortunes, and appears to have brought to a head a struggle for power between the family-based factions, resulting in a restructuring of holdings in 1991. Azcárraga and his family greatly increased their share in Televisa under the new arrangements, and also moved to take over the cable, video, radio, and dubbing divisions. As noted, Alemán left to join the Senate, but a son remaining within the administrative council was given the family's significant share, while O'Farrill entirely relinquished his 24 per cent interest ('Big Shuffle', 1991; Sánchez Ruiz, 1991).

One can only speculate as to the machinations which took place within the former triumvirate, but it appears that the consolidation of Televisa's control under the Azcárraga family was in preparation for a public float which was subsequently made on both the Mexican and New York stock exchanges in 1992. Perhaps Alemán and O'Farrill were not interested in adjusting to an era of public ownership, while Azcárraga had decided that going public was the only way he could raise the capital needed both to meet current debt and to fund his further ambitions for international expansion. Indeed, it soon became apparent that apart from dealing with the immediate liquidity crisis, Azcárraga was eager to finance a return to the strategic position in the US market that he had been forced to vacate in 1986, as well as to establish holdings in certain South American markets. It is worth recalling that these moves were taking place against the background of the then imminent signing of NAFTA (North American Free Trade Agreement). While unsuccessful in lobbying to have the

Emilio Azcárraga Milmo
(1930–97), master strategist
of Televisa's golden age,
known as *El Tigre* (The Tiger)

US broadcasting foreign ownership provisions modified in his favour (Fisher, 1992), Azcárraga was able to enter a partnership with a US majority owner and a Venezuelan network, Venevisión, to regain some direct control over the major Spanish-language television network in the US from which he had been disinvested, by then known as Univisión. This whole history of Televisa's strategic interest in the US, its prime international market, will be returned to in Chapter Five.

The public float did put Televisa in a strong cash position, not only to buy back into the US, but to make several new investments throughout 1992 and 1993. In July 1992, the same month as Televisa's return to its former US network was announced, also came the news that it had acquired 76 per cent of Compañía Peruana de Radiodifusión, Peru's second-ranked network, for around US$ 7 million ('Televisa anunció', 1992). Televisa had already bought 49 per cent of Chile's first private channel, Megavisión, at the end of 1991, for a similar amount, and entered an arrangement covering technical and commercial advice, programme supply, and co-production ('Televisa compro', 1991). Selective direct investments in other Latin American countries was something quite new for Televisa, evidently a tactic to strengthen links to its programming markets. Also in the Southern Cone in 1991, the state-owned ATC (Argentina Televisora Color), signed an agreement to take Televisa programmes, while in 1992, Televisa announced a non-competitive programme distribution and licensing agreement with Venevisión, also its Latin American partner in the US network (Morgan Stanley, 1992). Yet the most significant direct investment of 1993 was when Televisa paid US$ 200 million for a non-controlling 50 per cent share in PanAmSat, the international satellite venture it had initiated in the

1980s, but later had to withdraw from, as will be detailed further below. There were also some strategic alliances with international media corporations announced, notably an agreement to produce and distribute a Latin American version of the Discovery cable channel, and a program production and distribution arrangement with News Limited (Mejía Barquera, 1995).

FINANCIAL AND MANAGEMENT CRISIS

However, all this internationalisation of television services coincided with an economic reversal in Televisa's core business, the domestic market, which would leave both greatly weakened. Whereas the quincentennial year of 1992 marked a high point in Televisa's ability to fund international expansion, just five years later the company was in crisis. By 1997, Televisa was selling down prime assets to meet debts of almost a billion US dollars; its management had unravelled; it was facing serious private competition in its domestic market for the first time, and it was losing out to its foreign-based partners in its international ventures.

The financial crisis came at the end of 1994 when the Mexican Government devalued the peso, and then allowed it to float. This coincided with a spike in inflation. For all its international ambitions, Televisa's fortunes were still tied to its market dominance within a dependent nation, so both devaluation and inflation had drastic effects for Televisa, as for other Mexican companies. Apart from the drop in book value (Puig, 1997c), the devaluation plunged Televisa deeply into debt, at the same time curtailing its ability to generate income. Largely because of its international activities, Televisa had considerable operating costs and expenses in US dollars, but insufficient US dollar-denominated sales, and therefore had to earn that much more in pesos to meet its US dollar commitments. Domestic earnings were suffering from the so-called 'tequila effect', the adverse impact of government austerity measures on the domestic consumer market, and hence advertising revenues. Traditionally, most of Televisa's advertising revenues have been obtained under the 'French Plan', an up-front arrangement under which advertisers pay a year in advance at an agreed rate, with an option to acquire more time at the same preferential rate later. Obviously, such a system has been most advantageous to Televisa's financial planning and liquidity, giving it control over its income, and yielding around 80 per cent of annual broadcast revenues (Televisa, 2011). However, the crisis put Televisa in the position of trying to squeeze more income from diminished sources, testing the loyalty of its advertisers with steep increases each year (Grupo Televisa, 1997). This tactic was not sustainable in the more competitive environment which had been created by this time, as will be explained below.

Televisa had incurred large debts in the US and Spain, as well as Mexico, prior to the devaluation. In order to meet and service the costs on them, Televisa began to sell down its stake in some of its strategic assets. First, in 1995, was the sale of all of its interest in the Peruvian station it had acquired in 1992. The sale of 49 per cent of its cable division, Cablevisión, came next, made to América Móvil, owned by Carlos Slim Helú (Grupo Televisa, 1997). Then, towards the end of 1995, PanAmSat was converted from a limited partnership to a public company, thus diluting Televisa's former half-share to 40.5 per cent. Another significant international sell-down took place in 1996, when Televisa's former 25 per cent interest in the US Univisión network and 12 per cent interest in the corresponding station group were reduced in total to a less than 20 per cent interest in the restructured whole (Grupo Televisa, 1997). In brief, within two years of the 1994 devaluation, Televisa had given up most of what it had gained in the 1992–3 wave of expansion. The Peruvian channel was not a great sacrifice, but the dilution of its participation in Univisión meant that Televisa's toehold in the key US Spanish-language television market, which it had regained only in 1992, was once again weakened, even if a significant programme supply agreement was not affected. The reduction in its stake in Cablevisión diminished Televisa's position in the domestic cable market, vis-à-vis its competitor at the time, Multivisión.

While the PanAmSat restructure of 1995 was the least of Televisa's problems, there was more to come. In September 1996, PanAmSat merged with Hughes Electronics Corporation, the US-based satellite division of General Motors. This meant that, in effect, Hughes acquired most of Televisa's interest in the restructured and publicly-traded company that resulted, the 'New PanAmSat' (Grupo Televisa, 1997). Televisa applied most of the payout from Hughes to its debt of US$ 988 million, retaining a 7.5 per cent interest in the restructured PanAmSat, with the rights to acquire more equity in its DTH (Direct to Home) satellite television operation, Sky. Televisa explained the sell-down of its participation in PanAmSat thus: 'the fundamental business of the company has always been the production of programming, and it doesn't necessarily need to be the owner of program distribution companies' (As cited in Cardoso, 1997). This patently false gloss was trying to make a virtue out of necessity. Certainly, programme production for the domestic market has always been Televisa's stock-in-trade but, as this account has argued, production has been augmented significantly by its vertical integration with distribution systems. These have been principally its own networks in Mexico, but also, if unevenly, Univisión and its predecessor companies in the US, and PanAmSat at the intercontinental level.

Within Televisa itself, there was once again a management crisis. This time it was a problem of succession, following the retirement of Emilio Azcárraga Milmo as President of Televisa on 3 March 1997, and his subsequent death from cancer on 16 April. Since the 1991 restructure, Azcárraga had been able

Emilio Azcárraga Jean, who emerged as President of Televisa in 1997 after a boardroom struggle for succession, seen here under Televisa's logo

to consolidate all power and decision over Televisa within his own person. The feudal style of management which this encouraged, and which had earned him the nickname of 'The Tiger', left a vacuum on his death. On his retirement, he did name his son, Emilio Azcárraga Jean, to succeed him as President, but, at the same time, Guillermo Cañedo White became the Chairman of the Board. Cañedo White's father had been a significant Vice-President of Televisa, and instrumental in twice bringing the soccer World Cup to Mexico, and thus to Televisa. Furthermore, Miguel Alemán Velasco (son of the former Mexican President and Board member), who had left Televisa in 1991 to become a PRI Senator, now returned to Televisa and assumed a Vice-President's position on the Board. Generational change was in process here too, for his son was also on the Board (Puig, 1997a). The ensuing boardroom struggle was like a *telenovela* plot, the London *Financial Times* said ('FT: la batalla', 1997). For Televisa, this was no joke: regaining the confidence of the Mexican and New York stock exchanges in its management was essential to securing the capital that it needed to deal with its ongoing crises. Emilio Azcárraga Jean did emerge as the new President, and assert his authority as such, but clearly, rivalries within the organisation meant that it was not a foregone conclusion (Fernández & Paxman, 2000).

ADIOS MONOPOLY, HOLA DUOPOLY

As this chapter has explained, Mexican television has been run as a virtual monopoly for most of its existence. It was seen how the original licensees first merged to form Telesistema Mexicano in 1955, and then, when faced with the threat of government intervention in the industry, merged with a competitor to create Televisa in 1972. For the next two decades, Televisa flourished in an uncompetitive environment, effectively protected by the Mexican Government's merely spasmodic political will to assert regulatory control, and the lacklustre performance of Imevisión, the state television enterprise. All this changed drastically in 1993, when the government of Carlos Salinas de Gortari (President 1988–94), imbued with the policies of market liberalisation and privatisation which characterised the era, called for tenders to take over the two Imevisión networks, Channels 7 and 13, along with production studios and a cinema chain. The tender went to Ricardo Salinas Pliego and his partners in the Saba family, who relaunched the networks as TV Azteca, thus challenging Televisa with a commercial competitor for the first time ever (Prieto Bayona, 2011).

Like Televisa, TV Azteca is a Mexican company with an international orientation. Salinas Pliego (unrelated to Salinas de Gortari) is from the Salinas y Rocha family of retail store owners, and TV Azteca became an integral part of the development of the hundreds of electrical stores he owns throughout Mexico and Central America ('Azteca into El Salvador', 1997). Audiences found the new commercial channels refreshing. Before the government sold the former Imevisión, it was attracting only around two per cent of the ratings (Moffett & Roberts, 1992), whereas the new TV Azteca had about 14 per cent of the audience by 1995, rising to 22 per cent in 1996. By the end of that year, it was claiming 37 per cent of the prime-time audience, and 23 per cent of television advertising revenue ('Avanza TV Azteca', 1997). The initial audience and corresponding advertisers' interest in TV Azteca can be compared to the popular support gathered over the same decade for the PAN, the conservative opposition to the formerly unassailable PRI. In both cases, the attraction of the competition was not so much because it was better or even different, but just a change. However, TV Azteca has not been able to make much more of an impact on audience share ever since its honeymoon years: in prime time for all of 2008–10, it was struggling ever to gain more than 40 per cent (Informe Annual TV Azteca, 2011).

Initially, TV Azteca's competitive strategy was to offer a range of imported programming (Mejía Barquera, 1995), including some of the same programmes which aided the rise of the Fox network in the US, namely *Los Simpson* (*The Simpsons*), and *La niñera* (*The Nanny*) (Godard, 1997). In the first few years, TV Azteca also enjoyed the benefit of the programme content, technology, and prestige of a formal relationship with NBC, the major US network (Ramón Huerta, 1997). It continues to import programmes from US sources, which makes up about 35 per cent of its prime time schedule. However, we shall see that TV Azteca has followed Televisa in several respects, including the integration of its channels of distribution with the production of its own content, so 65 per cent of prime time programming is composed of TV Azteca's own news, sport, *telenovelas*, talk, music and reality shows (Informe Anual TV Azteca, 2011). TV

Azteca has invested heavily in production facilities, and although actual production is carried out by independent companies and freelancers on a co-production and advertising income-sharing basis, TV Azteca's quantity of output is now said to be second only to Televisa in the Spanish-speaking world (Prieto Bayona, 2011).

As one TV Azteca executive declared: 'We are doing what Televisa is doing – they are a terrific model' (As cited in Sutter, 1996). In addition to increasing production for the home market and for export, they have acquired stations in Central and South America, not to mention launching Azteca America in the US in 2001, in competition with Univisión. Like Televisa, TV Azteca has its own soccer team (to gain access to football transmission rights), a talent school, a recorded music division, an internet portal, and its own philanthropic foundation. Against Televisa's four networks, TV Azteca has two: Azteca 13 which competes with Televisa's flagship general channel, Channel 2; while Azteca 7 targets Televisa's Channel 5 audience with imported, mainly US, series and sports. Azteca also supplies programming to Channel 40, a more up-market channel available only in Mexico City, and has an international cable channel devoted exclusively to *telenovelas* (Prieto Bayona, 2011).

As for access to advertising revenue, which continues to be the principal source of income for both corporations, TV Azteca has its Azteca Plan and Mexico Plan, both schemes for advertisers to purchase advertising time in advance, modelled on Televisa's longstanding French Plan, but with more flexible rules on credit and better rates, which Televisa has had to match (Ramón Huerta, 1997). Azteca derives almost 90 per cent of its income from its sales of advertising (Informe Annual TV Azteca, 2011), but Televisa has become much less dependent on broadcast advertising revenue as it has increased its activities in cable and convergent delivery technologies over the last decade, as will be detailed below (Televisa, 2011). Nevertheless, it is Televisa which obtains the lion's share of what advertisers spend on broadcast television advertising. According to a 2006 investigation by the Mexican competition watchdog, the Comisión Federal de Competencia (COFECO), Televisa had 71.2 per cent of that market, and TV Azteca 28.2 (as cited in González Amador, 2006). It will be apparent that these figures correspond roughly to their relative share of the total audience.

The several global advertising agency groups active in Mexico buy up time at the annual upfront events on behalf of their advertiser clients. Such buying time in advance, on either Televisa's or TV Azteca's plans, tends to favour larger advertisers. Mexico is the region's second largest advertising market after Brazil and, in both cases, television attracts around 60 per cent of total advertising expenditure. The largest advertisers are the global marketers of 'fast-moving consumer goods' (FMCG) such as Procter & Gamble with its hundreds of brands of packaged goods for personal care and the household, but there are some substantial Mexican advertisers as well, notably Carlos Slim's group of companies. It is worth noting that Televisa and TV Azteca are themselves leading advertisers, advertising having become such a weapon in the competition between them (Sinclair, 2012b).

As will be explored in the next section, new technologies of distribution are beginning to have their impact on how television is viewed and by whom, but for the immediate future, mass market, free-to-air, terrestrially broadcast analogue television remains the ground on which TV Azteca is challenging Televisa. Although it does have significant telecommunication interests, TV Azteca has not been able to diversify into the new television distribution technologies (Prieto Bayona, 2011). This has meant that programming has become the basis on which competition in television is conducted, and quality, understood in the broad sense, has become an issue. For all the wealth which Televisa's productions have generated both at home and abroad in the past, this success has been on the basis of quantity rather than quality, that is, programmes with wide popular appeal. Televisa's prodigious output is legendary, but its production-line approach in the earlier years, in which, for example, actors merely repeated the lines fed to them over an earpiece, did nothing for its reputation as a producer of distinction. Nor did the heavy-handed control Televisa exerted over its talent in developing its star system (Paxman, 2003). The interior-only studio shooting, cheap sets and flat lighting of their *telenovelas* have often been compared unfavourably by aficionados to the trademark quality look of Brazilian ones in particular, but Televisa has been unapologetic on these scores. Many of the obituaries which appeared upon Azcárraga Milmo's death recalled this frank comment from a 1992 press conference:

> Mexico is the country of a modest, very wretched class, which isn't ever going to stop getting screwed over. There is an obligation for television to bring diversion to these people and take them out of their sad reality and difficult future. (As cited in Puig, 1997c, p. 15)

Correspondingly, in taking over control from his late father, the young Azcárraga Jean made even more explicit Televisa's philosophy of programming appropriate for such a target audience:

> This is a business. The fundamental thing, the face of this company, is the production of entertainment, then information. To educate is the government's job, not Televisa's. (As cited in Puig, 1997b, p. 30)

Logo of TV Azteca, challenger since 1993 to Televisa's hitherto virtual monopoly of Mexican television, but still distant rival

This comment is manifestly a rationalisation for the low intellectual and production values of Televisa's characteristic output, primarily the *telenovelas* which dominate the company's production and programme schedules, but it also alludes to the lack of credibility which has always dogged Televisa as a news and information source. This has been the price Televisa has always been prepared to pay for the close relations it has usually enjoyed with the PRI and the state, as discussed earlier in this chapter, and also of its willingness to commercialise the content of its information programmes (Zepeda Patterson, 1997). So long as Televisa was a virtual monopoly, audiences had no means of expressing their dissatisfaction with Televisa programmes, and Televisa could claim to be giving the people what they wanted. With the arrival of TV Azteca, their offer of news and current affairs programmes such as *Hechos* (*Facts*, 1994) and *Ciudad Desnuda* (*Naked City*, 1996), albeit with a popular 'vivid controversial tone' enabled the new competitor to draw audiences away from Televisa channels (Prieto Bayona, 2011). Similarly, TV Azteca was able to challenge Televisa's hegemony in *telenovelas* with an initial two offerings that garnered much critical success for having a political and social relevance that was welcomed as edgy and refreshing, and for their superior production values. These were *Nada personal* (*Nothing Personal*, 1996), and *Mirada de mujer* (*Gaze of a Woman*, 1997), both produced by an independent production company, Argos Comunicación. Although these and others were not necessarily commercially successful, they did have the effect of pushing Televisa towards more contemporary social themes in their own *telenovelas* (Paxman, 2003).

In terms of 'quality programming' as it is more conventionally understood, it is worth noting at this point that there is still a state-subsidised, public broadcasting sector consisting of two channels: the longstanding Canal Once (Channel 11), dating from 1958, and, from 1993, Canal 22. Although the state evacuated the ground of mass market television with the sale of the 7 and 13 networks to TV Azteca, it retains a commitment to the provision of cultural programming.

Indeed, the state continues to assert a role for itself in the television industry of Mexico, albeit at the margins. In 2011, Channel 11 was relaunched as Once TV, with a budget aimed to increase its national coverage and stimulate 'diverse and solid' content production (Young, 2011). For its part, Canal 22, under the auspices of the SEP (Secretariat of Public Education) and CONACULTA (National Council for Culture and the Arts) provides educational and cultural programming distributed by several means: free-to-air, basic cable and DTH in Mexico; and via international satellite to the US (CONACULTA, 2011).

CONVERGENT DISTRIBUTION

Although Televisa faces no domestic threat from TV Azteca in the realm of the new television distribution technologies, there are other quite serious competitors to be dealt with. Whereas the revenue model for free-to-air relies on presenting programmes that can attract large audiences for which advertisers pay to gain access, non-broadcast technologies operate on a subscription model, 'pay-TV', in which subscribers pay to be connected to services largely of their choice, which may or may not also carry advertising. Furthermore, because of the convergence of television distribution with telecommunications in the digital era, and the privatisation and internationalisation of such services, the relatively small, but growing and lucrative, market in convergent modes of television distribution is quite intensely competitive. A particularly powerful driver of new corporate alliances and entries to the field of television distribution is the advent of the marketing strategy of 'triple-play', the bundling of telephony with internet connection and cable television services.

Cable is the oldest non-broadcast, pay-TV technology, with a prehistory in Mexico dating back to 1954, but government regulation prevented the offer of commercial services until the 1970s. There are hundreds of cable companies in Mexico, but the largest are Megacable, Cablemás and Cablevisión. Megacable has its strength historically in the states of the Pacific coast, but has long since achieved nation-wide coverage. As of the end of 2010, Megacable had almost 1,800,000 television subscribers, but was also strenuously expanding the triple-play of telecommunication services it had begun in 2006. That same year, the Mexican shareholders had bought out the large minority share formerly held by the US RCN corporation (Megacable, 2010). Cablemás, the second-largest provider, with less than a million subscribers (Company Profile for Grupo Televisa SAB, 2011), began in Tijuana in 1968, and was developed to national reach by the Álvarez family, but in 2007, Televisa acquired a 49 per cent stake ('Mexico media regulator', 2007). This considerably strengthened Televisa's interests in the cable field, as it was already the majority owner of Cablevisión, Mexico's third-largest and oldest cable service, which had begun under TSM in

1966. Cablevisión, however, is restricted in its coverage to Mexico City and sur-
rounds, where it had over 630,000 subscribers as of 2009. Cablevisión offers a
range of digital video services, bundled along with internet and telephony
(Company Profile for Grupo Televisa SAB, 2011). Televisa also has a stake in
another cable company, TVI. As of mid-2011, Televisa was claiming over two
million video subscribers (Televisa, 2011).

Looking beyond cable as such, Televisa's main rival in the pay-TV field in
Mexico historically has been MVS Multivisión. In 1989, Joaquín Vargas Gómez,
another of Mexico's veteran broadcasting entrepreneurs (at one time manager
of TIM, a corporate ancestor of Televisa) launched Multivisión as a subscription
service delivered by both MMDS (Multipoint Multichannel Distribution
Service) and cable, and distributed by satellite. MMDS technology has lower
channel capacity, but also has lower installation costs in a field in which costs to
subscribers is the major barrier to expanding the market. Digital MMDS can
also provide high-speed internet access (Budde, 2006). By 1993, Multivisión
claimed to have overtaken Cablevisión in Mexico City. Furthermore, it had
begun to make direct investments in Latin American cable providers, and to
establish arrangements with US programme suppliers to package their programmes for the whole Latin American market, notably with their film channel,
Cinecanal (Mejía Barquera, 1995). In 2002, Multivisión launched a new venture, MASTV, a special low-cost pay-TV service available in 11 cities across
Mexico, with 570,000 subscribers as of 2008 (EchoStar, 2008).

Although continuing to compete with their cable services, both Televisa and
Multivisión have been more recently looking towards the satellite distribu-
tion/delivery technology of DTH, a field in which the Mexican services have
been establishing strategic alliances with major US-based and continental Latin
American companies. While not representing so great a qualitative leap as either
the advent of radio or television, with DTH there has been a similar pattern in
which the new technology is developed outside the country and then introduced
by local entrepreneurs. However, unlike the introduction of those previous technologies, DTH has lent itself to a complex history of joint ventures which have
cut across national, regional and global levels of finance, management and programming. While DTH satellite television transmission can be seen as just a new
mode of distribution similar in concept to other kinds of pay-TV systems, certain qualitative differences have been capitalised upon by the largely US-based
satellite and programming interests which have been promoting the medium in
Latin America and the rest of the world. In particular, digital decompression
technology permits many more channels to be carried than has been the case in
the past, a 'multi-channel environment'. Obviously, this allows for a greater variety of channels dedicated to certain kinds of programme, whether films, sport,

news, music or special interest, to be offered but, significantly, allows the same channel to be transmitted in more than one language. Thus, there is less of a technical impediment against the use of programmes produced in languages other than those in which they are transmitted, making the spread of DTH attractive not only to the US-based satellite industry, but also the major global programme suppliers. Another implication is that the natural language barrier which traditionally has protected Televisa against foreign competition in programming has been breached, at least in pay-TV.

Cablevisión and Multivisión have been the vehicles through which Televisa and the Vargas family (the founding patriarch died in 2009) have entered into global associations. The development of DTH in Mexico has been very much under the auspices of these two companies: however, it will become evident that their international links have been unstable, very much at the mercy of the shifting corporate strategies of their external partners, and the regulations to which they are subject in the US in particular. In November 1995, Rupert Murdoch announced that News Corporation, which already had a programme exchange agreement with Televisa, would lead a pan-regional DTH consortium. This was to include not only Grupo Televisa, but also its counterpart Organizações Globo in Brazil, and another US-based company, TCI. News, Televisa and Globo were to have 30 per cent each, and TCI the remainder. Televisa had previously been planning such a regional service in conjunction with PanAmSat, while News had already envisaged a similar venture in partnership with Globo, so apart from the hemispheric scale and the cross-cultural links that it brought into being, this initiative was remarkable for its decision in favour of global-regional corporate collaboration rather than competition (Francis and Fernandez, 1997). It also made it apparent that News Corporation recognised the strength of Televisa and Globo in their national markets and the region.

Whatever opportunities Televisa saw in the deal for its further internationalisation, it would have been motivated at the level of the domestic market by the fact that, previously that year, Multivisión had announced it would join a similar pan-regional project led by the US satellite manufacturer Hughes, and incorporating TV Abril in Brazil (TV Globo's main cable competitor), and Grupo Cisneros of Venezuela ('Country Profile: Mexico', 1996). Multivisión was to have 10 per cent of the venture, as would TV Abril in Brazil, while Grupo Cisneros would hold 20 per cent, and Hughes the controlling 60 per cent. By the end of 1996, Multivisión was signed up with this project, known in the region as Galaxy, and was set to launch the service in Mexico, which was to be known there as DirecTV, the same name as Hughes's DTH service in the US. It would be carried by one of Hughes's own satellites from the US. Of its 13 exclusive channels, nine were from the US, and only one was of Mexican production

(Toussaint, 1996). Around the same time, on 15 December 1996, Televisa's corresponding service based on Cablevisión began transmission, under the name DTH Sky, in line with News Corporation's satellite ventures in other global regions. It had more channels than DirecTV, including the Spanish and/or Portuguese versions of US-based channels such as Discovery (as modified by Televisa) and MTV, as well as News's own FLAC (Fox Latin Channel). Several of these DTH channels were already available through Cablevisión. Sky also carried Televisa's terrestrial network channels. For its part, the Mexican Government had cleared the way for all this DTH development by signing an agreement with the US in November, under which Mexican and US satellites could transmit into each other's national space (Francis & Fernandez, 1997).

However, as was noted previously, PanAmSat, the satellite venture associated with Televisa and Sky, and Hughes, the leader of the competing Galaxy group, in fact had merged in September 1996, under the name PanAmSat, just months before the launch of their respective services in Mexico. Both launches went ahead, but given that both Galaxy and PanAmSat were by that stage ultimately owned by Hughes, the US-based parent corporation, DTH in Mexico in effect began as a monopoly, at least at the global level of satellite hardware, while the programming partners competed at the national level. This proved not to be sustainable, particularly because the costs of signing up for DTH were prohibitive for the vast bulk of Mexican households, and so the market was very restricted and unprofitable. In any event, the corporate manoeuvres in the US were far from settled. In December 2003, News Corporation acquired DirecTV in the US and, within a year, merged the Sky and DirecTV operations in Latin America. Except in Mexico: Televisa took the opportunity to stabilise its position in the DTH field by buying out News's interest in Sky Mexico, giving Televisa 58.7 per cent, while DirecTV (indirectly owned by News) retained 41.3 per cent in the new management company, called Innova ('News Corp sells Sky Latin America stakes', 2004).

As for Multivisión, its parent company MVS Comunicaciones also allied itself with a US satellite provider, EchoStar Corporation, in a joint venture, Dish Mexico. Launched in 2008, this initiative coincided with Echostar splitting off Dish in the US as a marketing and satellite television division, while EchoStar concentrated on satellite manufacture and operation. The deal gave Multivisión access not only to DTH satellite distribution, but also to reception technology for consumers at a relatively modest price. For Dish/Echostar, Multivisión made an attractive partner, since it had its existing MASTV venture, as mentioned previously, with an established management structure and subscriber list that could be migrated to Dish immediately. The basic bouquet of programming of around 40 channels on offer includes all the major channels most popular with pay-TV subscribers internationally – Disney, Discovery, MTV, Sony, etc., with movie channels at an additional premium (EchoStar, 2008).

Official figures from Mexico's Comisión Federal de Telecomunicaciones (COFETEL) in mid-2011 make it clear that DTH is the ascendant technology in the pay-TV arena. Subscriptions had increased 45 per cent over 2010, very much at the expense of MMDS, which registered a 29 per cent decrease. Cable increased, but only by four per cent. On this basis, DTH subscriptions, at this time 5.09 million, can be expected to overtake cable's 5.50 million, while MMDS subscriptions continue to fall from the 2011 figure of 268,000 as DTH supersedes MMDS ('Mexico's satellite TV subscribers', 2011). The breakdown of market share between the two competitors in DTH puts Sky ahead, a little short of three million, with Dish having somewhat over two million. As Dish's no-frills service proved popular, Sky lowered its prices, and both have benefited from an expanded market (Barrera Diaz, 2011). To put these figures in perspective, there are fewer than 10 million pay-TV subscribers in total, regardless of delivery technology, yet there could be around 40 million individuals with access to pay-TV: subscriptions are per household, not per individual, and we might assume an average of four persons per household. This is within a population of 120 million, so around a third of the population has access to pay-TV. Traditionally, pay-TV has been limited as a medium for the elite – the more 'globalised' sector of the population, more educated (perhaps in US schools and universities) and cosmopolitan in worldview, more likely to speak English, and more receptive to international rather than Mexican television programming. The lower costs since the end of the decade of the 2000s appear to have opened up pay-TV to the emergent middle classes.

Televisa estimates pay-TV penetration at 37 per cent, and acknowledges that catering to this growing minority of the population has become increasingly profitable. As Table 2.2 shows, Televisa reported in 2011 that it was obtaining 24 per cent of its total income from Sky, 18 per cent from its cable interests, and seven per cent from its own pay-TV network (in rounded figures). This amounts to 49

Broadcast network TV	Televisa: four channels About 70% of market	TV Azteca: two channels About 30% of market
Subscription TV (cable)	Cablevisión, Cablemás and TVI 2.1 million households	Multivisión (Vargas Group) 268,000 MMDS households
Subscription TV (DTH)	Sky Mexico 3 million households	Dish Mexico (Vargas Group) 2 million households

Table 2.1 Televisa and its Competition (2011)

Operation	Extent	Percentage of operating segment income
Television production and distribution (domestic and international)	Four domestic free-to-air networks, plus foreign programme distribution to 58 countries	Broadcasting 43% and exports 7%, amounting to 50% of operating segment income
Sky DTH service (owned 58.7%)	Mexico and Central America	24%
Subscription television via cable: Cablevisión (owned 51%) Cablemás (49%)	Mexico City and regions	18%
Pay-TV networks	Eighteen channels in various genres, distributed nationally and internationally	7%
Magazine publishing	Largest in Spanish-speaking world: 158 titles under 107 brands, including many global titles	2%

Other businesses include related cultural industries such as radio production and broadcasting; music recording; feature film production and distribution; sports promotion; betting; as well as other activities.
Source: Televisa, 2011

Table 2.2 Extent of Televisa's Operations (2011)

per cent of income from convergent technology sources, compared to 43 per cent from its traditional core business of television broadcasting. The remaining sources, incidentally, are seven per cent only from its television exports, and two per cent for publishing. In other words, even if Televisa is celebrated as the world's largest exporter of television programmes and formats, exporting to 58 countries as of 2011, and even if it clearly dominates its domestic market with more than twice the audience of its competitor, the income from its several post-broadcast, convergent, subscriber-based television activities now almost equals the traditional sources (Televisa, 2011). In this respect, convergence has been a 'game-changer' for Televisa: only five years before, Televisa's proportion of income from network television was more like two-thirds (Dickerson, 2005). This trend does not represent a retreat from external markets, however, for Televisa also obtains income from its activities in convergent distribution in foreign markets. For example, Sky derives some of its income from Central American countries, and Televisa produces and distributes 15 of its own pay-TV channels, reaching more than 50 countries. Additionally, Televisa's income from supplying programmes to Univisión in the US is set to increase, following a renegotiation of their royalty and rights agreement (Televisa, 2011). However, in the next section we shall see how Televisa has become most determined to carve out a position for itself in pay and other convergent media in the domestic market, even to the point of creating an alliance with TV Azteca, its rival in the broadcasting sphere.

THE ULTIMATE MEXICAN STAND-OFF

Clearly, it is not pay-TV alone which has been the game-changer, but the whole deregulated convergent environment that opened up after 1990–1 with the privatisation of the former state-owned telecommunications carrier, Teléfonos de México, which, as noted earlier, was acquired as Telmex by the Mexican entrepreneur, Carlos Slim, usually described as 'the world's richest man'. Significantly, the television industry (that is, mainly Televisa at that time) was protected under the newly deregulated regime, in that Telmex was prevented from entering television broadcasting. However, since 2005, with the advent of triple-play as a marketing strategy, that is, the combination of telecommunications, internet and television connections, both Televisa (through its cable divisions) and the owners of TV Azteca (which also has a major mobile telephone company) have been able to offer such services, but Telmex and its subsidiaries can not. Thus, television interests have become aligned against telecommunication interests over the issue of who will control future market development of convergent services.

As of 2011, Televisa and TV Azteca became joined together in a struggle with Carlos Slim's companies over the right to offer triple-play. This situation will be outlined presently, but it should first be explained that this was not the first time that the common interests of Televisa and TV Azteca have caused these ostensible competitors to act in collaboration. In 2006, they combined to discredit a major pharmaceutical corporation headed by the since-deceased Isaac Saba Raffoul. This was because Saba was connected to an application by the US Spanish-language network Telemundo to obtain a broadcast television licence in Mexico (Malkin, 2006). News coverage on both Televisa and TV Azteca channels accused Saba's company of monopolistic price-gouging for pharmaceutical products, ultimately causing Saba to withdraw the application (Eilemberg, 2008). Such an ironic spectacle, of the duopolists joining voices to denounce a monopolist, has also characterised the campaign against Carlos Slim's interests.

Towards the end of the term of the neoliberal PAN President Vicente Fox (2000–6), a highly controversial law was passed which deregulated the digital spectrum in a way which effectively gave it to the incumbent broadcasters

Televisa and TV Azteca free of cost, but requiring new entrants to bid for spectrum at auction. The law passed easily through both houses of government, in spite of the outrage of public interest groups, who dubbed it 'La Ley Televisa' (the Televisa Law). Although TV Azteca was also a beneficiary, the epithet was attached to Televisa because of past decades of monopolistic practices and its continued dominance of Mexican television. Amongst the progressive intelligentsia and the Left in Mexico, Televisa's hold over the national political culture is seen as a fundamental stumbling block to democratic government. Indeed, the explanation at the time for the successful passage of the legislation was that 'in order to ensure favourable (or avoid unfavourable) coverage of their candidates in an election year, parties were willing to rubber stamp the "Televisa Law"' (Lettieri & Garcia, 2006). However, a sufficient majority of dissident legislators was able to secure a review of the legislation by the Supreme Court, which in 2007 struck down those offending provisions that would have given preferential treatment to Televisa and TV Azteca (Randewich, 2007).

This judicial decision reflects a growing concern over the degree to which oligopolistic control in several sectors of the Mexican economy, not just television, is seen as inimical to growth, development and diversity. It is interesting to contrast the Televisa Law with the strict anti-monopoly laws passed in 2011, the second last year of the PAN presidency of Felipe Calderón (President 2007–12), and a landmark challenge to concentration of ownership in Mexico ('Billionaires vie for Mexico's telecoms market', 2011). Calderón's successor in the 2012 election, however, was Enrique Peña Nieto, marking the return to power of Televisa's traditional political ally, the PRI, after 12 years. This was an outcome in which Televisa was widely believed to have played an active role (Carroll, 2012), presumably in the hope of enjoying a more favourable regulatory environment and competitive advantages during Peña Nieto's term (2013–8).

Returning to the confrontation between the television duopoly and the telecommunications mogul, and recalling that Televisa has an interest in triple-play via Cablevisión and Cablemás, it is important to appreciate also that TV Azteca is part of Grupo Salinas, the group which entered this battle as owner of Iusacell. This company has a small but significant stake in mobile, or cell, telephony, being the nation's third-largest mobile provider, though with only a five per cent market share (de Cordoba & Harrup, 2011). Carlos Slim's Carso group of companies dominates telecommunications: Telmex has 80 per cent of fixed lines; Telcel has 70 per cent of mobile telephony; and Infinitum has 95 per cent of internet service provision ('Billionaires vie for Mexico's telecoms market', 2011). Slim's case is that in the convergent environment, his companies should not be prevented from offering triple-play as Televisa and TV Azteca do. For their part, the television companies argue that Slim's dominance of telecommunications allows him to charge high interconnection rates – this prejudices competition but, more to the point for them, discourages the take-up of subscribers using mobile devices to view entertainment content.

Slim's counter-argument has been that television advertising rates are too high and, in February 2011, declared that he was cancelling all Carso Group television advertising, a blow aimed against both Televisa and TV Azteca. The boycott included not only Slim's telecommunication companies, but unrelated companies in the group, notably the venerable Sanborn's retail stores. The television duopolists retaliated by intensifying their involvement in telecommunications – in April, Televisa bought 50 per cent of the Salinas group's mobile telephone company Iusacell (de Cordoba & Harrup, 2011). By the end of the year, the deal had regulatory approval, and Iusacell was raising the stakes by getting ready to offer quadruple play; that is, by adding wireless access to the mix. Furthermore, Televisa reported that its advertising sales had increased, even in the absence of the big advertisers of the Carso Group (Castano, 2011). However, another front in the battle had been opened up in October by Slim's internet service providing the Pan American games as a live video stream. In spite of Telmex's insistence that 'Streaming on the Internet isn't TV', Televisa and TV Azteca filed yet another suit against Slim (Harrison, 2011). They already had taken action about the relationship between Telmex and Dish Mexico, the Multivisión/EchoStar DTH venture. This had also attracted the attention of the regulators, because although Telmex claimed that it was just providing billing services for Dish, prospective Dish subscribers were being offered a special deal with Telmex, and there was other marketing collaboration, leading to the suspicion that Dish was a front for Telmex (Rucker and Comlay, 2011).

CONCLUSION

These charges and counter-charges will be played out in the courts and chambers of government for some time to come, for, no less in Mexico than anywhere else, the legal basis for the commercial use of convergent technologies lags behind their implementation. Whereas Televisa's golden age of the 1970s and 1980s was characterised by a profitable domination of the domestic free-to-air/mass broadcasting market, which in turn supported Televisa's international ventures, the gradual take-up of cable and DTH subscription services has made it imperative for Televisa to increase and consolidate its position in this pay-TV/elite market. Furthermore, the convergence between television and telecommunication services has brought Televisa into confrontation with Telmex, a situation in which Televisa's mass market rival TV Azteca has become its ally in convergent services. In contrast to the certainties and relative stability of past decades, television as a medium is in a state of transition, as new business models and convergent modes of delivery proliferate. Yet notwithstanding current government attempts to break down the dynastic and oligopolistic character of the communication industries in Mexico, the future of television more than likely will be shaped by the outcomes of the continued titanic clashes of the current players.

3

The Dominant Markets – Brazil

Unlike Mexico, Brazil has not had the same dominant television broadcaster since the beginning, even though TV Globo has often been almost as powerful in Brazil as Televisa has been in Mexico. TV Globo did rise to dominance in the 1960s and has been pre-eminent since, but it built on the programming and production ideas of several other networks which had started in the 1950s. TV Globo has also been challenged more severely than Televisa has, in several phases starting in the 1980s. Instead of tolerating or even cultivating a quasi-monopoly, like Televisa, Brazilian governments have intervened several times to create new network competitors to TV Globo by issuing them packages of television station licences.

Television is still the dominant institution in Brazil for news, information and culture. TV Globo's evening news and prime time *telenovelas* still hold sway in over half the homes in the country. They have served as a unifying force in a nation with extremely diverse regions since the early 1970s; they are still the dominant means by which Brazilians imagine themselves as a country. TV Globo's strong base in the Brazilian market has also permitted it, like Televisa, to become a major exporter of *telenovelas*, particularly to the Lusophone (Portuguese-speaking) transnational cultural linguistic market, as well as Latin America, and much of the rest of the world, particularly in the global deregulation and expansion of commercial TV in the 1990s.

Brazilian television historian Sérgio Mattos (2000) described four phases in the history of Brazilian television. First, there was an elitist or takeoff phase between 1950 and 1964, when television was limited to upper and upper middle classes in cities. There were no true national networks, but TV Tupi had stations in many cities, was loosely dominant, and created the basic forms of programming, such as the Brazilian version of the *telenovela*. Second came the nationalist or populist phase (1964–75), when TV Globo started and quickly rose to dominance under a military government (1964–85). The audience expanded rapidly and the programming became more popularly oriented. In the third, technological development phase (1975–85), broadcasting expanded via microwave and satellite to cover nearly all the country, and the number of networks increased.

This was the high point of TV Globo's dominance and influence. In the fourth, transitional and international expansion phase (1985–90), civilian government returned and TV Globo and others began to export widely to the world (Mattos, 2000). A fifth phase (1990–2005) began the slow growth of cable, DBS and SMATV, and the further segmentation of the audience (Duarte, 1992). TV Globo adjusted to this with new channels and a partnership with Rupert Murdoch's Sky Latin America, but almost went bankrupt by overinvesting in cable infrastructure. With the rapid growth of the lower middle class since 2000, a new sixth phase seems to herald the increased access to and use of satellite TV, cable TV, and television over the internet.

THE TAKE-OFF PHASE OF BRAZILIAN TELEVISION (1950–64)

Television broadcasting was begun in Brazil on 18 September 1950. Assis Chateaubriand, of the Diários e Emissoras Associados (Associated Dailies and Broadcasters), a very large, but loosely organised media empire, opened a commercial station in São Paulo – the beginning of the TV Tupi network. He started the station almost on a dare, after he was told by an American engineer that television was economically unfeasible in Latin America (Raoul Silveira, 4 October 1975). Aside from adding it to his political influence empire, and to a lesser degree his advertising base, Chateaubriand was not initially sure what to do with television programming. On the second day, after the initial opening gala, he reportedly asked the RCA technicians who had helped set it up, 'Well, what do we do next?' (Straubhaar, 1981).

Television in Brazil in the 1950s and early 1960s was limited by its reach, market and resources. It initially reached primarily middle and upper middle classes in major cities with programming that was mostly locally produced. That initially tilted programming toward more elite interests, producing high quality dramas and music in what seemed to many a golden age of high quality programming. However, this limited market also restricted resources for production, so when importation of programmes from the United States became technologically feasible, due to the use of kinescopes and videotape, they flooded in.

The prospects for commercial television in Brazil in the long run were excellent. Potential advertising support was strong. J. Walter Thompson installed its first Latin American branch in Brazil in 1929. US advertisers, like General Motors in 1925, were setting up in Brazil, and opening advertising operations (Woodard, 2002). US agencies dominated, at least for national advertising, until the 1960s (Durand, 1993). Local markets for radio and newspaper advertising were developing well, which ironically may have inhibited national television, since several key companies, like the local owners of TV Tupi stations, preferred to focus on dominating local markets.

Assis Chateaubriand (right), founder of Brazil's first television station, reads the inaugural speech

TV Tupi was the largest network in Brazil for some time, covering 23 cities in 1976. It created some innovative television genres. It created a Brazilian version of the large variety shows common to much of Latin America. TV Tupi in the 1950s significantly affected the emerging Brazilian television programme formats: *telenovela*, music, comedy, news, sports and variety shows (*shows de auditório*). In virtually all these genres, TV Tupi was the primary arena for early experimentation and development. It functioned 'as a laboratory for an entire generation of technicians, artists and producers, oriented first by and through radio and after by cinema and theatre.' (*Veja*, 3 August 1977). Tupi shaped the *telenovela* genre in Brazil first with adaptations of imported scripts like *O Direito de Nascer* (*The Right to be Born*, or *The Right to Know Who Your Parents Were*). It gradually adapted the *telenovela* genre to Brazil, creating the first *telenovela* widely considered to really have the look and feel of Brazilian urban culture, *Beto Rockefeller*, in 1968, by Brazilian writer Bráulio Pedroso. *Beto Rockefeller* came out of a strain of mass mass culture that was very distinctly Brazilian, despite the protagonist's last name. The lead character was a charismatic "player" rising from the working class to make his way in Rio society. He wasn't always nice, or even honest, but he and the rest of the cast reflected a number of Brazilian archetypes.

> Beto Rockefeller was a classic Rio "rounder" (*boa vida*), a "classic Brazilian." The show was popular because it was very satiric and treated real national issues directly. It crystallized a moment of transition, raising our consciousness about treating our own national reality … After "Beto Rockefeller," the system of adapting foreign material diminished and the amount of national content in themes, plots and characterizations grew steadily (Porto e Silva, interview, 1979)

TV Tupi should have been the Televisa of Brazil. Joe Wallach, the Time-Life financial manager who helped raise TV Globo to dominance in the late 1960s and 1970s, said, 'The competition, like TV Tupi, could have wiped us out at any moment, at that time [1967], if they had been better organised' (Wallach, 2011). TV Tupi's primary problem was indeed organisational and structural. Its parent group, Diários e Emissoras Associadas, had very decentralised ownership and control. It was spread all over Brazil, first in newspapers, then radio and television, but was based in local commercial and political fiefdoms held by local partners, or *condóminos*, who never agreed to a fully fledged network with simulcast or even coordinated programming. According to *O Estado de São Paulo* (28 May 1970), 'A [Tupi] station in the State of Paraná, which was part of the network, could buy programmes independently from TV Record in São Paulo.' This happened even in the major markets. TV Tupi São Paulo could opt not to broadcast, or broadcast at a very different time, a major programme produced by TV Tupi Rio, and vice versa. That kept them from creating a national advertising market that could have given them the resources to create dominant programming, two things that TV Globo was doing by the early 1970s.

Throughout the 1950s and 1960s, various other entrepreneurs, usually those who already owned other radio stations and newspapers, started rival television stations in the hopes of making money from advertising. Examples were TV Rio and TV Record of São Paulo, TV Bandeirantes, TV Excelsior and, eventually TV Globo. TV Rio, TV Excelsior and TV Globo were more innovative in programming and network organisation than TV Tupi (da Costa, 1986; Straubhaar, 1981, pp. 79–223). TV Excelsior, in particular, has been seen by several media historians as the network which could have competed with TV Globo to become a dominant, modern network in Brazil (da Costa, 1986). Muniz Sodré (interview, 1978) observed that, 'Excelsior was a Brazilian network prototype. In 1964, they started to do programmes for a wide public because they started to be truly commercial, competing hard for advertising agency money. They offered advertisers a Rio-São Paulo package of coordinated programs and advertising, which was significant since no other network, not even TV Tupi with its national reach, offered simulcast or even well-coordinated programming or advertising. They developed popular *telenovelas* and popularized Brazilian singers.' The TV Excelsior management was aware of the structural problems of other groups, like the Diários Associados' TV Tupi.

TV Excelsior's advertising initiatives were significant because prior to their incipient coordination of ads in Rio and São Paulo, almost all advertising in Brazil was local. Media markets were very decentralised aside from a few national magazines, equivalent to the US *Look, Life* or *Time*, which sold national advertisements oriented to the small but growing national middle class. Some advertising agencies, particularly in São Paulo, wanted to focus on the national audience, which was to power TV Globo's later rapid rise to national dominance. Advertising agencies had long been influenced by US advertising practices and were increasingly making partnerships with US advertising agencies, attracting US and global clients, and national clients who envisioned a potential national audience, so the ground was ready for a national network that could sell national advertising. Much advertising in Brazil remains local, but as TV Globo, and later others, developed national advertising, television came to consistently take in over 60 per cent of national advertising investment (Bolaño, 1988; Sinclair, 2012b).

What went wrong for TV Excelsior remains a matter of controversy. The Brazilian government cancelled their licence to broadcast in 1970, after they had gone through a descending spiral of fires, financial crises and labour disputes. The problem started, ironically, with TV Excelsior's management. On that point, it is illuminating to compare TV Excelsior with TV Globo. 'TV Excelsior was bad at financial management, which TV Globo was superb at. Globo picked up on this idea [of strict planning and management] at the same time that the 1964 Revolution tried to increase governmental efficiency by creating a Planning Ministry. Planning, which had been neglected, became a new ideology' (Sodré, interview, 1978). However, many Brazilian observers believed that TV Excelsior's troubles were primarily caused by political disagreements with the post-1964 Revolutionary governments. Moya (interview, 1979) felt that 'TV Excelsior fell because of post-1964 politics. The new government liquidated other Simonsen Group holdings and TV Excelsior slowly died.'

TV Rio prospered for a while but TV Globo raided some of their top programming staff in 1966–8, which, combined with poor management, led to its decline. TV Record, owned by the same group as TV Rio, had similar problems. Sodré (interview, 1978) observed that 'TV Record was a feudal family enterprise, which had limited ambitions and was not really interested in developing a network.' However, all of these groups contributed some important genres and programme developments to the emerging shape of Brazilian television. TV Rio and TV Record developed music, variety and comedy genre traditions. TV Excelsior produced some well-received *telenovelas*, which helped shape the genre.

Several of these Brazilian networks were important in terms of the transition from the first, early phase of Brazilian to the next, more expansive phase. Paulo Moura, of the audience research firm IBOPE, summarised how the different Brazilian television stations and groups acted and created programming in the market structure of the 1960s (interview, 1979):

Up until TV Excelsior in 1960, Brazilian TV was in its pioneer phase. In São Paulo, TV Tupi and TV Record, and in Rio, TV Tupi and TV Rio were primarily adapting elements taken from Brazilian radio and copying and adapting U.S. methods. In their programming, they emphasized comedy, music and game shows. In the second phase, the years of TV Excelsior [1960–70], TV Excelsior imposed a higher level of quality, hired the best professionals available – including some from Argentina – and sent many people to the U.S. for training. Their programming used some U.S. themes but began some more distinctly Brazilian themes. The third phase was the final ascension to dominance of TV Globo. TV Globo uses American techniques but Brazilian themes. And that is partially due to political pressure about American influence. (Moura interview, 1979)

THE NATIONALISATION OR POPULIST PHASE OF BRAZILIAN TELEVISION (1964–75)

The military governments brought in by a coup in 1964 radically changed the circumstances of Brazilian television in a number of ways. First, the military intervened primarily to change the nature of Brazilian politics. They were concerned about left-wing political populism of the early 1960s, which they saw as moving toward socialism. Changing that also changed some key aspects of the television system, both in its political role and in its economic structure. In the 1950s and early 1960s television owners, like Tupi's Chateaubriand, made money both by selling ads and by playing politics, offering favourable coverage to politicians and others in return for financial support.

Chateaubriand knew how to use the media to make money and gain power. He had a hold on many important people, such as their desire to gain favorable publicity or avoid unfavorable publicity for some faux pas that Chateaubriand knew about, and he knew how to exploit that hold to his advantage. He was not alone in using this technique. Many reporters, columnists and media organizations of his day did exactly the same thing.

Chateaubriand was singularly skillful at the game, however, and when he went into decline due to ill health several years before his eventual death [in 1968], his media organization, the Diários Associados, also went into decline. None of Chateaubriand's lieutenants were nearly as skillful at the political game as he was. And their organization was not really rationalized in economic terms to compete in a market economy without a covering flow of money gained through political influence ... Besides, the field for the "dirty game" of political influence peddling became much less open after the 1964 revolution [when the Army pre-empted the roles of the political parties] (Valentini interview, 1978).

The military limited electoral politics from the 1960s to the early 1980s. They restricted parties, what offices were elected, and how media, particularly television, could cover politics and elections. Television stations could no longer make money by playing in electoral politics. Media allies of the military could, however, expect to receive some favours from direct government advertising and from government-controlled corporations. Media support was increasingly focused on commercial advertising. Until the mid-1960s, the advertising revenues actually invested in television were not sufficient to support all the television operations that were initiated (Raoul Silveira, 1975). Throughout the 1950s, the television audience was limited to an economic elite in a few cities so advertiser interest grew slowly. However, in many cases, television stations were seen as desirable for the prestige that they added to media empires, even if advertising income could not support them. After the 1960s, however, television became very profitable. The share of advertising investment given to television went from 25 per cent in 1962 to 59 per cent in 1981 (Duarte, 1992, p. 76), largely at the expense of radio and non-mass media advertising.

The second major impact of the 1964 military coup was the deliberate insertion of money into selected parts of the media system, particularly television. They directed advertisements by large government ministries and state-owned companies to preferred partners, which most prominently included TV Globo. They also used economic controls to hurt television stations that they thought opposed them, like TV Excelsior. (That also had the effect of removing one of TV Globo's major competitors at the time.) They subsidised consumer credit for television set purchases. 'After 1968, a lower class or lower middle class family could purchase a set over 36–40 months. This democratized set possession.' (Octávio Florisbal interview, 1979)

The military had a vision of accelerating consumer capitalism in Brazil, to draw people into that paradigm and away from the competing appeal of socialism, as they saw it (Salles, 1975). In this, they had the full-fledged co-operation of the middle classes and ownership class of Brazil, including Roberto Marinho of Globo, who was personal friends with some of the original military revolutionaries, particularly the Castello Branco group, which included the first and last two military presidents (Wallach interviews, 2011). The military saw television as a primary means of furthering and strengthening this kind of capitalist growth and economic inclusion. In practical application, this involved an increasingly close co-operation between advertisers, advertising agencies, and television networks with national reach, with facilitation by both government advertising and government investment in telecom infrastructure.

Third, the military vision of national security involved pulling the remote parts of Brazil into a tighter connection to the centre of the country. They wanted to use television to reinforce linguistic, cultural and political loyalty. Like many developing countries, they wanted to use television to reinforce national identity, but they also had a specific notion of what that identity should be: nationalistic, consumer oriented, and to quote a military government TV commercial from the late 1970s – 'a country that is going forward' (Riding, 1 December 1984). To enable television to reach all of Brazil, the military also invested massively in the telecommunications infrastructure required to create genuinely national television networks, first in microwave networks between cities, later in national communication satellites, such as BrasilSat. This did have the effect of pulling Brazilian audiences more strongly into a shared national culture (Kottak, 1990; Porto, 2008), despite the considerable regional differences which had always characterised Brazil, between a largely indigenous north, an Afro-Brazilian northeast, a mixed but largely European center-south, and a far south that had once tried to secede and which often had more in common with Argentina and Uruguay.

THE FORMATION OF TV GLOBO

Six factors kept the stations before TV Globo from becoming true national networks. First was a narrow focus on their local market, as in the case of TV Record. Second was poor discipline among stations belonging to networks, reinforced by a lack of network identity and distinction in programming products to inspire loyalty, as in the case of TV Tupi. Third was an orientation by some large stations, like TV Record, towards selling programmes instead of fully exploiting the revenue possibilities of network-wide advertising themselves. Fourth was an unclear idea of what the mass audience wanted in programming, except on TV Excelsior, which managed for a time to please both audiences and advertisers. Fifth were limited financial resources (except at first at TV Excelsior), confounded by bad financial management in all the stations (including TV Excelsior), which limited the accumulation of financial resources for reinvestment. Sixth was a failure by all the stations before TV Globo to reinvest sufficient of their profits to maintain equipment and adequately compensate their employees.

TV Globo overcame these problems and exploited the conditions that made a strong national network possible. Many critics have argued that TV Globo's success was largely due to its relationship with Time-Life Broadcasting, Inc. (Hertz, 1987; Brittos and Bolaño, 2005). While the explanation was more complex, TV Globo's success was undoubtedly dependent on Time-Life, particularly at first.

It is clear that Roberto Marinho, owner of the Globo Group, started television operations in 1964 heavily relying on capital and technical expertise from Time-Life, Inc. Marinho had obtained a licence for television in Rio in 1957. In

1962, his Globo Group (Organizações Globo) signed an agreement with Time-Life for an investment of over 6 million, which it used to buy equipment, facilities, staff and, initially, a large amount of US programming. In return, Time-Life was to receive 30 per cent of the profit from TV Globo's operations. This agreement was widely seen as violating the Constitution of Brazil, which prohibited foreign persons or companies from owning interests in Brazilian media. The implementation of the agreement also violated another rule, that foreigners not occupy top management positions in Brazilian media. Time-Life's main representative in Brazil after 1965, Joe Wallach, took charge of the financial and administrative operations of TV Globo, essentially becoming its executive director. After Time-Life withdrew from the agreement in 1970, Wallach became naturalised as a Brazilian citizen to overcome that objection and stayed on as executive director of TV Globo.

TV Globo's association with Time-Life powerfully reinforced the commercial pattern of the television industry, which had already developed in a more varied and ad hoc manner in Brazil. Several of the competing television networks were badly organised, subject to the whims of their owners, and sometimes more oriented to politics, as noted with TV Tupi above, than with commercial operations and commercial success. To a much greater degree than any of its predecessors, TV Globo (with Time-Life's help) introduced a sophisticated commercial network operation on the American pattern, which led in large part to TV Globo's subsequent success (Straubhaar, 1981; Straubhaar, 1984). Wallach re-organised Globo's finances, and got it to do solid budgeting and accounting. He developed a better sales team and started selling more ads. He developed upfront ad sales for TV Globo when it only covered the Rio and São Paulo markets, then he and his colleagues steadily expanded that relationship with advertising agencies (Wallach, 2011).

Even though Time-Life's financial backing and technological and financial expertise would prove critical to TV Globo, Time-Life's initial programming advice was disastrous. Wallach noted that when he arrived in Rio in 1965 to take over as Time-Life's representative to TV Globo, they were paying for several extensive contracts for quite a bit of imported US programming (2011). Based on that imported programming and a couple of live variety shows, TV Globo was fourth out of four television stations in audience popularity in Rio. Perceiving that this strategy could not compete well, Wallach broke some of Globo's contracts with US programme suppliers and instead used Time-Life's resources to hire away a couple of successful programming executives from other networks, first Walter Clark from TV Rio in 1966 and later José Bonifácio de Oliveira ('Boni'), who had been programme director at TV Tupi in Rio (Wallach, 2011). Besides Clark and Boni, they hired other advertising, sales and management people, as well as variety show hosts, *telenovela* scriptwriters, directors, actors, etc.

After these new hires, TV Globo started programming along lines that were locally successful: live music shows and live variety shows (borrowing from Clark's experience at TV Rio), and *telenovelas* (borrowing from Boni's experience at TV Tupi). Live local music and musical festivals were very popular in the 1960s, helping launch a number of well-known singers and groups. TV Rio had done particularly well with such programmes, so Clark started similar programmes at TV Globo. An annual music festival was one of its first big successes (Wallach interviews). Large-scale live variety shows were also very popular in Brazilian prime time in the 1960s. They had games, song contests, dancers, comedy, live music, etc. Globo hired some existing, well-known variety show host stars like Chacrinha and Silvio Santos. Even though they had to compete with and outbid other networks to get them, such stars improved ratings.

In the late 1960s, *telenovelas* and live variety shows were the most popular local genres. Globo hired several well-rated variety show hosts, but by 1971, the military government began to put pressure on television stations to either eliminate or more closely control live variety shows (Straubhaar, 1981). Chacrinha in particular often featured popular Brazilian musicians who were also frequently openly critical of the military (Straubhaar, 1983). Live shows sometimes opened up topics, like a live Afro-Brazilian religious ceremony, that military officers considered scandalous or inappropriate. Even though they were popular, the live programmes did not facilitate the degree of censorship and control that the military wanted. In 1968, there was a more hardline takeover within the military government and the military instituted Institutional Act Five, which provided for prior censorship of all media content, including television. Live television frustrated this intent. Under Boni's direction, Globo gradually moved their version of the large-scale, long Sunday evening variety show into a shorter, much more controlled, highly produced show, called *Fantástico* (Fantastic), which replaced Chacrinha in 1973.

The genre that rose on TV Globo as live variety declined was the *telenovela*. Wallach, Clark and Boni had observed how well TV Excelsior and TV Tupi had done with their most successful *telenovelas*. Boni in particular had the idea that TV Globo could dominate prime time if it consistently produced the shows with the highest quality. This came to be called 'The Globo Pattern of Quality' and was a major slogan in their promotion of their programming. In the early 1970s, Clark and Boni concentrated on creating predictable programming strips of three quality *telenovelas* at 6 pm, 7 pm and 8 pm and one evening news show (*Jornal Nacional*) every weekday and Saturday night in prime time (Borelli and

Priolli, 2000). That also created a strong programming flow between programmes and kept the audience tuned into TV Globo.

A demonstration of the development of *telenovelas'* popularity can be seen by listing the most popular programme in Rio de Janeiro of each year in the 1960s. Interestingly, the same list shows the transition in popularity from TV Rio, briefly to TV Excelsior, and then to TV Globo:

1960– [variety show] *Noite de gala*, TV Rio
1961– [variety show] *Noites Cariocas*, TV Rio
1962– [comedy] *O riso e o limite*, TV Rio
1963– [variety show] *Noites Cariocas*, TV Rio
1964– [imported series] *Peter Gunn*, TV Rio
1965– [*telenovela*] *O direito de nascer*, TV Rio
1966– [*show de auditório*] *Discoteca de Chacrinha*, TV Excelsior
1967– [game show] *Telecatch*, TV Globo
1968– [*telenovela*] *O homen proibido*, TV Globo
1969– [*telenovela*] *A Rosa rebelde*, TV Globo
1970– [*telenovela*] *Irmãos coragem*, TV Globo

(Source: Artur da Távola, *O Globo*, 9 April 1977)

TV GLOBO'S NETWORK REVOLUTION

TV Globo's management had begun to reorganise and adapt in US management practices. It had also begun to create an effective programming schedule. The next step in the making of the basis of its dominance was the creation of a national network. TV Globo had acquired a station in São Paulo in 1966. They gradually expanded in the late 1960s into the interior of the state of São Paulo, the country's second most lucrative advertising market (after the city of São Paulo itself), and into Belo Horizonte in 1968. As they expanded, Marinho, Wallach and Boni created a strongly centralised management system, which enforced the central programme production and uniform programming pattern for all Globo stations that José Bonifácio had envisioned and earlier offered to TV Tupi. This created the basis for further expansion toward national coverage.

THE TV GLOBO – TIME-LIFE CONTRACT AS AN ISSUE

Competitors and critics charged that the contracts in 1962 between Time-Life and TV Globo were illegal and dangerous to Brazilian society and politics. In fact, the original 1962 contract was a form of joint venture that probably violated the law. The agreement had powerful enemies. João Calmon, Rio Head of the Diários Associados [TV Tupi] and a Brazilian senator, crusaded against it, held Senate hearings about it, and wrote a book about it (Calmon, 1966). He was particularly concerned about the power of the Time-Life financial adviser,

Joe Wallach, since having a non-citizen in senior management also violated Brazilian law. The concern was prescient since Wallach's management role proved to be crucial in TV Globo's success, and adapting in foreign (US) influence in the form of management practice was part of that success.

The official government actions between 1962 and 1968 seem to reflect, in retrospect, a desire to permit Roberto Marinho and TV Globo to exploit what seemed to be an advantageous arrangement as long as it did not become too much of a public scandal and as long as TV Globo did not, in fact, seem to suffer any strong influence from Time-Life on its journalistic and programming policies. When the contracts did become a loud public issue in 1966, the government seems to have co-operated with TV Globo to permit them to delay breaking the contracts in order to derive maximum benefit from them. Investigations and pressure increased from 1966–68. So by 1969, Time-Life and TV Globo agreed to break the contract. Joseph Wallach, the business and financial advisor from Time-Life decided to stay and work for TV Globo, changing nationality to Brazilian in order to do so. He recalled that 'we finally nationalised the entire company in 1969 and liquidated the complete debt with the Time-Life group in 1971 … for me, the real history of TV Globo begins in 1969, with the departure of Time-Life, the launching of the news show *Jornal Nacional* and the boom in telecommunications which linked and switched on the country' (*Veja*, 6 October 1976).

THE GOLDEN AGE OF TV GLOBO

Between 1968 and 1985, in Brazilian television's second phase, TV Globo dominated both the audience and the development of television programming. It tended to have a 60–70 per cent share of the viewers in the major cities at any given time, and at some points in very successful programmes, had over 90 per cent TV Globo was acccused during this period of representing the view of the government, of being its mouthpiece.

In 1969, TV Globo began to programme simultaneously to all its operations in Rio de Janeiro, São Paulo, and Belo Horizonte, starting with a prime time news show, *Jornal Nacional*. It also began to sell coordinated advertising for them in 1969. As noted above, the idea of coordinated national ads that showed on multiple stations simultaneously was new to Brazil with the short-lived TV Excelsior. TV Globo moved into simulcast programming and advertising with the evening news in three markets, but then rapidly expanded its coverage of new markets, the number of programs simulcast, and the number of shows and markets available for simulcast, increasingly national advertising. TV Globo created a marketing journal, *Mercado Global*, which detailed its coverage This sealed TV Globo's dominance of the Brazilian market by creating the core of a genuine national network, which no other network had. Advertising revenue rolled in, which enabled Globo to increase its level of quality in *telenovelas*, shows, news, music and other programming even higher – a growth cycle that continued without any real competitors until the 1980s.

TV Globo's golden age coincided with the maturation of advertising in Brazil. A variety of national agencies, such as Dualibi, Petit and Zaragosa (DPZ) grew with television, from the 1960s on, and became increasingly dominated by local or national agencies, often working with international partners. The Brazilian government reserved its considerable ad funds for national agencies, which consolidated the strength of national agencies in their partnerships with foreign agencies (Durand, 1993). Major national agencies, including MPM, Lintas, DPZ, and Salles Interamericana, frequently topped lists of most profitable agencies, even more profitable than the global agencies operating in Brazil (Rodrigues, 2002).

TV Globo's desire to dominate the Rio and São Paulo audience ratings and advertising markets made the TV Globo production people work hard at creating programming that would be the most popular among the widest audience. They sold that programming to stations in areas where TV Globo did not yet operate, and used those programming sales to build up a group of stations that would later become affiliates to a more formal TV Globo Network. In 1971 and 1972, TV Globo added two more owned and operated stations in Recife and Brasília, reaching its legal limit of five. Three affiliates joined the network in 1972 and more came steadily after that.

TV Globo was also extremely innovative in the use of careful research to design their programming. Since 1971, TV Globo has used several kinds of research: audience interests in various types of programming, the differences between audiences for various days and time periods, and the importance of the various audience groups to advertisers as potential consumers. By 1977, Globo had differential profiles of the audiences for its various *telenovelas* at 6, 7, 8 and 10 pm (Rohter, 1978, p. 58). This also tended to keep advertisers loyal to TV Globo, since it was providing much more information to help advertisers target the markets they wanted than were any competing networks.

Unlike the situation in Mexico, TV Globo continued to have competition in different cities, particularly in the largest market, São Paulo, where TV Record, TV Bandeirantes, and TV Tupi had some audience success. However, production costs climbed as TV Globo reinvested heavily in increasingly production quality and audience tastes became more demanding. Independent stations, even those with a certain share of a big market like TV Record in São Paulo, could not afford to keep up with what audiences preferred. The most successful and most expensive formula was high quality Brazilian production (Dualibi,

interview, 1979), exactly where production manager and programme director
José Bonifacio (Boni) planned for TV Globo to be.

TV Globo started a national network in 1973, when they had five of their own
stations and three affiliates broadcasting a uniform programme schedule and
carrying the same advertisements (*Mercado Global*, October 1975). Brazilian
advertisers had long wanted a true national advertising vehicle. As late as 1973,
Ramona Bechtos (*Advertising Age*, June 1973) commented that there was still
no truly national advertising vehicle in Brazil. So advertising revenues were
increasingly highly concentrated in the Rede Globo network, which has usually
drawn at least 60 per cent of the television audience, nationwide, since the mid
1970s.

The rise of this golden age for TV Globo coincided with the rise of the *telenovela* as the pre-eminent prime time genre in Brazil. It was the cultural product
for which TV Globo became best known nationally and, starting with the export
of the novela *Gabriela* to Portugal in 1976, internationally. As Rohter (1978,
p. 57) observed, 'the emergence, growth and continued success of the *telenovela* is inextricably linked with the rise of TV Globo.' *Veja* (6 October 1976) noted
that, 'Globo did not invent the *novela* but from its studios came the decisive
contribution in the *novela*'s transformation into an almost cinematic genre of
Hollywood dimensions and yet [a genre] most typically Brazilian in its language,
plots and rhythm of production.' José Bonifácio and other production managers
for Globo put together an impressive production machine. They hired talented
scriptwriters from theatre and cinema. They hired producers from other stations. They brought over some existing stars, but began to work on creating their
own stable of actors, which turned out a national star system somewhat equivalent to that of Hollywood in the studio era. In fact, the Brazilian news magazine
Veja (6 October 1976) called TV Globo 'the Brazilian Hollywood.'

TV Globo hired *telenovela* writers who were noted for activism on the left,
but controlled its news very tightly. In part, this is because television news and
public affairs programming came under regular and strict censorship after 1968,
enforced by phone calls from censors telling them which stories not to cover.
The stations were responsible for keeping their own lists of proscribed subjects,
which encouraged self-censorship whenever doubt about a given news item or
interview arose. TV Globo was noted for self-censorship. In fact, some critics
accused it of being quite consciously the station of the government political line
(*Folha de Sao Paulo*, 18 November 1979).

Telenovelas, documentaries and comedies were also restricted by censorship.
TV Globo had at least two *telenovelas* already in production cancelled and one
finished documentary refused, all at considerable expense. That made the network producers cautious, while they complained that they could not treat issues

that appeared in imported American programmes, such as drugs, crime and other social problems (*Jornal da Tarde*, 6 November 1975).

While TV Globo dominated the national mass audience, other stations and networks were forced to come up with alternative strategies to pick off some portions of the audience and maintain some special appeal to advertisers. TV Tupi lost organisational coherence after its founder, Assis Chateaubriand, died in 1968, but TV Tupi still tried to challenge TV Globo head on, aiming for the same national mass audience with the same kind of programming: *telenovela* for *telenovela*, musical for musical, etc. But TV Tupi had fewer resources to finance and create programming as it lost advertisers and talent to TV Globo, so the network declined in the 1970s, and went bankrupt in 1980.

NEW COMPETITORS TO TV GLOBO SINCE 1981

Brazil's military government in the 1970s showed signs of being concerned about TV Globo's power over communication with the mass audience in Brazil. One of Globo's top executives, Walter Clark, had perhaps intemperately remarked that TV Globo was more powerful than the government. The government in Brazil moved in 1981 to create competitors. TV Tupi's licences were broken into two groups and given to TV Manchete, linked with the weekly magazine *Manchete* and to TVS (now SBT, Sistema Brasileira de Televisão), owned by Sílvio Santos, a variety show host who had worked on Globo and other stations. TV Bandeirantes also acquired more stations to become a major network.

This did create more competition. As of 1989, TV Globo reached 99.93 per cent of Brazilian homes with television. TV Manchete covered 90 per cent of TV homes, Bandeirantes 93 per cent, and SBT 90 per cent (Santos, 1989). However, TV Globo had by far the most presence and impact. TV Globo had a network of 79 owned or affiliated stations, including the dominant VHF stations in most markets. SBT/TVS (Silvio Santos) had 46 stations, TV Bandeirantes 30 stations, and TV Manchete 36 stations. There were also two regional networks. Rede Brasil Sul in the South carried TV Globo programming but supplied local news and other shows, and covered over 14,000,000 people in a wealthy region, who represented 12 per cent of the actual consumption in Brazil (Priolli, 1988). TV Record consisted of loosely affiliated independent stations in Rio and São Paulo and a few other cities in the heavily populated Southeast.

TV Manchete became the main competitor to TV Globo in the 1980s. It was owned by Adolfo Bloch, a prominent Rio publisher. TV Manchete created a competitive evening news programme and also created *telenovelas*, such as the ecological melodrama *Pantanal*, or the sexy political fable *Dona Beija*, which could compete in quality terms with those of TV Globo. However, TV

Manchete's strategy was probably flawed from the outset. It did not try to compete with TV Globo for a broad mass audience but aimed itself at the middle and upper classes. That was simply not a large enough advertising base to support the kind of programming they tried to create and sustain (Mattos, 1990). In 1991–2, TV Manchete was sold to Hamilton Lucas de Oliveira (IBF Group), since it was operating at a loss.

SBT was and is owned by Sílvio Santos, who started as a salesman, became a variety show host on TV Globo and other stations in the 1960s, and continued to host his own popular programme. He has also diversified into finance, land and sales operations. SBT took the opposite strategy from TV Manchete. It focused its programming strategy on the lower middle class, working class and working poor, with reality shows, game shows, and contests. Some of its reality shows reflect what might be called a Latin American tradition of television populism, in which hosts take call-ins and/or send reporters to examine business frauds or neglected government services, such as inadequate public hospitals. Similar shows can be seen in Bolívia and Peru. Brazilian television scholars refer to this tradition as *popularesco* – programmes with an exaggerated address to popular, or working class culture (Sodré, 1972). SBT had several notable shows in this genre, investigative shows like *Aqui Agora* (*Here, Now*) and slightly scandalous reality and game shows like *Ratinho* (the *Little Rat*) (Borelli and Priolli, 2000). This strategy was successful, raising SBT to a consistent second place behind TV Globo, given the increasing size of SBT's audience. SBT's promotional materials in the 1980s and 1990s stressed their success with this audience and the fact that this audience consumed many kinds of goods.

TV Bandeirantes was and is owned by the Saad family, who are also landowners and industrialists. It specialised in news and sports programming. It gradually evolved a national audience and advertising base in those areas. It attempted a couple of times to become a more direct competitor to TV Globo by doing *telenovela* production, but never succeeded in expanding into those kinds of genres, and retreated into doing what it did profitably, sports and news. Like TV Manchete and SBT, TV Bandeirantes ultimately wished to pursue a general audience with general appeal programming, such as evening serials (*telenovelas*), but tended to find that such efforts still did not gain enough of the audience to pay for the increased programming costs.

Some educational television stations also developed during this time. The most productive is TV Cultura run by the Padre Anchieta Foundation and financially supported by the State of São Paulo. The State of Rio de Janeiro also operated TV Educativa; and other states, such as Bahia, put together educational stations (Mattos, 1984). The Federal Government also owns stations in Brasília and other cities. These developed into a loosely organised public and educational network, TV Educativa, operating in many of Brazil's larger cities. (In the 2000s, the Lula government moved to create a more well-structured public television network, as will be discussed below.)

BRAZILIAN TV AFTER THE MILITARY GOVERNMENTS

The role of television, particularly TV Globo, as the military regime's banner carrier was also diluted by the creation and effective growth of new networks, like SBT, which targeted subaltern social classes with different, more opposition-friendly messages. Growing television competition was marked by market segmentation, where most other networks positioned themselves around the programming strengths of the dominant network, TV Globo. The military had already announced a gradual liberalisation of media censorship, starting in 1977 with elite print media and slowly moving to open up broadcasting.

Brazilian television after 1985 went through a third phase, marked by its role in the transition to a new civilian republic. In 1984, TV Globo initially supported the military government against a campaign for direct election of a civilian government, while other media, including other television networks, many radio stations, and most of the major newspapers supported the campaign for direct elections now. TV Globo went so far as to call a massive pro-democracy demonstration in São Paulo a city festival. Angry crowds at demonstrations began to throw rocks at TV Globo reporters and sound trucks (Straubhaar, 1988). Quite a few people began to watch other networks' news to get more favourable coverage of the direct elections campaign. Perceiving that it might lose its audience to the competition, TV Globo also switched sides and supported an early transition to a civilian regime which, in a compromise, was indirectly elected in 1985 (Straubhaar, 1988). The new civilian governments reduced political censorship and pressure on broadcasters, although some censorship on moral issues remained.

Despite the new competition that began in the early 1980s, TV Globo still had a majority share of the audience. As of 1991, TV Globo drew an average share of 66 per cent of the nationwide audience, SBT/TVS 18 per cent, TV Manchete seven per cent, TV Bandeirantes five per cent, and all others (TV Record, public TV and independent stations) four per cent (Marques de Melo, 1991). Other networks have had difficulty in competing with TV Globo. Efforts by several networks, first TV Tupi, then TV Bandeirantes and TV Manchete, to compete with TV Globo for a broad general audience have failed. So the oligopolistic, imitative competition among commercial networks for the general audience typical of the US never took place. Instead, other broadcast television networks found themselves pursuing smaller, more specific audience segments largely defined by social class. As noted, SBS (Sílvio

Publicity for *Carrossel*,
a youth-oriented telenovela
shown on SBT in 2012.
Originally a remake of the
Mexican *Carrusel*, SBT later
launched a cartoon version

Santos) targeted a lower middle class, working class and poor audience, that
gained it a consistent second place in ratings in most of the 1980s and early
1990s, but advertisers were not always attracted to that audience segment
(Mattos, 1990).

In the 1980s, other networks attempted to break into *telenovela* production
to compete with Globo for a broader general audience. Neither SBT nor TV
Bandeirantes had commercial success with producing *telenovelas*, but TV
Manchete achieved fairly high ratings for *Pantanal* set in Brazil's western sub-
tropical region of that name. SBT resorted to importing *telenovelas* from Mexico,
instead of producing them. TV Globo had also begun co-production of *telenovelas* with international partners to lower costs and reach other markets. In July
1991, eleven *telenovelas* were being shown on four networks: TV Globo (2
reruns, 2 international co-productions, 2 national), TV Manchete (1 rerun, 1
national production), SBT (2 imported from Mexico), and TV Bandeirantes (1
rerun) (Festa and Santoro, 1991).

INTERNATIONALISATION

The fourth phase of Brazilian television was its internationalisation. The importation of television programmes into Brazil declined in the 1970s–80s
(Straubhaar, 1984; Straubhaar, 1991) and continued to decline more slowly in
the 1990s and 2000s, particularly on broadcast television (Straubhaar, 2007). As
in many countries, opening a new network, station or cable/satellite channel
often leads its managers to look for cheap imported programming. That was particularly true of satellite television in its initial offerings in the 1990s, when
pay-TV in particular was almost entirely filled with imported channels. But we
will see below that that drew a very limited audience, so when TV Globo wished
to expand its audience on pay-TV, it had to expand its offering of national channels in film, news, documentary, etc. Brazilian exports of programming to the

rest of the world became a significant phenomenon, which will be discussed further below (Marques de Melo, 1988).

Telenovela quality steadily increased at TV Globo throughout the 1970s–90s. They increasingly drew on popular novels, such as those by Jorge Amado. The dominant themes were upward mobility, consumption goals and lifestyles–messages that appealed broadly to the mass audience in a growing consumer society. At TV Globo at least, the production values in *telenovelas* became high enough to best all Latin American *telenovelas*, except perhaps those of Mexico, and rival programmes imported from the US or Europe. The Brazilian *telenovelas* were good enough, as commercial television entertainment, to be exported throughout Latin America and then into Europe and Africa (Antola, Rogers *et al.*, 1984) (Rogers and Schement, 1984).

In the 1980s and 1990s, Brazilian television networks, particularly TV Globo, not only emerged as major exporters of *telenovelas* to the rest of Latin America and the world, but also other programming, such as music videos, variety shows, comedies and mini-series. TV Globo started in 1976, exporting the *telenovela Gabriela* to Portugal, followed by *telenovelas* dubbed into Spanish for the Latin American market. Despite dubbing costs, around $150,000 per series, Globo already earned over $1,000,000 in 1977 from exports. By 1991, TV Globo exported programming to 130 countries. The group was also investing internationally. The Globo Group acquired control of Telemontecarlo in Italy for several years (Netto, 1987) and in 1992 acquired one of the new private channels in Portugal (Rattner, 1992). While the Montecarlo investment was an expensive failure (Wallach, 2011), the Portugal station was very successful, in part by monopolising the import of TV Globo's own *telenovelas*, analogous to the situation of Univision in the US Hispanic audience – dominating a culturally proximate and popular import. By 1992, Globo earned about $20,000,000 per year from exports – modest in light of roughly $700,000,000 gross yearly sales revenues that year (Marques de Melo, 1992).

TV Globo's programming was sufficiently successful in Italy, Portugal and France that some European scholars examined its productions, particularly *telenovelas*, as potential models for European production (Mattelart & Mattelart, 1990). Italy in particular imported *telenovelas* on a large scale in the 1990s, as new private networks there also looked abroad for cheap but interesting television to import. As Italian ability to produce domestic melodrama grew, they did in fact adapt aspects of the Brazilian *telenovela* to their own serial drama production (Buonanno, 2004). Portugal also imported *telenovelas* on a large scale for a number of years, first on national public television, then later on the new private channel partially owned by TV Globo. Eventually the Portuguese also created their own melodramas, based in large part on Brazilian

Logo of TV Global
Internacional, which operates
satellite television channels
around the world, including
some direct feeds from Rio
de Janiero

models that had become familiar to the audience (Ferrin Cunha *et al.*, 2011). Brazilian *telenovelas* were also exported with considerable success to other parts of the Lusophone world in Africa. For other territories, Brazilian *telenovelas* were dubbed into a number of other languages, including English.

In 1979, TV Globo tried to move beyond *telenovelas* in its overseas sales. TV Globo began to produce a few series (self-contained one hour episodes with a continuing cast and theme, patterned on the series that the US exported.) A crime reporter focused on abuses of *favela* or slum dwellers, truck drivers traversed Brazilian roads and encountered Brazilian character types and situations, a newly separated woman tried to be independent in Rio. TV Globo exported these series, particularly the one about the 'unmarried' woman, which was shown on Spanish International Network in the US as *Malu Mujer*. TV Globo and TV Manchete also produced and exported a number of mini-series. The most successful of these, particularly for export, have tended to be historical in focus and like *telenovelas*, have often adapted literary works by authors such as Jorge Amado or Guimarães Rosa. After TV Manchete failed, TV Globo kept producing mini-series, both for domestic viewing and export. A Brazilian children's variety programme, *Xuxa's Show*, which originated on TV Globo, had been produced in syndication in Spanish in Argentina for Latin America. However, an English-language adaptation of *Xuxa* produced by a leading Hollywood studio failed in the US market in 1993, even though it was carried by one of the major networks. Global also began to experience troubles in Brazil where it faced growing competition. In the late 1990s, Globo therefore began to refocus on ensuring the quality and competitiveness of its national productions, since its international earnings were actually quite modest compared to its domestic profits.

Television imports into Brazil had declined overall since the 1970s (Straubhaar, 2007), but the availability of foreign films and, to some lesser degree, foreign television programmes, increased somewhat with new television technologies. The first new technology to open up a new stream of imports was the videocassette recorder (VCR). The proportion of homes in Brazil with a VCR increased from less than 1 per cent in 1980 to about 8 per cent in 1989 (IBOPE, 1989). That growth was slower than in many other Latin American countries, but seemed to accelerate in the late 1980s, with an estimated 250 per cent growth in 1989 to a total of 5,300,000 VCRs (Maiello, 1990). The number of video rental outlets increased from 200 in 1982 to 4,669 in 1989 (Maiello, 1990). Nearly all of the videos available in various rental catalogs surveyed by the author were from the US. A survey of rental stores to establish the ten most widely rented video tapes of 1989 showed that all ten were from the US: three adventure films, three police dramas, three comedies and one drama (Camargo, 1990). However, many Brazilian viewers remained loyal to national television channels and did not use VCRs extensively. Data from the Brazilian Video Association in 1990 showed that roughly 40 per cent were not actively used.

NEW TELEVISION SYSTEMS

The recent fifth phase of Brazilian television is marked by the appearance of some new video distribution systems. The first new technology to diffuse widely in Brazil was the home videocassette recorder (VCR), as noted above. Other new video technologies entered the Brazilian television market in the 1990s, offering focused or segmented programming through additional advertising-supported UHF (ultra high frequency) channels or pay-TV systems, like subscription television (STV), cable TV systems, multichannel multipoint distribution systems (MMDS) and direct to home satellite broadcasting (DTH). These main systems are competing with conventional VHF television and with each other, in terms of both programming and technological platforms.

However, the new technology with most effect on Brazilian electronic media is the microwave and satellite distribution of television, either to repeaters or direct to homes. First microwave towers and then BrasilSat took national television channels into the rural areas and small towns of the Brazilian interior and Amazonian North. In the 1980s, thousands of small towns in rural Brazil purchased satellite dishes and low power repeaters to bring in television. Local mayors or political candidates often purchased the systems as public works projects for the town in order to get (re)elected. In one month (15 April–15 May) in the local and state political campaign season of 1990, 600 such systems were installed in just one state, Bahia, all purchased by local politicians (Camargo, 1990). So the first and most lasting impact of satellite technology in Brazil was not to bring in foreign television channels (although that also took place), it was to bring national channels to people who would not otherwise have had them.

After small towns bought antennas and repeaters, as the cost of satellite dishes continued to go down in the 1990s and 2000s, millions of households in rural Brazil or the peripheries of towns where reception was poor, bought their own DTH satellite dishes, not to get imported signals, but to get a national signal or perhaps a better quality one. One ethnographic study of television viewing in the mid-1990s found such systems popular as a way to get access to national television channels, but residents actually longed to have a local signal with local news and local advertisements (La Pastina, 1999).

Brazilian television stations used first Intelsat, then the first and now fourth generation of BrasilSat to extend the reach of telecommunications and television across all of Brazil. The first BrasilSat was constructed by the US and Brazil, and launched by the French in 1984. BrasilSat One was followed by three other generations of BrasilSat, with the fourth generation launched in 2007. The third and fourth generation satellites are still in service.

It was hoped that opening up new technological channels in television would let in some new companies that had been frozen out of broadcast television for either political reasons (especially under the military), technological reasons (not enough easy to use VHF broadcast channels left), or economic reasons (pursuing a large conventional television audience with mainstream traditional programming required very large resources). With all of these barriers to entry lowered, a variety of traditional Brazilian media companies in print and radio thought anew about trying to enter some aspect of television. In fact, the opening up of new licences for UHF, STV, cable and satellite channels has admitted some new companies into 'broadcasting', but a number of the companies involved are familiar, like TV Globo. The major new entrant with UHF and STV was the dominant publishing house, Editora Abril, owned by Victor Civita, which eventually also scaled up into cable and satellite television as well.

A number of UHF licences were issued and several different kinds of UHF TV operations entered the market, from new advertising-supported national channels to regional channels to encrypted pay-TV. The first one was a licensed Brazilian adaptation of MTV (Music TV), owned by the Editora Abril group. It used a great deal of programming from the US MTV, with local announcers, local advertisements and some Brazilian music videos. One of the first major pay-TV systems, TVA, started on scrambled UHF/SHF/MMDS. It was a combination of earlier separate offerings by the TVA Group, Editora Abril, and the Machline industrial group. In 1992, it offered five channels: films, news (CNN), sports (ESPN), a super-station type channel, and TNT, targeted at individual upper middle class households in major cities (Schwartsman, 1991). It expanded its programming in the 1990s primarily by bringing in European and US channels in the original languages.

GloboSat was a DBS/DTH and SMATV (satellite master antenna TV – aimed at distribution systems within apartment buildings) satellite channel aimed at some rural viewers and condominium owners in major cities (Athayde, 1991), owned by the Globo Group. It initially had a programming line-up similar to TVA's, with four channels (films, news, sports, shows). GloboSat expanded its programming by offering international channels and a national all-news channel, GloboNews (in 1996) (Reis, 1999).

Cable TV and satellite pay-TV were initially very limited in their growth in Brazil. In 1993, less than one per cent of Brazilian households subscribed to cable, even though over 80 per cent had television then. By 1996, after extensive promotion of cable to middle class households, only five per cent had cable, much lower than the Latin American average of 11 per cent (Hoineff, 1996; Reis, 1999). Some observers felt that TV Globo was deliberately stalling cable television and pay-TV in order to protect its hold on the national television audience. That included holding a central role but not developing it very far, perhaps in order to not cannibalise its own audience, as well as apparently trying to limit the issue of licences to other potential competitors (Paxman, 1998; Reis, 1999; Fernández and Paxman, 2001). However, the Globo Group steadily increased its operations in cable and satellite TV. In 1996, it opened an all-news channel, Globo News.

The Globo Group went into cable TV in 1993 with NET (Net Serviços de Comunicação SA). They started with laying their own subterranean cable network in Rio de Janeiro. They incurred a great deal of expense, including foreign currency debt, which threatened to drag the company down financially, despite the continued profitability of much of the rest of the operations of the Globo Group, including TV Globo, *O Globo* newspaper, magazines and radio. Initially, they had a hard time convincing people to subscribe for $40–60 a month for limited programme options (Wallach, 2011). To have a chance to reduce its exposure and losses in telecommunications infrastructure, Globo lobbied for a change in Brazilian government foreign ownership rules, represented in the 1995 Cable Law, to permit it to sell part of NET to foreign investors. Eventually NET was co-owned by Globo and Embratel/América Móvil, owned by Carlos Slim, until a new 2011 pay-TV law prohibited broadcast companies from majority ownership of cable or telecommunications companies (Aquino, 2012). So Globo sold most of its half of NET to América Móvil. By 2012, Globo owned only 12 per cent of NET, which operated in 93 cities across Brazil, connecting over 10 million homes, including 4 million subscribing to pay-TV. In a very parallel development, Grupo Abril's TVA sold their pay-TV assets to the Spanish telecom firm Telefónica with approval from Brazil's telecommunications regulator, ANATEL (UOL, 2011). America Móvil and Telefónica/Vivo both now offer what are called triple-play services: cellular, VOIP (voice over internet protocol) capability, internet access and television. In the long run, two of Brazil's largest communications companies ended up having to sell their cable television interests to foreign conglomerates from Mexico and Spain, after having largely lost money in the market.

In a similar vein, the Globo Group stabilised and expanded satellite DTH through a partnership with Rupert Murdoch. Although the audience remained very limited until the middle 2000s, satellite, DTH and pay TV all expanded gradually in Brazil as the two major operations there became parts of competing transnational or regional satellite television groups. In 1997, TVA (Editora Abril) joined a consortium with DirecTV Latin America (then owned by Hughes). In 1996, GloboSat (Globo Group) joined Murdoch's Sky Latin America group, along with Televisa and Venevisión (Duarte, 2001). Initially, in the 1990s, pay-TV's audience was limited to the upper and upper middle class (Borelli and Priolli, 2000), in part because much of the programming was imported, not of much interest to an audience that had a fairly large supply of relatively well produced, culturally proximate national programming from several channels. Pay-TV suffered a classic cultural discount effect (Hoskins, McFayden *et al.*, 1997), being less relevant to the mass audience and mostly relevant to the kinds of people who were very familiar with US and European cultures and actively wanted to see television from there. The UHF and cable-based MTV Brasil offered a very clear analysis of this strategy: they consciously aimed at the richest and most internationalised 30 per cent of Brazilian youth, by programming imported music (Lobo, 1991). MTV Brasil researchers were aware that to reach beyond that 30 per cent, they would have to programme much more domestic music, which they saw as their long term strategy, but the initial segmented niche was a profitable beginning (interviews with author, 1991, 1994) Both TVA and GloboSat slowly expanded their offerings, both in terms of channels offered and how many of them were dubbed into Portuguese, seeming to offer the minimum localisation required to gradually expand the audience beyond the elite into the middle class (Straubhaar and Duarte, 2005). Globo joined with Murdoch in 1996 to form Sky Brasil, which was joined with other Latin American operations in Sky Latin America in 2000. TVA ultimately sold its interest to DirecTV, whose Latin American operation merged with Murdoch's Sky Latin America. Globo continues to be a minority partner with Sky Brasil.

NEW BROADCAST TELEVISION COMPETITION

TV Globo's broadcast dominance began to decline in the 1990s. Competition increased with the existing television networks, like SBT and TV Bandeirantes, who began to effectively segment the market, winning parts of the audience

away from Globo. Part of the competition was new television groups and channels that had slowly acquired specific niches, like Bandeirantes, which was
competitive in sports and news, or SBT, which aimed more popular (*popularesco*)
programming at lower middle class and working class audiences. Accentuating
this competition was the entry of new kinds of media groups with different
motives, some primarily political, some completely or partially commercial, and
some religious and/or partially commercial.

Both democratisation and growth tended to open up television to the entry
of new groups in the late 1980s and 1990s. This led to increased competition,
particularly in São Paulo, but eventually opened up local and regional competitors around the country, too. The main new force in the long run was a network
affiliated to a religious group. Edir Macedo, the bishop of the Universal Church
of the Kingdom of God, a Brazil-based evangelical group, had participated in
the Brazilian branches of US evangelical and Pentecostal churches and observed
US televangelism broadcast in Brazil. He decided in classic hybrid fashion that
he could glocalise and improve Brazilian televangelism. So in 1975 he created
the Universal Church of the Kingdom of God, usually considered part of a larger
neo-Pentecostal movement in Brazil, (the "neo" difference is in their move to a
much large scale of action, larger congregations and nationwide organisation, as
well as a much more aggressive profile in growth and public presentation)
(Birman & Lehmann, 1999). It grew rapidly in the 1980s–2000s. Macedo
bought the TV Record Network, based in São Paulo, in 1989 and gradually built
it into the number two television network in Brazil. Birman and Lehmann note:

> TV Record seems to have a dual religious and secular/commercial agenda: it is
> evidently aiming to be a commercially viable, professional TV station, attracting a
> nation-wide audience and carrying advertising and mainstream non-religious
> programmes, broadcasting preaching and the testimony of converts during off-peak
> hours and all through the night. Although on occasion, its management has
> interfered to influence news or current affairs programmes in the Church's
> interests, these incidents have been few and declining in number, and the company
> has proved able to attract top-ranking newscasters and presenters (1999, p. 4).

Although some of TV Record's late night programming was overtly religious,
its daytime and prime time programming followed the *popularesco* lines laid
down earlier by SBT. That programming, now expanded in the 1990s by both
SBT and Record, made major inroads into TV Globo's audience, creating a segmentation, partially along social class lines (with the populist emphasis of SBT
and Record), but also along interest lines (like Bandeirantes' sports and news
emphasis) among the broadcast television audience (Borelli and Priolli, 2000).

Logo wars: being out-rated
by TV Record is a poke in the
eye for TV Globo

The competing channels opened up new emphases, which segmented the audience by interests. For example, while TV Globo programmed largely to children in the afternoon, TV Record could pull away a substantial audience with a women's show in the afternoon. Stations accentuated the competition with Globo by targeting more specific groups: sports fans, news fans, women, children, and by bringing back programme genres, like big variety shows, at which both SBT and Record excelled, and which Globo had given up as inconsistent with its emphasis on high quality in prime time and elsewhere.

The opening up of the UHF spectrum in the 1990s also allowed in a number of channels segmented by interests, such as MTV (youth and music, as mentioned, started by Editora Abril in 1990), Rede Mulher (for women), and Redevida (Catholic Church). Other channels came in that were more localised (as in a community channel in São Paulo) or regionalised, like Northeastern culture programmes in the afternoon on TV Itapoan in Bahia or Southern Brazil programming on Rede Sul de Comunicação (RBS) (Borelli and Priolli, 2000).

Political interests and powers came into broadcasting strongly, too. Most of the radio and television licences granted in Brazil since the late 1980s have been to local or state level politicians with national influence who saw media outlets in their political domains as part of their overall power (Amaral & Guimaraes, 1994; Matos, 2011). Matos notes that 'in the mid 1990s politicians controlled 30–40 per cent of the total number of radio [40 per cent] and television [31 per cent] stations in the country' (2011, p. 189, 196). As time went on, these stations were also a way to diversify their incomes with commercial revenues. Some of these groups have become more commercial, some more political, but they are different from the traditional family empires, like Globo, although a number of them are affiliated with the TV Globo or other national networks. The Brazilian national government, under President Lula, finally created a national public network, TV Brasil, in 2007, by combining parts of a national radio service, RadioBras, and a largely defunct national educational television service (TVE). It focused on regional programmes, carried programmes made by university and educational stations around Brazil, and is intended to serve as the flagship of a planned national interactive digital television service.

TV Globo began a slow steady decline in audience ratings, starting in the 1990s. For example, TV Globo had an average annual rating in prime time of 51.5 per cent in São Paulo in 1979, and 53.5 per cent in 1987. Its share of households actually watching in 1988 was in the 70–80 per cent range, depending on the show. By 1997, its average rating in a national average of state capitals was 37 per cent (Borelli and Priolli, 2000). Both TV Globo's journalism and *telenovelas* declined in popularity. This resulted in internal debates and struggles that led to the dismissal of some of the founders of the Globo formula, like Boni, in 1997 (Borelli & Priolli, 2000). In the 2000s, TV Globo's total audience share for all programmes combined (7 a.m. to midnight) dropped from 55 per cent in 2004 to 44 per cent in 2008 (Grupo de Mídia, 2009; Thomas, 2010). In 2008, TV Record had climbed to a 16 per cent share, SBT 14 per cent, Bandeirantes 5 per cent, Rede TV 2 per cent and all other channels combined, 18 per cent (*Mídia,* 2009; Thomas, 2010). As TV Record grew, it acquired a parallel network of stations in many cities that carried more clearly religious programmes. The main Record network shifted its program line to try to compete more directly with TV Globo, which has responded by attacking Record and its parent church (Birman & Lehmann, 1999). In the 2000s, TV Record met this challenge by launching a series of high-quality *telenovelas* that struck right at the heart of Globo's dominant position in television drama. Earlier attempts by Bandeirantes and SBT to compete in *telenovelas* had generally failed, but TV Record's parent organisation, the Universal Church of the Reign of God, has deep pockets and seemed determined to compete directly in even the most costly genres. However, rising costs finally led them to cut back original programming in 2013.

The Globo Group, despite severe losses in cable TV infrastructure, still saw its overall fortunes increase. TV Globo remained highly profitable, if not as dominant as it once was. *O Globo* became the dominant newspaper in Rio and one of the two major papers in Brazil. The Group's twenty-seven magazines, record sales (label Som Livre) and radio stations (over 160) were profitable. Globo Group also became a major player in film production and distribution. TV Globo stars, such as Xuxa and the Trapalhões (the Three Stooges of Brazil), had long starred in popular films, which Globo Group frequently distributed on video. Starting in 1998, Globo Filmes became a major producer, involved in around 15 per cent of the films produced. It was even more powerful in promotion and distribution. In one study of national films 2001–05, Globo Filmes productions had 80 per cent of the box office for national films (Thomas, 2010).

In the 2000s, a number of complex economic developments began to change the face of Brazilian television. The economy grew rapidly, bringing almost 40

Avenida Brasil (Brasil Avenue) is a gritty tale of intrigue which was a commercial and critical success for TV Globo in 2012

per cent of the population from working class (class D in Brazilian market analysis) and working poor (class E) into the lower middle class (class C3), according to several economic analyses (Barros, de Carvalho *et al.*, 2010). Since almost all of those people and households already had a television set, one result was to increase their pursuit of other entertainment and information options. The number of television sets tuned in during prime time went from 66 per cent in 2000 to 59 per cent in 2009 (Thomas, 2010). Those who still wanted to watch television had more options. Market studies in the late 2000s onward showed steadily increasing interest in cable television among the new middle class (Folha, 2012). As regional economic disparities decreased, local and regional television stations and groups grew in their ability to programme locally at an attractive level of quality and attracted more of the local and regional audience away from national broadcast networks. Overall, several participants in a panel discussion for the industry report *Mídia Dados Brasil 2011* reported that the overall trend was to growth in the television sector through increasing diversity of technologies, channels and audience choices (Grupo de Mídia, 2011).

CONCLUSION

Brazilian television is shifting from a long era presided over by a few broadcast networks, principally dominated by TV Globo alone in the 1970s–80s. During that time audiences were remarkably loyal to TV Globo, but segments of the audience began to shift to competing broadcast networks, such as SBT and TV Record, starting in the 1990s. Brazilian audiences, outside the elite and upper middle class, showed little interest in cable or satellite television until the mid 2000s. An opening up of a new television scenario came as many more Brazilians became part of the middle class, where cable or satellite pay television was a realistic ambition. It also depended on GloboSat, and new UHF and cable channels, beginning to create a series of segmented channels with more extensive national content that could also draw in an audience that was used to seeing national programming on television. Unlike Mexico, Brazil's main television channels, both broadcast like TV Globo or cable/satellite like TVA and GloboSat/NET, lost their attempts to be major players in the new triple-play world of combined cable, telephone and internet access. TVA sold its interests to Telefónica of Spain and Globo became a minor partner with América Móvil of Mexico in NET. However, GloboSat does remain a growing power in cable programming, demonstrating that perhaps it was better to remain in new services related to its core competence, since it lost a lot of money in the 1990s trying to build cable infrastructure.

4

Emergent Producers and Markets in Latin America

As argued in the previous chapters, the television industries of Mexico and Brazil came to dominate the trade in their respective cultural-linguistic regions because they are the largest domestic markets in those regions. So, size does matter, but that is not the whole explanation. Dominance within the domestic market is clearly another factor – the cases of Televisa in Mexico and TV Globo in Brazil each show how one large producer-distributor can derive profit from their programmes in the domestic market, then go on to reap the benefit of export revenues on top of that, all the while keeping competition at bay. Other related factors which are evident in our accounts of Mexico and Brazil include the early acceptance and successful local adaptation of the commercial model for broadcasting and its institutionalisation in the radio era; the capacity to attract investments from broadcasting networks and similar interests in the United States at strategic stages of development; a favourable regulatory environment permitting both vertical integration of production and distribution and horizontal integration of related media interests; the development of programming that gained audience approval and loyalty; and the shrewd management of relations with the government of the day.

Looking further afield in Latin America, there is a second tier of countries in which large producer-distributors of television programming have emerged and become active in the regional trade. These are Venezuela, Argentina, and more recently, Colombia. Some of the same factors as identified in Mexico and Brazil are to be found in these cases, though they are very much shaped by discontinuities of government control, and each in their unique way, which is what this chapter will examine. In addition, the case of Chile is considered, where the history and structure of its television industry exhibits some strikingly exceptional features. It will become evident that the development of television in Latin America has been, and continues to be, highly politicised. The chapter concludes with a look at a major production, distribution and trading centre outside of Latin America: Miami, where US and Latin American companies collaborate in feeding both their respective markets, and finally, a review of some data on patterns of programme exchange within the Iberoamerican world as of the end of the first decade of the 2000s.

VENEZUELA

Decades of dictatorship and military government in Venezuela prior to World War II restricted the spread of radio, but it nevertheless became established before then on a commercial basis, as occurred elsewhere in Latin America. By 1953, when the military government of the time granted two licences for the transition to television, Radio Caracas, Venezuela's first radio network, centred in the capital and dating from 1935, was well-placed to launch Radio Caracas Televisión (RCTV) as Channel Two. The other licence, for Channel Four, went to a company known as Televisa, by no means related to the Mexican behemoth (Giménez Saldivia & Hernández Algara, 1988; Fox, 1997). These two companies in effect formed the infrastructure of television in Venezuela for the rest of the century – a virtual duopoly, with weak domestic participation by the state, not unlike 'the Mexican formula' referred to in Chapter Two. In 1960, the Televisa name was changed to Venevisión, when the licence was purchased by an industrial corporation owned by Diego Cisneros, originally a Cuban immigrant. Cisneros was backed by an initial investment of 43 per cent from the US network, ABC, while, for its part, RCTV was owned 20 per cent by NBC. This was during the period when the US networks thought there was some value for them in fostering the development of television in the region. A further arrival came in 1965 with Cadena Venezolana de Televisión (CVTV) Channel 8, owned by another of Venezuela's industrial groups, in conjunction with the then-exiled Cuban entrepreneur Goar Mestre, and with the participation of US capital from Time-Life and the CBS network. As mentioned in Chapter One, the revolution in Cuba had displaced capital, management and talent from its television industry, and Venezuela clearly was a major beneficiary. The RCTV/Venevisión duopoly shook off the competition from Channel 8, which was acquired by the state in 1974, and made into its national network. It remained a losing concern, with inadequate production facilities and a heavy reliance on imported programmes, which in those days mainly meant from the US (Giménez Saldivia & Hernández Algara, 1988; Fox, 1997). For this reason, the era came to be subsequently denounced for its 'cultural imperialism' via television.

Whereas the television activities of Televisa in Mexico and Globo in Brazil are integrated into fully-fledged media corporations, the television networks of Venezuela, and, as we shall see, Colombia, have formed part of consolidated industrial corporations, also including some relatively marginal sports and entertainment companies. Diego Cisneros was the founding patriarch of an industrial group which had its origins in the 1940s, when it was based on transport, refrigeration, food, and drink, notably bottling franchises for Pepsi Cola (Giménez Saldivia & Hernández Algara, 1988), although Venevisión became the most profitable division of the group. Just as Emilio Azcárraga Milmo restructured

Televisa in the 1970s on the death of the founding father, just so did Gustavo Cisneros, the son who succeeded Diego in 1970, undertake a major restructure at that time, in the process naming the group as Companías Grupo Cisneros, or Cisneros Group of Companies (CGC). At its greatest extent, the group's activities have ranged over mining, supermarket chain operation (in the US and Puerto Rico as well as Venezuela), sports and electronic goods manufacturing, and telecommunications. While CGC still retains a strong presence in several industries, it has been media and communication where it has now concentrated its efforts (Cisneros, 2012).

Like TV Azteca in Mexico, where the parent company can use television to promote its electrical goods stores, Venevisión has been able to provide advertising for CGC's manufactured and franchised goods and services on its television network. Yet also like Grupo Televisa and Organizações Globo, CGC is a conglomerate in which media are integrated vertically, notably through the television network and an international sales arm which distributes its programme production; and horizontally, incorporating companies ranging across a number of media fields. These include radio broadcasting, publishing, branded entertainment, music recording, and film production and distribution. Venevisión has a significant offshore presence in the form of Venevisión Internacional, part of the Cisneros Television Group located in Miami, where it has studios producing *telenovelas* and other programming both for the US Latino market (on Univisión) and internationally, distributing its own and other Latin American productions to 90 countries. One particular export success, for example, has been its *telenovela* from 1992, *Cara sucia* (*Dirty Face*), a characteristic tale of danger and deceit, and love across class barriers. Venevisón also has pay-TV channels it markets to subscribers in both Latin America and the US. Again like Televisa and Globo, it has other interests in sports and entertainment (notably the running of and broadcasting rights for Miss Venezuela, the national passion), and a philanthropic foundation, in CGC's case, run by Gustavo Cisneros's wife, Patricia Phelps de Cisneros (Cisneros, 2012).

Both Venevisión and RCTV have considerable incentives to look outside their domestic market to expand their businesses. Firstly, Venezuela has the smallest population of the four countries being considered here: just over 31 million, compared to 42 million for Argentina, 49 million for Colombia, and less than 18 million for Chile, according to United Nations 2010 estimates of 2015 populations. Thus, the Venezuelan companies have the least opportunity to build on domestic market strength: Mexico by comparison has 120 million, and Brazil 203 million (United Nations, 2011). Secondly, it would be an understatement to observe that economic stability and prosperity in Latin America is highly variable, not only from time to time and country to country, but within each country.

For example, Brazil's booming economy stands in stark contrast to Venezuela's protracted economic crisis. The third factor is that with the accession to the presidency of Colonel Hugo Chávez in 1998, and the subsequent implementation of his populist policies to address the nation's problems (what he called 'twenty-first century socialism') and shore up his own power, the national television networks were put under extreme pressure. As will be explained, Venevisión's domestic service did buckle down to Chávez, but RCTV in fact was taken off the air indefinitely in 2007 and the frequency taken over by the government ('Chávez changes channels', 2007). Chávez seems to have been prepared to bear the unpopularity of this action, perhaps because some of RCTV's *telenovelas* had controversial, contemporary plots. The classic example is *Por estas calles* (*On These Streets* 1992–4) which dramatised life in the *barrios* (slum communities). Furthermore, while RCTV subsequently made a tactical retreat to concentrate on its cable channel RCTVI, the government extended its authority in 2010 to block such a move, effectively eliminating any access to RCTV for Venezuelan audiences other than via the internet (Alvarado Miquilena & Torrealba Mesa, 2011). Chávez's interest in television extended to him conducting his own talk show, *Aló Presidente* (*Hello, President*), compulsorily aired every Sunday since 1999. As well, his government backed the production of historical dramas, celebrating the original Bolivarian revolution which achieved independence for Venezuela, and in the news arena, took a leading role with the establishment of Telesur, as explained below.

Venevisión's international activities did not begin with the Chávez era, however; nor was Chávez the first Venezuelan president to seek to control the media. Already in the 1990s, Venevisión's parent company was deriving about half its earnings outside of Venezuela, much more than the corresponding level for Televisa or Globo at that time. Apart from its international programme sales, Venevisión became active in acquiring direct interests in television networks in other Spanish-speaking countries. As will be explained in Chapter Five, Venevisión entered a deal to purchase a share of Univisión in the US as equal partners with Televisa and, like Televisa, bought into a newly-privatised channel in Chile, in its case Chilevisión. Venevisión also has had interests in channels in Puerto Rico and the Caribbean media group, CCN (Smirnoff, 1994b). Venevisión was the largest of the Latin American partners in the former Hughes Galaxy DTH consortium, which ultimately became DirecTV. Cisneros was active in signing up other Latin American countries to the venture, and was developing programming for it in Miami. In new media, he partnered with AOL Time Warner (Hoag, 2000).

The personalised, patriarchal control and dynastic continuity we have seen in the history and structure of Televisa and Globo can also be found in CGC.

Gustavo Cisneros is the fourth of Diego Cisneros's eight sons. Educated in the US, he sits on the boards of US businesses and universities, and cultivates a cosmopolitan international standing which was never achieved by his Mexican peer, Azcárraga Milmo, who was known more for his conspicuous consumption of luxury yachts and women (Fernández & Paxman, 2000). It has been said of Cisneros that he 'has always found his own country too small for his talents and too insecure for his accumulated fortune' (Gott, 2006). However, while the Azcárraga dynasty has always enjoyed a relatively stable position within the domestic political structure of Mexico, the Cisneros family has not had such good fortune, at least in that regard, or perhaps has lacked the political skills.

Even before the accession of Chávez, Gustavo Cisneros had political problems. He and his brother Ricardo were publicly discredited when an arrangement that they had with President Carlos Andres Perez (President 1973–8, and 1989–93) to allow greater media concentration in return for political support became undone (Fox, 1997). Perez's successor, Rafael Caldera, was unable to resolve Venezuela's continuing financial crisis, and was ousted by Chávez in the 1998 election. When Chávez subsequently proved resistant to Cisneros's influence, Cisneros and his Venevisión network publicly opposed him, and privately participated in an attempted coup against him in 2002 (Gott, 2006). Yet, as it has since turned out, because Venevisión eventually became compliant and dropped its on-air opposition to Chávez, it became RCTV which stood its ground and was punished with the loss of its broadcast licence, in 2007, and then by being restricted from participation in pay-TV in 2010, as noted above.

Until Chávez thus cleared RCTV from the field, Venevisión had been facing much more substantial competition from RCTV, both in the domestic market and internationally, than either TV Globo or Televisa have to deal with in their markets. As explained, RCTV still exists, but has been removed from domestic free-to-air broadcasting, and although it then consolidated itself for a time as a cable and satellite pay-TV network, it is now restricted to international programme production and distribution from its base in Miami. Very much like Venevisión, RCTV is owned by a family-based industrial group, Grupo Phelps, also known as 1BC, which has had interests in property, construction, retailing and manufacturing, but increasingly has become focused on its media and communications companies. In both cases, the non-media industrial activities mark the Venezuelan variation on the Latin American model of media ownership. The founding father of the group was William Henry Phelps, who, after his return from being educated in the US, went on to establish Venezuela's first commercial radio station in 1935, and subsequently RCTV in 1953 (Giménez Saldivia & Hernández Algara, 1988). RCTV began producing *telenovelas* in the 1950s, but these were broadcast live, and it was not until 1961, with the advent of videotape, that such programming could be packaged and thus become tradeable. An early success of this year was *El derecho de nacer* (*The Right to be Born*), a *telenovela* based originally on a 1948 Cuban *radionovela* which, with its controversial abortion theme, has been made in several national versions elsewhere in the region, such as Mexico in 2001. It is worth noting, incidentally, that such remaking from country to country, and updating from one decade to another, is a common feature of the genre, by which some titles become classics.

Since 1982, RCTV's international activities have been centred on programme production and distribution through Coral Pictures Corporation, which, like Venevisión International, is based in Miami, the virtual media capital of the Spanish-speaking Americas (Sinclair, 2003). Mirroring its competitor, in 2005 Coral was renamed RCTV International. Just as RCTV once offered strong competition to Venevisión in the domestic market before its banishment by Chávez, this is still the case in programme export activities. Coral has been a major distributor of programming, with its number of hours sold annually comparable to that of Televisa and Globo, both of its own programming and that of other producers. Its most internationally popular *telenovela* has been *Cristal* (1985), a drama set in the fashion industry. Coral was responsible for opening up Spain to Venezuelan *telenovelas* in 1991, although it was soon followed there by Venevisión, and both became involved in co-productions with networks in Spain at that time.

As of 2012, RCTV International was exporting out of Miami to forty-eight countries in a dozen languages, and claiming the title, 'the *telenovela* people'. A particular international success, reminiscent of that of RCN's *Betty la fea*, has been *Mi gorda bella* (*My Sweet Fat Valentina*; literally, *My Fat Beauty*). First shown in Venezuela in 2002–03, this *telenovela* has been shown in many countries, including the US (on Telemundo), and remade in Mexico as well as more remote countries like India and Malaysia (RCTV International, 2012).

One quite different aspect of television in Venezuela, and symptomatic of the former Chávez regime, which deserves a closing mention has been the advent of Telesur. Launched in 2005, Telesur is an initiative of the Venezuelan Government, founded in conjunction with several other Latin American governments, including Argentina, Cuba, and Uruguay. Its focus is to give those governments a renewed voice in television, over against private commercial television networks, which dominate the audience. It is a satellite-to-cable news and information service transmitting out of Caracas, and in principle, available throughout Latin America, and also in the US and Europe. In fact, Telesur has had difficulty in gaining access to the major privately-owned cable systems of the region (Kozloff, 2007), although it is carried by the US-based international

Logo of Telesur, *La nueva televisora del Sur* ('the new television channel of the South'), a joint initiative of regional Left-wing governments

subscriber service DirecTV in some countries (Telesur, 2012). Its official name is *La nueva televisora del Sur* ('the new television channel of the South', in the sense of 'global South'), and dedicated to Latin American integration, consistent with Chávez's project of the 'Bolivarian Revolution'. This mission thoroughly colours Telesur's news values, and positions it as a counter-force to services such as CNN en Español. Its declared aim to build 'a new communication order' recalls the Cold War rhetoric of the Non-Aligned Movement in UNESCO against 'cultural imperialism' in the 1970s and 1980s (Thussu, 2006).

ARGENTINA

Like Venezuela, a complex history of populist dictatorship and military intervention in Argentina prevented the development of a relatively stable and mutually supportive relationship between the state and private television owners of the kind which has favoured the incumbents in Mexico and Brazil. On the contrary, Argentina's first television station, set up in 1951, was at the instigation of the President, Juan Perón (President 1945–55 and 1973–4) at a time when radio and press were already under the direct control of his government, or given into the hands of his supporters. When the military overthrew Perón in 1955, they purged the Perónists from the media, and granted a number of city-based commercial television licences, just before allowing civilian rule to resume. This was 1958, the beginning of the US network investment era. However, the military had been careful to forbid foreign investment, and to prohibit the channels from building themselves into networks. These provisions were circumvented in the first instance by having the foreign partners invest in production companies rather than the channels themselves, and then by joining affiliated stations to the production companies. Notable was Channel 13, established by Goar Mestre, the leading figure of the Cuban television diaspora, discussed in Chapter One. Mestre was backed by Time-Life and CBS, who invested in Channel 13's production company, Proartel. However, Perón was returned to power in 1973, when he nationalised all of the channels and their production companies. Nevertheless, even throughout the years of grim repression after 1976, when the military once again returned to power, television continued to be run on a commercial model. It was not until the 1980s that Argentine television became free from very direct government control, and because state-owned television had been associated with long decades of both civilian and military dictatorship, the democratically-elected regimes of Raúl Alfonsín in 1983 and especially Carlos Menem in 1989 progressively turned television over to private ownership (Fox, 1997).

This history makes the television industry of Argentina quite different to the others considered so far in this book, which have been built on the manoeuvres of one or two dominant national broadcasting networks. In particular, the historical absence of terrestrial free-to-air networks and the relative recency of privatisation has made satellite and/or cable modes of distribution especially important in Argentina. While cable television was first used to distribute the signal from terrestrial antennae to remote towns in the 1960s, the liberalisation of satellite transmission in the 1980s facilitated the take-up of cable in the cities. Thus, from serving as a mere rural relay system for broadcast channels, cable came to offer a mix of domestic and international programming to urban dwellers. As of 2010, more than 60 per cent of all television households in Argentina are cabled (Argentina Broadband Overview, 2011). Furthermore, the incidence of cable links Argentine television into the convergence of the media and telecommunications industries and their technologies on a global scale, with major Spanish, Mexican and Italian companies being involved. Thus, quite apart from the fact that it is generally one of the more active exporters and co-producers of programming amongst the Latin American countries, Argentine television also deserves our attention because of the relationship which it bears to regional and global telecommunications corporations in the age of media convergence.

Although historically, Argentina has had no television networks as such, the privatisation process has nevertheless favoured media concentration, as television channels are now in the hands of companies which are either based in print media, or have more diversified media ownership. Significantly, it was not just the sell-off of the former government-owned channels, but the removal of a previous restriction on cross-media ownership which created new media corporations. Notably, in 1989, Channel 13 was awarded to Grupo Clarín, owners of the newspaper which claims the largest circulation in the Spanish-speaking world, *Clarín*. Like Televisa and Globo, this is a public company under the control of a single family, though in this case being directed by the founder's widow, with interests across a wide range of media industries. It has a history of attracting capital investment from the US, most recently with a Goldman Sachs consortium holding around 10 per cent of shares (Grupo Clarín, 2012). In addition to the press interests and the television division, called Artear (Arte Radiotelevisivo Argentina), Clarín has companies in traditional media such as radio, and in new media, notably internet service provision and cable.

Except in the earliest years outlined above, Argentine television owners have tended not to vertically integrate production with distribution as their counterparts elsewhere have done so profitably, but rather, they have horizontally integrated broadcasting with cable. In Clarín's case, they first bought a cable company in 1992, Multicanal, and then Cablevisión in 2006. Not to be confused with Televisa's company of the same name in Mexico, Clarín's Cablevisión has about a quarter of the broadband market in Argentina, the region's third largest after Brazil and Mexico. Cablevisión is a player in telecommunications as well as media, since it is able to offer triple-play (TV, telephone and internet connection). It dominates pay-TV in particular, providing value-added services such as high definition and video-on-demand (Argentina Broadband Overview, 2011).

Artear is still the licensee for Channel 13, *El Trece*, in the capital, Buenos Aires, but the channel has national coverage through its affiliate stations and its own relay system – effectively a national network. It claims leadership in format and genre innovation and in defining the aesthetic style of television fiction in Argentina. Its variety show *Showmatch* (2004) is one of the country's most popular programmes. However, unlike Televisa and Globo and its Venezuelan counterparts, Channel 13 does not produce its own serial drama, but commissions it from independent producers. Nevertheless, it exports to a number of other Spanish-speaking markets, including Spain and the US, and engages in co-productions, notably of *Amas de casa desesperadas*, the Latin American version of *Desperate Housewives*. Artear also has a strategic content alliance with Disney, under which it has exclusive access to Disney product (Grupo Clarín, 2012).

In the privatisation of 1989, the Channel 11 licence was awarded to Telefé (Televisora Federal), a consortium of television stations and industrial conglomerates led by a book and magazine publisher, Editorial Atlántida (Fox, 1997). Telefé soon became the most popular of the new commercial channels, a position it held until 2010, with Channel 13 being its only real competitor. Like Channel 13, Telefé is a network in practice, with national coverage through a system of affiliate stations and repeaters, but as well as cable in some parts. It shows mostly its own productions, though along with the occasional Brazilian, Mexican, or Colombian *telenovela* as well as US fare such as *Los Simpson* (*The Simpsons*).

Since 2001, like its main competitor, Telefé has been more inclined to rely upon acquiring independent productions (Telefé, 2012). This shift coincided with the buyout of Telefé by the Spanish telecommunications giant Telefónica in 2000, which around that time also became the owner of the international production house Endemol. Predictably, Telefé produced and aired *Gran hermano*, a local version of the Endemol standard *Big Brother*, and continues to co-produce it with Endemol, but there is also a stream of other productions in a wide range of genres which Telefé shows and exports. These include Sony Pictures remakes of US series like *The Nanny* (*La niñera*, 2004–5) and *Married with Children* (*Casados con hijos*, 2005–6). Since 1998, Telefé has operated an international satellite service that offers a selection of news and entertainment programming which they claim reaches over five million subscribers worldwide. In addition, there is a division responsible for the commercialisation of formats and scripts, as well as others in film production and music recording (Telefé, 2012).

There are two other private channels. They are networked over broadcast and cable, but do not have complete national coverage. These are Channel 2, América TV, operated by the Argentine-owned América Medios and Uno groups, which also have other media interests; and Channel 9, which in 2007 became a part of Albavisión, a unique media corporation owned by a mysterious Mexican, Ángel González (Aprea & Kirchheimer, 2011). Based in Miami, Albavisión dates back to 1948 in Guatemala, but, as of 2012, boasted a network of twenty-six owned or affiliated television stations throughout a dozen Latin American countries, as well as a similarly dispersed radio network, and film distribution and exhibition interests (Albavisión, 2012). González is nicknamed 'the phantom' (*el fantasma*) because he keeps such a low public profile ('¿Quién es el empresario Ángel González, *el fantasma*?', 2007). Most of Channel 2's programming is live, while Channel 9 is strong on foreign *telenovelas*, films and other entertainment. The one remaining state-owned channel is Televisión Pública, Channel 7, which has a mix of entertainment and public-interest programming. It has the most extensive coverage of the nation, but trails well behind the two commercial leaders in audience share (Aprea & Kirchheimer, 2011).

Building on the original arrangement under which the Buenos Aires television channels formed production companies to make programmes that could be distributed to their provincial affiliates, and the strong preference that audiences have since shown for Argentine programmes, the era of privatisation has encouraged domestic production and, in turn, motivated a strong drive to establish distribution arrangements and co-production partners abroad. These have principally been in other Latin American countries, but also in Europe, Asia and the Middle East, as well as the US. 'Independent' production houses have greater or lesser links to the networks – the case of Endemol and Telefé has already been mentioned. By contrast, in 2010, two top flight programme directors of long standing at Telefé surprised the industry when they left to form their own company, ON TV. The ten most-viewed titles on Argentine television that year, incidentally, were all Argentine productions, eight of which were *telenovelas* (Aprea & Kirchheimer, 2011). The 'glocalised' domestic versions of foreign formats have also proven popular with audiences. Waisbord and Jalfin (2009) examine some cases in which Argentine producers, drawing on their own cultural sensibilities, act as gatekeepers to ensure that adaptations are in line with audience mores and expectations.

COLOMBIA

With a population predicted soon to reach 49 million, Colombia has the third largest populace in Latin America, after Brazil and Mexico (United Nations, 2011). Yet whereas the commercial television industries in the larger nations have thrived on the basis of their large domestic markets, this did not happen until the 2000s in Colombia. Rather, for decades, the television market in Colombia remained fragmented, and although there were companies actively involved in programme production, Colombia was very much behind the other second-tier producers of the region. However, with the eventual privatisation of television in the 1990s, and over the first decade of the millennium, Colombia gained much ground in its production profile and output, particularly after the exceptional international success of *Yo soy Betty la fea* (*Ugly Betty*), first aired in Colombia over 1999–2001. Colombian networks are now becoming more involved in regional co-productions with US Hispanic network Telemundo and others, which increases both their productive capacity and their export presence.

Each Latin American country has its own peculiarities. Colombian broadcasting was established in the radio era on a unique public-private model, which endured almost to the end of the century, in which the government owned the stations but leased out the provision of programming, and the sale of advertising, to private companies. Commercial radio flourished under this scheme, but because successive military and civilian governments were determined to contain *la violencia* (the violence) which plagued Colombia in the 1940s and 1950s, broadcasting was frozen out from political influence. Consequently, Colombia did not develop the kind of accord between government and broadcasters seen in Mexico and Brazil.

Television was introduced under the military regime of Rojas Pinilla in 1954, but it was not until the 1960s that the television system stabilised under a public institution, Inravisión, which implemented the public–private model for the new medium. Inravisión owned and controlled the infrastructure of national broadcasting, and charged private programming companies for the use of the facilities and access to airtime on a finite lease basis. These companies either

Publicity for the original
Columbian version of *Yo soy
Betty la fea* (*Ugly Betty*)

commissioned or produced the entertainment programming, and sold time slots to advertisers, but the ruling parties maintained oversight of news (Fox, 1997). This was a system designed so that the state was able to control information content at the same time as it could recover costs from private interests. Furthermore, because programmers were not able to own networks, the state was preventing the emergence of a class of media owners who might become political players in their own right. As in Argentina, but in a different way, this was a regulatory framework which separated television distribution, or broadcasting, from the production of programming, at least until privatisation in the 1990s.

Nevertheless, there has been strong corporate continuity in Colombian broadcasting. The owners of both the now-privatised national channels are former programming companies (*programadoras*) that can trace their corporate origins back to radio days. This fact is reflected in their names: Caracol, which is a contraction of Cadena Radial Colombiana (Colombian Radio Chain); and RCN, which stands for Radio Cadena Nacional (National Radio Chain). Caracol became a television programmer when the government developed its first national network, and RCN when it opened a second. Other major programmers with a similar history are RTI (Radio Televisión Internacional), and Punch, except that these two, having no broadcasting licence of their own, still concentrate exclusively on programme production. These four programmers dominated the supply of television entertainment content throughout the 1970s and 1980s, for the most part with programming they made themselves, as distinct from brokering it from other sources, national and international (Fox, 1997).

In the wake of a new constitution promulgated in 1991, the authority of Inravisión was superseded by CNTV, the National Television Commission, which began a process of privatisation, first with provincial and local channels, and ultimately with the two national channels just mentioned that began in 1998. Although there are two quality state-owned public channels and a commercial one with national coverage, the private channels garner the mass audiences. Caracol and RCN are fairly evenly matched, each of them being able to attract over ten times the audience of any other competitor (Aranguren *et al.*, 2011). In effect, Colombian broadcast television is a duopoly, very broadly comparable in that respect to Artear and Telefé in Argentina, or formerly, Venevisión and RCTV in Venezuela.

Also as in Venezuela, the owners have come from non-media industrial sectors, but have gone on to build themselves up into integrated media groups. The principal owner of Caracol is the Grupo Santo Domingo, which acquired its wealth from brewing, banking and civil aviation under the late Julio Santo Domingo, from whom control has now typically passed to a son, Alejandro (Molinski, 2011). As noted, both Caracol and RCN have long histories in radio, where they have maintained a similar duopoly as in television, and as *programadoras* for both media. Although Santo Domingo in fact sold its interest in the broadcast radio network to the Spanish media conglomerate Prisa in 2003, it retains its interests in television, as well as having digital radio, print, cinema, and auxiliary media companies. Caracol has extensive studio facilities in the capital, Bogotá, where it produces *telenovelas*, reality shows and other programming for its network, as well as for international distribution. It claims to be one of the five biggest producer/distributors in Latin America, exporting to fifty countries, and also runs a cable channel for international subscribers, offering *telenovelas* such as the regional hit, *Sin tetas no hay paraíso* (*Without Breasts there is no Paradise*, 2006) (Farandula.com, 2008). Caracol has an ongoing arrangement with Sony, co-producing *telenovelas* and adapting Sony programmes for local broadcast in Colombia, as Sony is also doing in Argentina (Hecht, 2011).

Since the early 1970s, RCN has been owned by Organización Ardilla Lulle, a major Colombian industrial conglomerate with companies in diverse fields such as brewing, soft drinks, agribusiness and textiles, a broader range of industrial sectors than any of the other media owners being examined in this chapter. Like Santo Domingo, Carlos Ardilla Lulle is not only one of the richest men in the country but the region, on a par with Diego Cisneros of Venezuela, although he seems not to have Cisneros's strong personal handle upon the development of media interests. Nevertheless, in addition to media companies ranging from its traditional radio interests to a digital content initiative, the group has integrated the RCN national television network with its own production studios, a recording company, a dubbing unit, a regional twenty-four hour news channel, and an international entertainment channel, these last both available on cable and DTH (RCN, 2012).

As elsewhere in Latin America, the *telenovela* is by far the most popular programming genre, occupying over 60 per cent of prime time and 100 per cent of morning time in Colombia (Aranguren *et al*., 2011). One of RCN's most successful *telenovelas* of recent decades has been *Café con aroma de mujer* (*Coffee with the Scent of a Woman*), a torrid drama set in the coffee plantations of Colombia, written by Fernando Gaitán, and first shown in 1994. Building on this initial success, RCN produced another Gaitán script, *Yo soy Betty, la fea*, over 1999–2001, which English speakers later came to know in its US version as *Ugly Betty*, and which has also been remade and reversioned in many other countries (Mikos & Perrotta, 2012). Another ongoing regional success by Gaitán is *Hasta que la plata nos separe* (*Until Money us do Part*, 2006) but, as already suggested, the exceptional international success of *Betty* considerably lifted the profile of RCN, and Colombia, in the international television industry beyond Latin America. Yet although the *telenovela*, and fiction in general, certainly predominates in Colombia's output, production of a wider range of genres does take place, with both the domestic and export markets in mind. Nor is all its source material as original as the work of Gaitán. For instance, amongst RCN's most successful programmes of the 2000s have been remakes of US or UK reality shows, namely *La isla de los famosas* (2004–7), a version of *Celebrity Survivor*; and *El factor-X* (2006–12). In 2010, the most popular programme on Colombian television, and throughout the Iberoamerican world, was *A corazón abierto* (*Open Heart* – as in open heart surgery) on RCN, a *telenovela* based on *Grey's Anatomy* (Aranguren *et al*., 2011).

Because only two licences were granted under the privatisation scheme of the 1990s, not all of the major *programadoras* active at that time were as fortunate as Caracol and RCN in obtaining their own network: as noted, RTI and Punch were left out in the cold. Although the government has since conducted a tender process for a third network, this has been without result. Tenders were opened in 2008, and extended into 2009, but the interested parties objected to flaws in the process, and it was abandoned. These included the Grupo Cisneros from Venezuela; the Spanish Prisa group, mentioned above as the new owner of Radio Caracol; another Spanish media group, Planeta, which is the majority owner of Colombia's largest newspaper, *El Tiempo*; and most interestingly in this context, the *programadora* RTI (Mozzo, 2008).

In September 2009, it was announced that Telemundo, the second largest Spanish-language network in the US, had acquired a 40 per cent interest in RTI. As will be explained in the next chapter, Telemundo is owned by NBC Universal, whose ultimate parent company is General Electric. A major challenge for US mainstream corporations with investments in US Spanish-language television has been securing access to supplies of programming, and although both Univisión, the largest network, and Telemundo are both substantial producers in their own right within the US, connections with Latin America remain invaluable. Even prior to the 2009 arrangement, RTI had produced programmes for and with Telemundo, and RTI had sold their studio in Miami to their US partner, but the deal strengthens Telemundo's security of supply, as well as enhancing its opportunity to sell the rights to the programming into other markets. For RTI, it ensures an outlet for their product in the US, the world's largest export market for Spanish-language programming (Alsema, 2009). With Telemundo, Sony and others now co-producing *telenovelas* in Colombia, the country is emerging as a key producer, or co-producer, for the transnational Latin American and US Hispanic market.

CHILE

With the smallest population amongst the countries considered here, estimated at less than 18 million (United Nations, 2011), it should not be surprising that Chile occupies a third tier of production below the second-tier nations (Orozco Gómez & Vassallo de Lopes, 2011). Nevertheless, Chile exhibits certain similarities with them, as well as some strikingly unique features in the history and structure of its television industry, and there are also interesting links in ownership to other main markets of the region. As in the other cases, the form of the television industry has been shaped by discontinuities of government control, followed by eventual privatisation, but each in its own exceptional way.

The most remarkable feature of Chilean television has been the fact that the original licences were granted to universities, and remained under their administration until the era of privatisation. Chilean television had been a late starter by regional standards. Unlike Mexico or Brazil, but more like Colombia, there were no commercial radio entrepreneurs powerful enough to hasten governments into the introduction of television. Indeed, and again like Colombia and also Argentina, the mode of its eventual establishment was designed to ensure that no class of private television owners would emerge to challenge the authority of the state and upset the balance of party politics. Thus, in granting the licences to selected universities in the main cities of Santiago and nearby Valparaiso, and in restricting television to those cities, President Jorge Alessandri (President 1958–64) aimed to ensure that the new medium was politically neutralised. Furthermore, this strategy discouraged unwanted foreign investment and imbued the new medium with a public service character, even if in fact the channels had to attract commercial advertising and run large amounts of US programming for their economic survival. In 1969, television reached the provinces with the opening of a national network, this time funded by the state and controlled by a government-appointed director (Fox, 1997).

However, with the election of Salvador Allende (President 1970–3), television fell victim to a bitter struggle for control between Allende's Left-wing government and the conservative forces ranged against him, including advertisers. This was resolved abruptly by a military coup in which Allende was killed and a dictatorship established under General Augusto Pinochet. All of the television channels were obliged to run on a wholly commercial basis with no state subsidies, and under a repressive regime of censorship that furthered the dependence on foreign (mainly US) programming and banished political commentary. This situation endured until 1989, when free elections brought Chile back to democracy with the victory of Patricio Aylwin (President 1990–4), and the subsequent privatisation of television in Chile. The process attracted investors from around the region: as mentioned in Chapter Two, Televisa of Mexico acquired 49 per cent of Megavisión, the first private channel to be licenced. Also with the initial privatisation, CanWest of Canada invested in another new channel, La Red, in conjunction with a Chilean print-based media corporation, Copesa, while Cisneros's Venevisión bought the maximum 49 per cent of Chilevisión, the channel originally licensed to the University of Chile (Fox, 1997).

By the end of 2010, a new pattern of ownership had emerged. Megavisión, by then known as Mega, had been acquired entirely by Televisa's original Chilean partner, the Grupo Claro. A year later, it had been bought out by another Chilean conglomerate, Bethia. A Mexican connection remained in the case of La Red, held for a time by Mexico's second largest network, TV Azteca, and then by Ángel González, whose Albavisión group was noted above in connection with its interests in Argentina. González, '*el fantasma*', is also believed to have ties to another private channel, Telecanal. Since its original privatisation, Chilevisión had had a chequered history, having passed wholly into Chilean hands, but eventually into those of Turner Broadcasting System, part of Time Warner. Another of the original university channels, UCTV Channel 13, became 67 per cent owned by the Luksic Group of Chile (Fuenzalida & Julio, 2011). Rather like Cisneros in Venezuela and Lulle and Santo Domingo in Colombia, the Chilean television entrepreneurs had come from other fields of business. The late Andrónico Luksic had initially built up his corporate interests in manufacturing and brewing, while Ricardo Claro, also deceased, but former principal of the Grupo Claro and long-time owner of Mega(visión), had grown his group's wealth from the wine and shipping industries. The new owner, Bethia, comes from the fields of real estate and agricultural production. These discontinuities of ownership in Chilean television suggest that it is seen by corporations and entrepreneurs there as a business, rather than as a base for power and social influence as in Mexico and Brazil.

So, in spite of its unique origins under university administration, television in Chile ultimately became privatised and has come to look very much like that of other countries in the region. However, there is one more feature which should be remarked upon, and that is the fact that the most popular network in Chile is Televisión Nacional de Chile, known as TVN or TV Chile, the public channel first launched as a national network in 1969. Mega is not far behind, however, with CHV (Chilevisión) and Channel 13 soon following. TVN is the network that shows most locally-produced fiction, mainly *telenovelas* produced or commissioned by the channel itself, but other genres as well, notably historical dramas examining the nation's troubled past. There still is a substantial presence of US programming on Chilean television, mainly on CHV and Channel 13, but this is much less attractive to audiences than fiction programming produced in Chile, or other Spanish-speaking countries, as the 'cultural proximity' concept would predict. This includes *telenovelas* and docudramas from US Hispanic networks and production houses. Notably, given their Mexican associations, Mega and La Red show a lot of Mexican imports, while Brazilian material can be found across all the major channels (Fuenzalida & Julio, 2011). Thus, with its record of occasional export successes in the past, and the high level of self-sufficiency achieved by the end of the 2000s, Chile can be categorised as holding its own as a 'small producer' (Orozco Gómez & Vassallo de Lopes, 2011).

MIAMI AS MEDIA CAPITAL

As explained in the Introduction, a cultural-linguistic, geolinguistic or geocultural region exists above and beyond geographical space, and in the case of the Spanish-speaking such region, not only the various nations of Latin America, but also the US and Spain are included. The next chapter will examine the relevance of these very different markets in some detail, but for the present, we return to the unique role played within the Spanish-speaking cultural-linguistic region by the US city of Miami. Already referred to above as 'the virtual media capital of the Spanish-speaking Americas', we have seen that Miami is home to both Venevisión International and RCTV International from Venezuela; Albavisión, the Mexican owner of stations in Argentina and Chile; and RTI of Colombia, which owns studios in conjunction with the US Hispanic network, Telemundo. Both Telemundo and its massive US competitor Univisión have their production studios in Miami. In addition to the Latin American producer-distributors and the US Spanish-language networks, Miami has attracted some of the major US-based global cable and satellite services which since the late

Publicity for *Cristal*, one of the Venezuelan RCTV's successes, distributed internationally by its distribution company based in Miami

1980s have offered channels in Spanish and/or Portuguese for the US Hispanic and Latin American markets, notably MTV Latino.

Both the major US Spanish-language networks, Univisión and Telemundo, now produce around half of their original programming in Miami, across a range of genres, and catering ever more to the interests of US Spanish-speakers. However, there is also a history of co-production with Latin American producers, with the productions being distributed in both directions, that is, into both the US and Latin America. Univisión has had a long and close association with Televisa and Venevisión, while Telemundo has had arrangements at various stages with the network TV Azteca and independent producer Argos of Mexico; Caracol and RTI of Colombia; and Globo of Brazil. Both US networks also have or have had dealings with RCN of Colombia. So in some ways, a Miami – Colombia axis of production is also emerging as a component of the Latin America audiovisual space and television market (Piñon, 2011).

Michael Curtin has theorised the notion of 'media capital' with regard to Asia, but his principles can usefully be developed in application to the case of Miami. A fundamental point is that a media capital is 'geographically relational', meaning that it 'holds sway' over a certain territory, in Miami's case the 'dispersed but loosely coherent' Spanish-speaking cultural-linguistic region of the Americas (Curtin, 2007, p. 285). Miami as a media capital is a central node 'in the transnational flow of culture, talent, and resources' (Curtin, 2009, p. 111), flows which are virtual, but located in space which is real as well as imagined. Physical location still matters, but it is always mediated by other factors – in this case, including historical, political, demographic and linguistic as well as economic considerations. Thus, the fact that Miami is the US city closest to Caracas or Bogotá, a direct flight over the Caribbean, is a necessary but not sufficient condition for its special status vis-à-vis the region.

Curtin's first principle is 'the logic of accumulation', which gives focus to the economic incentives motivating companies in Spanish-speaking television production, distribution, and exchange to locate in Miami. For the Latin American companies, the prime incentive is to give access to the US market, which, as will be outlined in the next chapter, is large and lucrative. Miami provides them with a foothold in that market, and opportunities to produce programmes that can be sold not only in the US, but back into their domestic markets, and elsewhere in Latin America, and also internationally. Additional incentives are that corporate income taxes are low, and for Latin American companies from the less stable and inflation-prone countries in particular, Miami offers the relative political and economic security of the US, including currency stability (Reveron, 2001).

Although it was the 'Golden Exile' generation of refugees from the Cuban Revolution of 1959 which gave Miami its definitive character as a Spanish-speaking city, that in turn has since attracted other immigrants from Latin America, including creative and technical personnel who could find employment, initially with the US Spanish-speaking networks in the late 1980s. With the arrival of the Latin American companies, a critical mass or 'creative cluster' has formed as production and technical personnel, directors, writers, actors and other creative talent have come to live there. As well, the diverse technical and other support services required by television production have become established, such as casting agencies and post-production facilities (Sinclair, 2003). All of this amounts to a 'trajectory of creative migration', Curtin's second criterion.

Above all, the dominance of the Spanish language as a cultural marker in Miami and the city's Latin-cosmopolitan ethos makes it uniquely in, but not of, the US, and gives it a special place in the Latin imaginary. It has its own celebrity culture, *la farándula*, or the 'glitterati' of the region's television and music industries, who make their homes and work in Miami, and who, revealingly, say they like it because they never feel like second class citizens there. The fact that these celebrities live in Miami becomes part of the city's attraction for Spanish-speaking audiences as much as for the producers and the 'multinational bazaar of talent' who work in the television industry (Sinclair, 2003). Curtin's third principle, 'forces of sociocultural variation', is palpable in Miami, a city with a skilled, bilingual, hybrid workforce and an urban setting which forms a strategic cultural-linguistic fulcrum for the whole hemisphere of Spanish-speakers in the Americas.

PROGRAMME EXCHANGES WITHIN THE IBEROAMERICAN WORLD
A snapshot from the first decade of the privatisation of television in Latin America is provided by a study of the audiovisual trade flows of the Iberoamerican cultural-linguistic region, drawing on 1996 industry-supplied

data from Mexico, Brazil, Venezuela, Argentina, and Chile, as well as Spain and Portugal (Media Research and Consultancy Spain, 1997). Television programmes were found to be by far the largest sector of all audiovisual exports (76 per cent), with satellite and cable services a distant 17 per cent and cinema mustering only seven per cent. With over half of these exports (54 per cent) going to other Iberoamerican countries, the study acknowledges the region even then as 'a true economic space' of audiovisual exchange. Significantly, the US was the second largest destination (20 per cent), a revealing measure of the importance of the Univisión network there to its principal Latin American suppliers at the time, Televisa and Venevisión. European countries were taking 11 per cent of Iberoamerican exports, with 15 per cent going to the rest of the world (Media Research and Consultancy Spain, 1997).

Just as US-based television production and international distribution has become dominated by a few major players who price their products according to each national market, the same study found that in television programming exports from the region, only five companies accounted for 94 per cent of programmes exported. These were Televisa, Globo, Venevisión, RCTV, and the Spanish public broadcaster RTVE, in that order. However, although it does not cite any figures, the study also reports that export sales represent only a small percentage of the income of these companies. It is interesting to note that just as the US was the most important market outside the Iberoamerican region for the main Spanish-language producers, Portugal had particular importance for Globo: half of its regional sales were going to SIC, then the leading private channel, in which Globo had an ownership stake at that time (1997).

The 1997 study can serve to some extent as a useful comparative baseline for data from comprehensive studies of the trade in television fiction between the Iberoamerican countries in the period 2007 to 2010, conducted by the Iberoamerican Television Fiction Observatory, or Obitel. Obitel is a network of researchers representing all the major Latin American countries, plus Spain, Portugal, and the US. They have been collecting data on the production, distribution, circulation, and consumption specifically of television fiction on an annual basis since 2005, in effect tracking specific trends over time (Obitel, 2011). 'Fiction' includes not only *telenovelas*, but also series, miniseries, TV movies, and docudramas. Although there have been several reality programmes running on Latin American channels, and being co-produced and exchanged with both global and regional partners, this genre is not included in Obitel's data. By definition, news and information programming is also excluded, but it is fiction programming in the *telenovela* and other popular genres that forms the basis of Latin America's participation in the international television trade, and that is our interest in this book. It is worth noting in passing that, as elsewhere in the world, major international exchange takes place in sport and feature films in the Latin American television industry, but the countries of the region participate more as importers than exporters of these forms of programming. There is also a tendency for sport and film to gravitate towards pay-TV, while the *telenovela* remains the staple fare of free-to-air broadcast television. News is another area in which global services in Spanish and Portuguese, such as the US-based CNN, provide strong competition for pay-TV audiences in the region.

Ever since 2007, Brazil has been the Iberoamerican country which has produced the most of its own television fiction, and conversely, imported the least. The same conclusion comes from a multi-country study of television imports and exports from 1961 to 2001 (Straubhaar, 2007), which also showed Brazil as the highest producing country in the Latin American countries studied, and one of the most self-sufficient producing countries among all those studied in Asia, Africa, Europe and Latin America. Not only TV Globo but also its rivals are active in the export of their material, and in co-production. Traditionally, Brazil has been distinguished by its quality *telenovelas*, but there has been a more recent expansion and internationalisation of the range of genres produced, notably to include sitcoms and miniseries, on familiar US models. Remembering that Brazil is unique in Latin America for being the sole Portuguese-speaking country amongst Spanish-speaking neighbours, there is a linguistic barrier which would explain its relative self-sufficiency, and also the fact that Brazil's main partner in programme co-production and exchange is Portugal, rather than any country in its geographical region. For its part, Portugal is also one of the leading countries in the production of national fiction hours, though the market there is more for series and miniseries rather than *telenovelas*. This Lusophone connection reinforces the parallel importance of geocultural and geolinguistic markets like Latin America and more spatially dispersed cultural-linguistic markets like the Lusophone cultural space in Africa, Europe and Latin America.

As will be more fully explained in Chapter Five, the Globo corporation of Brazil played an active part in the privatisation of the television industry in Portugal, even helping create one of the first private channels, SIC (Sousa, 2002). This became the leading channel of the 1990s, not least because of a programming agreement which gave it exclusive access to Globo *telenovelas*, which had previously been imported only by the public channel RTP. By 2010, SIC and Globo still had such a mutually-advantageous agreement, and RTP1, the main public channel, had a similar agreement with one of Globo's main competitors in Brazil, TV Record. However, SIC's leadership had been eclipsed by its sole commercial competitor, TVI, which does not show Latin American productions (Ferin Cunha *et al.*, 2011). This turnabout would suggest that as the Portuguese market has matured from its initial privatisation and the national fad for

Brazilian *telenovelas*, audiences now have more of a taste for Portuguese material, and in a wider range of genres. This reinforces one of the original predictions of cultural proximity (Straubhaar, 1991), that audiences would tend to prefer first national programming, but would look next to culturally similar producers, if their national or local television system could not produce the genres they preferred. So if national producers are eventually able to produce a preferred genre, then audiences would probably prefer that, even to productions from within the same cultural-linguistic group. The *telenovela* nevertheless remains the most popular genre, and dominates in prime time.

Meanwhile in Spain, there are relatively few *telenovelas*, and these are mainly Spanish productions to be found on second networks, while prime time on the leading networks is given over to series and miniseries. National productions predominate across all genres. Indeed, Spain leads the Iberoamerican world in terms of the hours of national productions shown in prime time, and although its overall level of production decreased towards the end of the 2000s, its imports from other Iberoamerican nations increased correspondingly. Looking specifically at the *telenovelas* shown in Spain, very few are imported, and in 2009–10 at least, most of these came not from Latin American, but US Hispanic networks (Orozco Gómez & Vassallo de Lopes, 2011).

It is notable that although Portugal and Spain remain markets for Latin American *telenovelas*, their own domestic production tends more to series and miniseries, some of the most successful of late which favour historical themes drawing on their respective national cultures. As will be explained further in Chapter Five, the television industries in each of the Iberian nations have a similar history: originally state-controlled under dictatorship, then reformed on a public service basis, and eventually privatised in part, yielding dual public/private systems. In Spain, the public channel leads a series of private competitors in audience share, while in Portugal, one private channel dominates, on the basis of strong production of national fiction, leaving the public channel to compete with the other for second place. In terms of ownership, there is a degree of integration across borders, insofar as the Spanish media conglomerate Grupo Prisa is majority owner of the dominant channel in both Spain and Portugal. As noted above, Prisa also has active interests in broadcasting in Latin America.

Over the period covered by Obitel's research, from 2007 to 2010, Brazil, Mexico, and Portugal have maintained their place as first-tier producers, with Argentina, the US, and Spain forming the second tier. However, there are interesting year-to-year variations. In 2010, Argentina recorded a strong decrease in production. This was attributed to a crisis in the industry, as local fiction, particularly *telenovelas*, struggled for audience attention against comedy, sport and US material of the kind mentioned above (Aprea & Kirchheimer, 2011).

Publicity for *A corazón abierto* (*Open Heart*). Based on *Grey's Anatomy*, this was adapted to a *telenovela* format by Columbian writer Fernando Gaitán

Another of the emergent producers to experience a marked decrease in 2010 was Venezuela. This can be largely explained by the elimination of RCTVI from the pay-TV market there, as explained earlier, as RCTVI formerly showed a great proportion of its own productions, though also because of the amount of screen time commandeered by government (Alvarado Miquilena & Torrealba Mesa, 2011). The slack was taken up with programming imported from other Iberoamerican nations, the largest amount ever recorded by Obitel.

On the other hand, first place for national production of fiction hours that year went to Colombia. Notably, RCN's *Corazón abierto*, also noted above, was the most-watched fiction programme across all of the Obitel countries. This is a singular case in the globalisation of programming, unprecedented in Obitel's research, as it is a co-production with a script from a US production company, based on *Grey's Anatomy*, but given a *telenovela* format. This transnational hybridity may yet prove to be a model for the future, but it was certainly exceptional in 2010, as Colombia figured prominently as the source of scripts for many of the most-seen titles that year, second only to Brazil (Orozco Gómez & Vassallo de Lopes, 2011). Outside of the fiction trade, RCN in particular asserted its increased regional significance when a new network for US Hispanics was announced in 2012, MundoFox. This is a partnership of RCN with News Corporation's Fox network, which gives RCN an outlet for its programming in the US, where it will also be producing original programming (Messmer, 2012).

To sum up: the leadership of Mexico and Brazil in the television trade of the Iberoamerican world is unchallenged, as the fortunes of the emergent producers wax and wane. While there are some superficial similarities, such as dynastic entrepreneurship in oligopolistic markets, there are decisive historical and structural differences between, and amongst, the first and second-tier producers. Historically, we have seen how restrictive versions of the commercial model of broadcasting were set up in Argentina, Colombia, and Chile, with governments deliberately preventing the rise of an influential caste of media owners, such as occurred in Mexico and Brazil. Those restrictions tended to be loosened over time, permitting private networks to emerge in those countries. However, even in the current era of increased liberalisation of competition and privatisation, contingencies of political control can have great influence in the shaping of television markets, as seen in the case of the Chávez era in Venezuela. Structurally, domestic market size works differently for the emergent producers than for the countries which hold the largest populations in their geolinguistic regions. In Venezuela, a small national market has given a spur to off-shore production for export, while in Chile, it has allowed a degree of self-sufficiency to develop. On the other hand, Colombian and Argentine producers have yet to take full advantage of their relatively large domestic markets, having been hampered by the structural separation of production and broadcasting. All this underscores the point that market size does not in itself make for successful production for export.

Just as was evident in the previously cited study from 1997, the Obitel data from the end of the first decade of the 2000s demonstrates the high degree of programme exchange that continued to take place within the Iberoamerican world, at least for fiction. Across all of the Obitel countries in 2010, more than twice as many hours were imported from other Iberoamerican countries as were produced nationally, 69 to 31 per cent. As noted, the *telenovela* was the most common genre in this exchange (68 per cent of most-watched programmes were *telenovelas*), but there is a slight tendency discernible towards greater diversity of traded genres (Orozco Gómez & Vassallo de Lopes, 2011). Spain and Portugal are distinct from the Latin American countries with regard to preferred genres and in other important respects, as we have seen, while the Spanish-language networks in the US are emerging as significant partners in co-productions with the rest of the Iberoamerican world. The next chapter will examine the particular character of these Iberian and US Hispanic markets in relation to the major Latin American producer-distributors.

5

Iberoamerica and the Lusophone Space as Global Television Markets

We have seen that Spanish-speaking Latin American audiences in a whole host of nations can be addressed by virtue of their more or less common linguistic and cultural heritage as a kind of 'imagined community' on a regional scale. Brazil is a large national market, but shares its language with Portugal and its former colonies. Thus, the Latin American televisual space needs to be seen in the context of a wider 'Latin' or, more correctly, Iberoamerican space, and in addition, the Lusophone, or Portuguese-speaking world beyond Latin America. This transnational scale has emerged in the process of new distribution technologies, strategic investments, and productive capacities being utilised by those in a position to exploit cultural and linguistic similarities on a global basis, on both sides of the Atlantic. Significantly, the United States also has to be included as part of this region, with its over 50 million 'Hispanics' or 'Latinos'. For Brazil, given its position as the world's dominant cultural producer in Portuguese, there are also small but important markets outside Iberoamerica in the Lusophone cultural-linguistic spaces of Africa, Asia, and Europe.

However, the exploitation of their comparative advantage within these extensive cultural-linguistic spaces, or geolinguistic and geocultural regions, and the cultural proximity which accompanies it, does not offer a total explanation for the success of companies such as Televisa, Globo, Venevisión, and RCN in building their export markets, because of the enthusiastic take-up of the *telenovela* in Eastern Europe, Russia, China, Africa, the Middle East, and elsewhere far beyond the boundaries of the Latin world. Different kinds of explanation can be given for this phenomenon: the universal appeal of the melodramatic narrative mode; the appeal of the particular way that *telenovelas* treat somewhat universal themes like social mobility; the economic fact that *telenovelas* offer an affordable option with which to fill expanding schedules in poor markets with relatively little production capacity of their own; and the habitual everyday shared ritual quality of watching continuing serial narratives and discussing them in specific social settings. This chapter will examine the development of the Spanish-speaking and Portuguese-speaking cultural-linguistic regions respectively as television markets, and consider the various reasons given for the apparent success of Iberoamerican programming outside its natural language constituency. As well, an interesting contrast will be explored between the various difficulties which Televisa has had in securing a place for itself in Spain, and the considerable influence which Globo has wielded in the television market of Portugal.

It was already suggested in the Introduction that Mexico and Brazil, as exporters of television production, stand in a similar dominant relation to their respective cultural-linguistic regions as the US does to the English-speaking world. Looking firstly at the Mexican networks as exporters, we saw in Chapter Two that the Mexican domestic market, the largest in the Spanish-speaking world, is effectively a duopoly, though one in which the longstanding network, Televisa, has more than two-thirds of the market, leaving scarcely a third to its more recently-arrived competitor, TV Azteca. It was also noted how Televisa and its corporate ancestors had taken a series of international initiatives from quite early days: opening up stations in the US in the 1960s; adopting satellite transmission to the US and Spain in the 1970s; mounting an international news service in the 1980s; and in the 1990s making direct investments in stations in other Latin American countries and buying into international satellite services. That is, more than exporting programmes as such, Televisa used satellite transmission as a technological strategy to deliver directly to new markets, as well as making selective investment in actual foreign stations. For its part, TV Azteca has also made such direct investments, both in Central and South America, and with its Azteca America network, it competes with the Televisa-linked Univisión in the US market. As noted in Chapter Four, Venevisión too has made strenuous efforts to exert its influence in continental Latin America and, as we shall see, also has played a part in the US.

For Brazil, we first saw one network, TV Globo, dominate mass audience programming, surrounded by several smaller networks programming to segmented audiences. In that scenario, up through the 1990s, TV Globo was also almost the only exporter, had the main satellite channels for subscription, and was the only company that contemplated investment abroad. Its *telenovelas* became very popular exports from 1976 on. Its satellite channel became de rigueur viewing for the Brazilian diaspora abroad and other Portuguese speakers as well. It had a major investment in the first successful private network in Portugal, as well as a failed investment in Italy. The Brazilian television brand in the world market was TV Globo, up through the 1990s, which meant that TV Globo dominated the initial explosion of Brazilian *telenovelas* into world markets in the 1990s. That has evolved into a scenario where TV Globo is still the dominant exporter, but TV Record (and its parent, the Universal Church of the Reign of God) is an increasingly strong second in exports, has its own satellite channels abroad, and is currently more dynamic as an investor in channels abroad than is the Globo Group. TV Record has gone from populist niche programming for the working class, to competing with Globo across the board for the mass audience with *telenovelas*, shows, and news. Its *telenovelas* now export well, as an alternative to Globo's in many markets where *telenovelas* are still appealing. Furthermore, TV Record's parent organisation now owns the number two television network in Mozambique and several networks in Central America.

THE SPANISH-SPEAKING US

The population of Spanish-speaking origin in the US, customarily referred to by the collective term 'Hispanic', was estimated by the US Census Bureau in 2010 to be over 50 million in a total population of over 300 million: that is, more than a sixth of it. Another generic expression now preferred by many of these persons, incidentally, would be 'Latino', which is generally used in the following discussion. Note that neither name is meaningful outside of the US context, in the same way as English-speakers worldwide are not normally identified as 'Anglos'. The population of Hispanics or Latinos is very diverse, not only in terms of their nation of family origin, but also their length of residence in the US, and indeed whether or not they still speak Spanish. Again, according to the US Census Bureau, more than half of those people who speak Spanish at home say they also speak English 'very well'. Astroff has argued that, at least since the early 1980s, there has been a discourse about US Hispanics/Latinos developed by such 'cultural brokers' as market researchers, advertising agencies, and the Spanish-language media (1997). In fact, writers such as Rodríguez (1999) and Dávila (2001) go further to argue that advertisers, Spanish language broadcasters, and audience research corporations such as Nielsen have constructed a sense of essential commonality among Latinos, constituting them not as an imagined community in the political sense (Anderson, 1983) but as a commercial subject, a community of potential consumers who share the Spanish language. This commercialisation is happening because in spite of the generally lower socioeconomic indicators for Latinos relative to the mainstream US population, these various commercial interests see the Latino population as a market, arguably the richest Spanish-speaking market in the world, particularly in comparison to Latin America (Rodríguez, 1996). It is also one of the largest, perhaps second only to Mexico, by recent UN estimates. Thus, the size and wealth of the Latino population in the US has major strategic significance within the Spanish-speaking world as a whole, a point not lost on Latin American broadcasters such as Televisa, TV Azteca and Venevisión, and one which eventually came to be recognised by US mainstream programme providers, investors, and also advertisers, as this chapter will show.

As in Latin America and elsewhere, television broadcasting for the Spanish-speaking minority in the US was built up from the institutional and industrial base already laid down by radio. Even before radio, there were newspapers which dated back to when most of the Southwestern US, from California to Texas, where much of the Spanish-language population, particularly that of Mexican origin, is still concentrated today, was part of Mexico until 1848. By the 1930s, Emilio Azcárraga Vidaurreta was broadcasting across the border from his Mexican radio stations (Rodríguez, 1997). This began a long involvement by the Azcárraga dynasty in the development of Spanish-language broadcasting in the US, and established the model whereby entertainment programming generated for a commercial audience in Mexico and already paid for and proven there, could do double service by attracting a culturally and linguistically similar audience on the other side of the border. Then and now, the majority by far of the US Latino population is of Mexican origin, and this is a demographic and cultural-linguistic fact, which the three generations of Azcárragas have used to considerable advantage in this, their largest international market.

In 1961 the founding Azcárraga acquired a pioneering Spanish-language television station in San Antonio in the name of the Spanish International Communication Corporation (SICC) (Rodríguez, 1997). SICC was the corporate vehicle through which Azcárraga subsequently built up a chain of stations in the US. At the same time, the Spanish International Network (SIN) was created as the network management vehicle, wholly owned by Azcárraga, which was there to supply the stations with programmes and sell time to advertisers. Broadcast station ownership in the US is restricted to US citizens, and 'aliens' or persons acting for them may not control more than 25 per cent of shares in a television station. However, there is no such restriction on the ownership of the networks which supply programmes to and sell advertising time for the stations (Gutiérrez, 1979). For this reason, the fact that Spanish-language television in the US was a virtual extension of Mexico's predominant network and run from there, had to be concealed behind a legal fiction. Thus, Rene Anselmo, a US citizen originally working for Azcárraga's TSM network in Mexico, became the *prestanombre* (borrowed name) for the Azcárragas in the US for the next 25 years, as President of both SICC and SIN (Maza, 1986). Originally, Azcárraga had sent Anselmo to sell TSM's programmes to the major US networks, but he had been rebuffed with their disdainful view that such specialised 'ghetto time' programming was not appropriate to the mass medium which they then saw television exclusively to be. The acquisition of the station in San Antonio represented Azcárraga's strategy in response: to distribute TSM programmes via his own niche network in the US (Bagamery, 1982).

SICC/SIN built itself into a truly national network through astute application of new distribution technologies as they became available, notably in 1976, when it fully interconnected all its stations and affiliates via satellite so that they could air the same programming at the same time – programming which itself was being transmitted via satellite from Mexico on a weekly basis (de Noriega and Leach, 1979). This put SICC/SIN ahead of the mainstream networks, ABC, CBS, and NBC, in being the first US network to be interconnected via satellite. SIN subsequently added cable distribution and LPTV (Low Power Television) to its network so that, by the end of 1983, it had coverage of the vast majority of the US Spanish-speaking population (Valenzuela, 1986). Commercially, this meant that however widely dispersed the target community might have been, they could still be reached and presented to advertisers as a national audience.

However, because of a long-running legal suit by a SICC shareholder, the true relationship between SICC and SIN and the Azcárragas was being brought out into the open. This triggered an investigation by the US broadcast regulatory agency, the Federal Communications Commission (FCC), which found that SIN had eventually achieved its profitability at SICC's expense, by billing SICC for more programmes than were actually supplied (Critser, 1987). In January 1986 an FCC-appointed judge determined that SICC was in breach of US foreign ownership provisions, and ordered that the licences of the SICC be transferred to US owners. This launched a bidding competition, won by the greeting card/financial services consortium, Hallmark Cards. Emilio Azcárraga Milmo, who had succeeded his father in 1972, was able to minimise the disastrous impact of the judgment by negotiating a long-term distribution deal with Hallmark for Televisa programming to be shown on the US network, soon after known as Univisión (Sinclair, 1990).

Meanwhile, another US-owned Spanish-language network had emerged, Telemundo, developed by a Wall Street investment group. Telemundo initiated a competition for audience share on the basis of programming which it was producing specifically for US Latinos. However, this created a war of attrition, because of the high costs of US domestic production, so that both networks were soon making heavy losses (Besas, 1990). Telemundo's financial situation became so bad that in 1992 it defaulted on its debts and was acquired by another finance capital group. For its part, Hallmark cut its losses and sold out of Univisión that same year, thus creating the opportunity for Televisa's return. However, the new ownership was carefully structured to meet FCC regulations, with a US majority owner, media veteran Jerry Perenchio, and minority shares held equally by Televisa and a new Latin American entrant, Venevisión. Televisa had survived its exile from the US over the Hallmark years by building up its

Logos of the two major
national Spanish-language
networks in the US,
Telemundo and Univisión

Galavisión cable subscription service there, and with its initiative with PanAmSat, the world's first privately-owned international satellite system. Although it had had its initial impetus in the politics of satellite development in Mexico, as was noted in Chapter Two, PanAmSat came into existence as a US company through Azcárraga having Rene Anselmo and other connections in the US. PanAmSat assumed enormous significance, not only for Televisa's international activities, and for the various US cable channels that were then entering Latin America, carried by PanAmSat, but also for the globalisation of television more generally (Subervi Vélez *et al.*, 1994).

It was in the interest of both the networks to commission Nielsen Media Research, the major US audience measurement company, to set up a ratings measurement service for Spanish-language television in 1992, but the ensuing competition made it clear that Telemundo was losing ground. A major reason was that Telemundo could not obtain material from either the world's largest or even its second-largest producer of Spanish-language programming at that time, because they were its competitors: namely Televisa and Venevisión, who were both locked in to Univisión. By August 1997, Telemundo's market share had fallen to 18 per cent, and the finance capitalist owners sold the network to a co-venture of Liberty Media and Sony. This was relatively short-lived, however, for in October 2001 a completely new era began when Telemundo was acquired by what is now NBC Universal, owned by Comcast and General Electric. This brought Spanish-language television fully into the corporate mainstream of US broadcasting, and posed the strongest ever challenge to Univisión from its traditional competitor.

However, the duopolistic situation which had prevailed into the new millennium had already been broken that same year when TV Azteca launched Azteca America. This was announced as a joint venture with a US partner as the owner of the stations, while TV Azteca owned the network and supplied the programmes (Piñón López, 2007). By the end of 2011, Azteca America was claiming on its website that its coverage had grown to 94 per cent of the US

Spanish-speaking population, through seventy affiliates, but in terms of actual market share it was well behind Univisión, still by far the market leader, then Telemundo following at a distance, and even Telefutura, the second network which Univisión had launched in 2002. Telemundo also by that time had a second network, Mun2 (a pun in Spanish for 'two worlds', *mundos*), available on cable, but even in that sphere Univisión still dominated with its Galavisión service, acquired from Televisa in 1992 (Hispanic Markets Overview, 2010).

It is worth noting that the new networks have been bringing about a diversification of programming through linguistic hybridity. That represents a significant change in the definition of what was once thought to constitute an Hispanic television audience. Previously, 'Hispanics', for the television industry, were only those who still spoke Spanish. People who still thought of themselves as Hispanic but wanted to watch in English were assumed to be completely acculturated, no longer Hispanic in the eyes of television programmers. As more second, third and further generations of Hispanic immigrants wanted to see their culture on television, Spanish-only programming began to miss audiences of significant size (Piñón and Rojas, 2011). Whereas Univisión in particular has always kept a strict policy of correct Spanish only (even advertising slogans have to be rendered in Spanish), Telefutura is aimed at younger and less Spanish-dominant audiences. In this respect, they are competing with Telemundo's Mun2 which has made considerable concessions to the widespread use of the bilingual vernacular of Latino youth, the hybrid, code-switching patois often referred to disparagingly as 'Spanglish', thus goading Telefutura in the same direction (Sutter, 2003).

It was noted earlier that the Spanish-language media have a vested interest in the perpetuation of Spanish-speakers as a language community in the US, and so make their appeal to Latin-origin people on the basis of a vague discourse of pan-Latin identity and their speaking of Spanish. However, to remain relevant to an ever more diverse population, the reality is that the networks have to balance, on one hand, classic Spanish cultural-linguistic programming, like *telenovelas*, for the most recently-arrived, Spanish-dominant sectors of the population; and on the other, programming for those who are English-dominant or bilingual in their own vernacular. The most extreme shift towards the latter side of the balance came in 2012, when Univisión announced that it was launching a 24/7 cable news channel in English, thus breaking its former rule, and, furthermore, that it was doing so in conjunction with ABC News, a division of the major US free-to-air network ABC, which is owned by the massive Walt Disney Company (Turner, 2012).

Nevertheless, in both historical and structural terms, as this chapter has indicated, it was the strategic link with Mexico which enabled Spanish-language television to become established and built into a national network in the first instance. For Televisa, as the main driver and beneficiary, what remains crucial is not so much its level of ownership in a network in the US as such, but its capacity to ensure that Univisión continues to provide it with a secure and extensive distribution outlet for its programming: 'if content is king, distribution is King Kong' (Eilemberg, 2008). In the 1992 ownership deal, Televisa had made a programming arrangement with Univisión under which Univisión had first option over all Televisa (and Venevisión) programmes, in exchange for which the Latin partners received a percentage of Univisión's advertising revenue. This arrangement, intended to prevail until 2017, actually benefited Televisa more than Venevisión, because over half Univisión's programming was coming from Televisa, given the preponderance of Mexican-Americans in the US Latino population (Merrill Lynch Capital Markets, 1997). Furthermore, when Perenchio and the Latin partners acquired Univisión in 1992, imported programming had been around 55 per cent, but that proportion had climbed to 94 per cent by 1997 (Avila, 1997). As noted, ownership of Galavisión had been transferred to Univisión as a cable-only service in the deal, but it too continued to source its programming from Televisa.

However, these mutually advantageous arrangements were not to last. In 2005, a feud broke out between Perenchio and Televisa. By this stage, Televisa was under the leadership of Emilio Azcárraga Jean, the son of 'El Tigre', as explained in Chapter Two. Perenchio had made some senior management changes at Univisión, not least the appointment of a new President, without any consultation with Televisa or Venevisión. Televisa responded by banning its talent from appearing on any Univisión-produced shows and specials. In turn, Univisión retaliated with a lawsuit listing several grievances about Televisa's programme supply, including overcharging and neglecting to edit programmes in accordance with US standards. Televisa filed a countersuit, accusing Univisión of failing to pay royalties due, unauthorised editing of programming, and certain copyright infringements. Significantly, there was also the issue of whether Univisión had the right to stream Televisa's content over the internet in the US. In all, these actions revealed 'a poisonous working atmosphere between the two managements' (de la Fuente, 2005), confirmed when Azcárraga resigned his seat on the board.

Against this background, Perenchio put his holding in Univisión up for sale, in February 2006. At first, this seemed to be an ideal opportunity for Televisa to seize control. Azcárraga publicly declared that he was prepared to cross the foreign ownership barrier by becoming an American citizen, just as Rupert Murdoch had done in acquiring the Fox network. However, he decided instead to ally Televisa in a consortium with two private equity firms, Cascade

Investments and Bain Capital. Venevisión chose not to participate. Meanwhile, a competing consortium was formed, Broadcast Media Partners, led by an Israeli-American billionaire entertainment industry investor, Haim Saban, and consisting of four private equity companies: Madison Dearborn Partners, Providence Equity Partners, Texas Pacific Group, and Thomas H Lee Partners. Over a dramatic weekend in June, Univisión allowed the Saban syndicate to increase their initial bid, and accepted it without giving the Televisa group any opportunity to increase theirs, nor to negotiate any further. Majority ownership in Univisión thus changed hands for over US$ 12 billion, compared to the US$ 500 million Perenchio had paid in 1992 (Sorkin, 2006). By the end of the year, a bitter Azcárraga had sold Televisa's 11.4 per cent stake, although still with the programme licensing agreement (PLA) in place ('Televisa to sell stake in Univision', 2006).

It appears that Azcárraga had been trying to end the PLA. While in the past it had provided certainty as an outlet for Televisa programming, it was never particularly profitable: although Televisa productions were generating 40 per cent of Univisión's revenue, the income returned to Televisa was a mere fraction of all that company's income. As noted in Chapter Two, Televisa earns only seven per cent of its total income from programme exports, but the US market represents 65 per cent of that (Moreno Esparza, 2011). Furthermore, in the mid-2000s, two significant changes in the television market made the PLA less attractive to Televisa – the exclusive PLA meant Televisa could not sell programming to the rejuvenated Telemundo or the few other Spanish-language services at the margins of the market; and the growth of the internet, especially strong amongst Latinos, had opened up a new digital mode of programme distribution and reception not covered by the PLA (Eilemberg, 2008). Televisa believed they should have a separate right to commercialise digital distribution in the US; Univisión insisted programming rights were theirs, regardless of distribution platform.

The legal confrontation continued until January 2009, when an agreement was signed to settle the first issue, how much Televisa should get for its programming. Univisión had to pay Televisa US$ 25 million in back-payments, give it free airtime for advertising, and 'clarify and expand' the method of calculating royalties for the future. However, the PLA remained in place (Wentz, 2009). The terms were a hardship for Univisión, which had a debt of US$ 10 billion, thanks to the inflated price at which the Saban consortium had bought into the company (de Cordoba, 2010). The digital rights issue was resolved by a court ruling in July 2009 which went against Televisa but, little more than a year later, the companies were reconciled under a completely new arrangement in which Televisa was able to buy back into Univisión, paying US$ 130 million for a five per cent stake. In addition, under the agreement of October 2010, Televisa had the option of acquiring a further five per cent direct investment, and another 30 per cent in the form of convertible debt. It also gained three seats on the board. As for digital rights, these went to Univisión, but in return for higher royalty payments to Televisa. On this basis, the PLA has actually been extended now, from 2017 to 2020 (Wentz, 2010).

The agreement brought to a close several years of uncertainty in the US Spanish-language television market, at least as far as Televisa and Univisión were concerned. Televisa once again had a foothold in network ownership, while Univisión was guaranteed the supply of its most popular programming. However, the business model in which the two networks had now restored their mutual interest was under strain, as differences which had always existed in the Latino community came out more into the open. Typical Mexican programming, characterised by *telenovelas*, may be popular with the two-thirds of the Latino population of Mexican origin, especially those most recently arrived, but it has never appealed equally to all Spanish-origin Americans, such as those from Cuba and Puerto Rico. Furthermore, however much some still identify with their actual or putative country of origin, Latinos are Americans, a point illustrated by various past actions by community groups who have protested about the Mexican dominance over Univisión management and employment opportunities (Cantu, 1991) but, more generally, by their demand for US-made programming. This is not a question of who owns the network, though Telemundo's string of owners – Wall Street, Sony, NBC – do not seem to have attracted the opposition which Televisa/Univisión has done from time to time.

Although there have been some spectacular past failures in providing Latinos with US-made information and entertainment programming that they can genuinely relate to and enjoy, such as Telemundo's remaking of successful US series like *Charlie's Angels* (1990) into flops in Spanish, there are also some long-standing successes. Univisión does have a strong line-up of its own programmes, the best-known of which would be their morning show, *Despiérta América* (*Wake Up America*, 1997), variety show *Sábado gigante* (*Huge Saturday*, 1986), and the talk show *El show de Cristina* (1989). As noted above, in Telemundo's chequered history there has been less continuity of management and programming, but under the NBC Universal regime, Telemundo now rivals TV Azteca's claim to be the second biggest producer of Spanish-language programming in the world – after Televisa, of course (Wentz, 2007). Yet while the increased amount of US-made programming is the dominant trend, there is also a notable interest in material from countries in the Spanish-speaking world other than Mexico, including co-produced formats and reality genres (Sutter, 2003). In particular, keen competition for international sources of programming followed the success

Publicity for Univisión's
Sábado gigante (*Huge Saturday*),
possibly the world's longest-
running variety show, having
begun in Chile in 1962

of the unconventional, globally successful *telenovela*, *Betty la Fea* (*Ugly Betty*), which was shown on Telemundo (2000), but Univisión moved in quickly to secure the rights to the second series from RCN Televisión of Colombia. The growth of intercontinental co-production arrangements, particularly Telemundo's deal with RTI of Colombia, has been commented upon in Chapter Four. Such internationalised sourcing of programmes goes some little way to meeting the diversity of backgrounds amongst Latinos.

However, more than variations of national origin, the most significant dimension of diversity amongst Latinos now is the fact that the fastest growing segment is US-born, not the immigrants of the past (Lopez, 2011). It was already noted above how the 'second networks', Telefutura and Mun2, were making their pitch to younger, English-dominant or bilingual Latinos. Similarly, the youthfulness of the contemporary Latino population helps to explain why their use of the internet has grown at a rate up to three or four times faster than that of the general population of online users ('Hay 20 millones de usarios hispanos de internet en Estados Unidos', 2009). It also explains why digital rights was such an issue in the Televisa-Univisión dispute, and why all the US Spanish-language networks have been developing content especially for the internet, including mobile, distribution, and incorporating interactive and product placement features. One of Telemundo's *telenovelas*, for example, was about teenagers whose social life revolved around a Subway sandwich outlet, built as a permanent fixture on the set (Chozick and Vranica, 2010).

As the nationally-established Spanish-language television networks – Univisión, Telemundo, and Azteca America – thus pursue new ways of segmenting and commercialising a changing audience via new distribution platforms, they do so in an increasingly intense competitive environment. Each is aiming to build their share of the richest Spanish-speaking market in the world which, according to Televisa, within the Americas is greater than Mexico, Colombia, Argentina and Canada combined (Televisa, 2011). Yet in spite of the excitement generated amongst advertisers and their agencies by the findings of the 2010 Census, the Spanish-language media still have not been able to command advertising expenditure in proportion to their reach: while Latinos constitute over 16 per cent of the population, they attract only four per cent of advertising dollars ('Telemundo hires Cristina', 2011). A major reason for this apparent discrepancy is that many advertisers believe that they can reach Latinos using the same mainstream media through which they reach everyone else. And with good reason: as noted at the outset, a majority of Spanish-speakers also speak English. Consequently, it is not just as if the Spanish-language networks are competing against each other for the Latino market, but they quite rightly see themselves as up against the mainstream networks.

In this respect, Univisión at least can hold its own: in 2011 it was rating its usual fifth behind CBS, Fox, ABC, and NBC, and closing the gap (Andreeva, 2011), while its second network, Telefutura, was equal to Telemundo several points behind. Univisión garners 60 per cent of all Spanish-language media advertising income (Morena Esparza, 2011). On cable, Univisión has two assets derived from Televisa: Galavisión, which leads in the Spanish-language market, while several of Televisa's cable channels are supplied over its TuTV (Televisa, 2011). Since 2012, Univisión also has its 24/7 English-language news channel with ABC. Meanwhile, Telemundo has its Mun2, the youth-oriented cable channel mentioned above, which broadcasts programmes in English and the vernacular Spanglish, as well as Spanish. Conversely, competition on cable comes from the major US-based global cable channels, which have developed Spanish-language versions of themselves. Although CNN's services in Spanish and Portugese are also distributed in Latin America, most of the others are provided specifically for the US Latino market, including Discovery, History, ESPN, Fox Deportes and MundoFox, Fox's joint network with RCN of Colombia begun in 2012. MundoFox, which will be broadcasting some material in English, can be expected to upset the status quo, challenging not only Telemundo's vulnerable status, but also the pre-eminence of Univisión (Messer, 2012). Thus, the television landscape of Latinos, which forms the largest and wealthiest market in the Iberoamerican world, is no longer even necessarily Spanish-speaking, but it is very much American.

THE IBERIAN METROPOLITAN NATIONS

The television industries of Spain and Portugal, the one-time colonial rulers of Latin America, are incorporated into the same cultural-linguistic regions as their respective historical worlds, although each in a quite different manner. These nations share great similarities in the development of their television industries, including how they deviate from the common pattern found elsewhere in Europe. The most striking instance of their differences, however, is the contrast between the difficulties experienced by Televisa in establishing a foothold in Spain, and the exceptional influence which Globo has achieved in Portugal. Also of interest is the attention which Portugal gives to cultivating its diasporic populations in Brazil and its former colonies in Africa and Asia, often in acute competition with Brazil in terms of selling cultural products to and creating cultural influence in the latter areas.

The television systems of both Spain and Portugal were established during the long periods of dictatorship they endured during the twentieth century. Both were two-channel monopolies – of the government in the Spanish case, and a government-private consortium serving the functions of church and state in the case of Portugal – but neither had deep commitment to the public service ideal prevalent in most other European countries, and both were principally funded through the sale of advertising time. Thus, even before the privatisation which was introduced in both cases under the auspices of Leftist governments in the late 1980s to early 1990s, these systems had a strong trend towards entertainment programming, with a consequent appetite for international sources of such material. In the era of privatisation and deregulation, relations in each country between governments and media groups, notably newspaper-based conglomerates, have been decisive in the subsequent shape of the systems. Both the broad structural characteristics of the resulting systems, and even the time scale in which the transition took place, show close parallels between Spain and Portugal, perhaps something like an 'Iberian model' of private television institutionalisation.

TELEVISA IN SPAIN

Televisa's frustrated experience in its efforts to gain some share of the television market in Spain illustrates the political realities. It was seen in Chapter Two how Televisa is accustomed to having its own way in its home market, even when the government is opposed to it, but this has certainly not been the case in Spain. For instance, when Spanish television was first privatised by the PSOE (Partido Socialista Obrero Español) government in 1989, Televisa was not able to find Spanish partners, as the government guidelines required, with whom to bid for a licence, and a subsequent attempt to buy in to one of the successful licensee companies also failed. Televisa seems never to have found favour with the PSOE government. An attempt by Azcárraga Milmo in 1994 to buy Silvio Berlusconi's share of the major private network Tele 5 was rejected because Televisa was not considered to have a commitment to the Spanish public television model – as if Berlusconi's Fininvest did (Martínez, 1996). Furthermore, Televisa's stock-in-trade programming of Mexican *telenovelas*, however popular they may have been in the US, did not find the same ready-made audience in

Spain. There was an initial vogue for such programmes in the late 1980s to early 1990s, but the novelty of these *telenovelas*, or what the Spanish called *culebrones* (snakes, because of their unaccustomed length), soon passed. A trade journal survey in 1996 found that Spanish productions, particularly of comedy, were still the most popular form of programming, and quoted a private television source who said that *telenovelas* 'are no longer seen as culturally relevant to the Spanish public', particularly in the role models they presented for women (Quoted in Akyuz, 1997, p. 52). This is an interesting case of how cultural differences can still represent a barrier even when there is little or no cultural discount for linguistic differences.

Televisa had been allowed to introduce its Galavisión satellite service to Spain in 1988, which was some compensation for not obtaining a broadcast licence. Yet, having announced its arrival as 'the conquest of Spanish-speaking space in Europe', Televisa could hardly conceal the venture's abject failure by 1992. In spite of the comparative advantages of its own programme supply and satellite facilities, and hence its competitive advertising rates and relatively low costs in gaining market entry, Galavisión was not able to gain an adequate audience. In spite of installing thousands of free dishes, it was reaching fewer than 20 per cent of Spanish television homes by 1992, at best. By this time, satellite dish owners already had about 20 channels to choose from, including European and US-based services (Hernández Lomeli, 1992–3).

With the opening up of the digital DTH (direct to home) field, Televisa took up a 25 per cent interest in Vía Digital, in conjunction with Telefónica, Spain's pre-eminent telecommunications corporation, and RTVE (Radio Televisión Española), the public broadcast entity. It was mentioned how Televisa's ambitions in Spain had been frustrated by the PSOE government's negative attitude towards it, but in 1996 the conservative PP (Partido Popular) came to power. Thus, in addition to its association with the blue-chip Spanish institutions of Telefónica and RTVE, Televisa was then able to cultivate excellent relations with the PP government, particularly through Luiz María Ansón, a Televisa board member who was also the director of *ABC*, the Spanish newspaper most supportive of the PP, and the Right in general (Martínez, 1996).

The government supported Vía Digital's DTH initiative, particularly when a rival project, CSD (Canal Satélite Digital), trading as Sogecable, was mounted by the government's enemies, notably the media corporation Grupo Prisa, amongst many other things publisher of the influential newspaper *El País*. Both projects were launched in 1997, but apart from having the distraction of running disputes over issues such as soccer rights and technical standards, the rival services soon found that the DTH market was not growing quickly enough to support both of them, so by 2002 were compelled to merge. In effect, Sogecable absorbed Vía Digital, and Prisa went on to take up 95 per cent of shares in the merged entity, subsequently known as Prisa TV (Sogecable, 2008).

Thus, Televisa was bumped out of its apparently secure foothold in DTH, but another opportunity, in free-to-air television, arose when it joined with Spanish partners Globomedia and Mediapro to take up the licence for a new network, La Sexta, in 2006. Originally analogue, La Sexta began converting its offerings to DTT (digital terrestrial television) in 2009. However, given the already abundant supply of television in a country suffering from economic crisis, La Sexta was struggling to establish market share (MAVISE, 2010). Late in 2011 came the news that Televisa was exchanging its 40.8 per cent share in La Sexta for a 14.5 per cent stake in Imagina Media Audiovisual, described as 'the main provider of audiovisual content and services for the media and entertainment industry in Spain and one of the most important in the Spanish-speaking world'. This should be interpreted as a strategic change of corporate effort, out of broadcasting and into production, although Imagina in turn now owns 92 per cent of La Sexta ('Televisa acquires piece of Spain's "La Sexta" production company', 2011). For the present at least, Televisa's stake in Imagina gives it an Iberian beachhead for television production which can be distributed on both sides of the Atlantic.

TV GLOBO IN PORTUGAL

In spite of the albeit relatively mild cultural discount which applies between Spanish and Portuguese cultural-linguistic territories in television programming, TV Globo was a pioneer in exporting programmes to other Latin American countries, beginning in the early 1970s. The Globo *telenovela*, *O bem amado* (*The Beloved*) of 1973 was shown in Mexico that year, and Uruguay in 1976. More of a breakthrough in export sales for Globo was the *telenovela*, *A escrava Isaura* (*Isaura the Slave*, 1976), which was a hit not only in a number of Latin American countries including Cuba (where Fidel Castro himself was a fan) but also the world market (Brittos & Kalikoske, 2009). However, as noted already in Chapter Three, regarding the case of TV Globo's ill-fated investment in Italy, Brazilian producers in their internationalisation strategies also look to Europe, but particularly to Portugal, and the rest of the far-flung Portuguese-speaking countries. Brazil's rise to dominance in television in this Lusophone world has been more complete than Mexico's equivalent niche in the Spanish-speaking sector of the Iberoamerican cultural space. Compared to Televisa's difficult experience in Spain, the success of TV Globo in Portugal shows important contrasts in Brazil's relative position in the Lusophone world. First, perhaps most importantly, this has been because Portugal went through a more severe period of post-colonial decline, compared to Spain. By the late

Portuguese *fotonovela* (magazine) version of *Gabriela*, the successful *telenovela* from TV Globo, based on the novel by Jorge Amado

nineteenth century, after only fifty years or so of Brazilian independence, Portugal had lost its prestige in Brazil, and Portuguese immigrants there were often considered less educated and less productive than others from Japan, Europe or the Middle East (Lesser, 2005). The change of fortunes was accentuated during the Salazar dictatorship in Portugal from 1932 until 1968, which de-industrialised Portugal in general and de-emphasised the development of urban media.

Secondly, Portugal's decolonisation process outside of Brazil, and especially in Africa, was marked by revolutionary wars in the 1960s and 1970s, culminating in Portuguese withdrawal under hostile conditions and a loss of prestige and contact, including in media. By contrast, Brazil by the 1960s tended to be seen as sympathetic to the independence of Portugal's remaining colonies, maintaining positive contacts with the parties that emerged to govern Angola, Mozambique, Cape Verde, Guinea-Bissau, and East Timor. Thirdly, Brazilian cultural industries already had a foothold in Portugal and its other (former) colonies in publishing, music, and film. While Spain, for example, retained a publishing industry of great prestige in Latin America, Brazil tended to have a favourable imbalance in selling books and magazines to Portugal. So TV Globo was following a well-explored, favourable trail when it began, at a fairly early point in its history when it was still expanding to cover all of Brazil, to export *telenovelas* to Portugal, starting with *Gabriela* in 1976.

Thus it was that TV Globo started its Lusophone export drive, with its greatest success in Portugal, the former colonial centre. This coincided with the fall of the Salazar-Caetano dictatorship, the subsequent democratisation of Portugal's institutions, and the eventual move to the privatisation of the television industry. The new democratic regime inherited a state broadcasting entity, Rádiotelevisão Portuguesa, or RTP, from the era of dictatorship, which was already running on a commercial basis. Under the legislative structure set up in 1990, RTP was created as a private company, but with government-appointed directors and charged with public service obligations, while bids for two new private licences were called for. These duly went to Sociedade Independente de Comunicação (SIC) and Rede Independente (TVI). SIC was headed by Pinto Balsemão, a former prime minister and print media owner, but with a 15 per cent (the maximum allowable to a foreign owner) share held by Globo Participações, a company wholly-owned by the Globo organisation. TVI was a venture which included both the radio network of the Catholic Church, and other organisations directly or indirectly linked to the Church, along with international shareholders involved in Spanish TV (Sousa, 1996).

Prior to the advent of the private channels, Globo's links had been with RTP, and although Portuguese companies produced some of their own *telenovelas*, and there were some imported from the other Brazilian networks as well, *telenovelas* from TV Globo always were the most popular, so RTP felt that it had a trump card in the programming battle which was to come. However, RTP had not anticipated the Globo corporation becoming a shareholder in one of the new channels. In spite of Globo's failure to gain a European foothold with Telemontecarlo in Italy, and the heavy loss it sustained there, Roberto Marinho had been convinced by his son, then heir apparent Roberto Irineu Marinho, and also Pinto Balsemão, head of SIC, that this was an ideal strategic investment. For Balsemão's part, it was not just a question of getting access to Globo programming, but to their entire repertoire of commercial and technical expertise, since his own experience was with the press. As was explained in Chapter Three, Globo had acquired its initial commercial television know-how from Time-Life in the 1960s: now Globo was in a perfect position to take on the same role with its own apprentice. Yet for the first two years, Globo walked on both sides of the street, assisting SIC with every aspect of commercial television from engineering to marketing, but continuing to sell its coveted *telenovelas* to both RTP and SIC. SIC objected that this was devaluing the product with overexposure, and obtained an exclusive deal with Globo in September 1994. Within a matter of months, SIC overtook RTP's former market leadership, and sustained it for years to come

Logo of TV Globo Portugal.
Globo's own premium channel
in Lisbon, operated in liaison
with an agreement with SIC

(Sousa, 1997). Meanwhile, just as Spanish cultural elites had denounced the Latin American *telenovelas* as all-devouring serpents (*culebrones*) during the fashion for them in that country, Portuguese nationalists ceased to joke about 'cultural imperialism in reverse', and began to fret about the adoption of Brazilian Portuguese words into everyday language, and the spread of Brazilian names, fashions, festivals, and social behaviour into popular culture in general (Sousa, 1997).

TVI was sidelined by this competition between RTP and SIC around this time, but in its subsequent development, TVI became more commercially aggressive, playing down the influence of the Church, and attracting capital investment from European telecommunication industry sources. Like the other channels, TVI had its international connections through which to source programming, notably in the UK and US, and it was also acquiring Brazilian *telenovelas* from TV Globo's competitors in Brazil, SBT and Bandeirantes (Sousa, 1996). By 2011, TVI had become wholly under commercial control, owned by the Media Capital group, which is almost totally controlled by the Spanish media conglomerate, Grupo Prisa. TVI now strongly leads both SIC and RTP. For its part, SIC has become fully integrated into Balsemão's Impresa media conglomerate, and although there no longer appears to be any financial connection, SIC maintains an agreement giving exclusive access to TV Globo programming. RTP now obtains its Brazilian *telenovelas* from TV Record. Although *telenovelas* continue to dominate prime time as a genre, TVI's supremacy is now based on Portuguese productions: seven out of the top ten programmes in 2010 were *telenovelas* or mini-series from Plural Entertainment, Prisa's television production company (Ferin Cunha *et al.*, 2011). Looking beyond its Lisbon activities, Plural Entertainment operates out of several offices in Spain, and also Buenos Aires and Miami for Latin America and Hispanic USA.

TELENOVELAS AND INTERNATIONAL SERVICES IN THE LUSOPHONE WORLD

As noted, TV Globo has been selling *telenovelas* to Portugal since 1976, but also to the other Lusophone countries for nearly as long. Both TV Globo and TV Record are currently selling or licensing *telenovelas* and other programmes in Africa. For example, a blog report from 2002 noted that TV Mozambique was showing two *telenovelas*, plus a variety show (*show de auditório*) from TV Record. It also noted that DVDs of Brazilian *telenovelas* are widely available for sale and rental in Mozambique (Felinto, 2002).

The influence of Brazilian television, particularly the *telenovelas* of TV Globo and, since the 2000s, TV Record, in Lusophone Africa is very strong. We have seen some of this firsthand. Straubhaar, visiting Mozambique several times since 1992, has met people named after *telenovela* stars, been in markets and stores named after *telenovelas*, and found people eager to talk about favourite *telenovelas*, when they found that he was familiar with them. Just as in Brazil itself and, as noted above, in Portugal, people are eager to buy fashions and clothes they have seen on *telenovelas* (Borges, 2007). A GloboReporter story from Angola noted, 'The enormous interest in [Brazilian] television programs is a thermometer of Brazil's influence in the African country. "The Angolans, particularly those of lower social classes, idolise Brazil," says Professor Carlos Serrano of the Center for Africa Studies at the University of São Paulo' (Borges, 2007). From a quite different point of view, a Mozambican novelist, Paulina Chiziane, speaking at the 2012 Brásilia Biennal, criticised the negative impact on Mozambican racial self-image of Brazilian *telenovelas,* which showed Brazil to be a country populated by white, or 'at best mixed race' people, not blacks (Cited in Rodrigues, 2012).

Both the Globo and Record corporations have international television services, competing for influence in the Lusophone world with the international services of the Portuguese networks RTP, SIC and TVI. One of the current ways in which TV Globo addresses Brazilian and Portuguese emigrants abroad, reaching Portugal and the rest of the Lusophone world, is through TV Globo Internacional. It is a Portuguese-language satellite/cable TV channel that is sold à la carte, as a premium channel through various delivery systems to at least half a million people worldwide (Maio, 2009). It carries a similar line-up to that of TV Globo in Brazil, with small, localised changes for some markets, like the addition of a few news items or specials about Brazilians living in the US, for example. It is available in 115 countries: most of North, Central and South America; in most of Europe, Africa and the Middle East; and in Japan, Australia, and New Zealand. Beyond those who legally subscribe, the channel is widely pirated both directly and via DVD, particularly in Africa, so the actual direct reach of Globo via satellite is hard to calculate.

TV Record, in contrast, has two open, non-paid or non-restricted satellite channels, a general channel, TV Record Internacional, and a news channel. It began its general channel service in 2001, planning to reach a larger number of viewers than Globo by offering a free channel and by targeting countries where its parent church, the Universal Church of the Reign of God, was also expanding. As in Brazil, they also target a large audience of poorer people (Moura and Bolaño, 2007), who are also the church's likely converts (Chestnut, 1997). It claims to reach 150 countries via satellite and have terrestrial stations or repeaters in 17 countries. In Europe, it has channels of its own in Portugal, Spain and the UK. It is the only Portuguese channel on basic cable in several countries. In Africa, it covers all countries by satellite. It also has terrestrial stations in Angola, Mozambique, Cape Verde, Uganda and Madagascar, and has production studios in these countries, plus Japan. In Angola, Record claims to be the number one station in audience, according to its website. In Mozambique, where Record is the number two network after the government owned TV Mozambique, it has 10 stations covering the whole country. Asia and North America are covered by satellite channels (Record, 2012). This is how a New York cable operation describes the channel: 'TV Record Internacional (TV Record) is a 24-hour Brazilian general entertainment TV channel dedicated to providing a variety of high-quality television entertainment that meets the desires of different segments of the Portuguese-speaking public at different times. Programming includes soap operas, news, sports, comedy, talk shows, and musicals.' (Cablevision, 2011)

In contrast to Globo, Record's strategy seems to be to gain as much coverage as possible instead of maximising revenue. Since it is owned by the Universal Church of the Reign of God, that makes sense, but Record is clearly a Brazilian and Lusophone world phenomenon, not literally 'universal'. With a primary focus on religion rather than commerce, they are mainly concerned to reach large numbers of people (Moura and Bolaño, 2007) more than they are with revenue maximisation per se. (Although they do run their main networks in Brazil in such a way as to be quite profitable.) Probably to maximise audiences, versus controlling costs, they create a great deal more local content than Globo does in several of the African countries they serve (Maio, 2009). They also say they are creating at least 50 per cent local content on their stations to meet national requirements, particularly in Europe (Maio, 2009), where regional regulations do require this of satellite channels (although not all comply). In this sense, they have gone much further toward differentiating and localising their transnational services than Globo has, in the terms described by Straubhaar and Duarte (Straubhaar & Duarte, 2005). But Record is not interested in audiences that don't speak Portuguese, so they do no dubbing or subtitling. Globo, more in the mode of maximising profit with its existing products, had done relatively little localisation in terms of local production for its channels in Portuguese. However, it does do considerable localisation in another direction: massive dubbing and subtitling of the programmes that it licenses for broadcast on other stations.

TELENOVELAS BEYOND THE IBEROAMERICAN AND LUSOPHONE WORLDS

Previous chapters have shown how the commercialisation of popular culture in the media of Latin America is deeply entrenched and longstanding. The *telenovelas* which form the backbone of television programming in Latin America today have descended from the *radionovelas* which were expressly developed as cultural vehicles for advertising in the region by sponsors such as Procter & Gamble and Colgate-Palmolive in Cuba in the decades between the World Wars, and subsequently diffused to continental Latin America, ultimately migrating to television (Luis López, 1998). Although the *telenovela* was fostered by the same companies who created and sponsored the soap opera in the US, scholars are careful to distinguish between the two genres: whereas the soap opera can run for years, the *telenovela* is finite, usually running for six to twelve months, and having a discernible narrative structure of beginning, middle, and end. There are also thematic distinctions: *telenovelas* often take dramatic motivation from contemporary social conflicts and issues, while the soap opera rests more on individual characters and conventional plots. As well, aficionados like to draw attention to national differences in *telenovelas* – Brazilian ones are thought to have relatively high production values and more complex plots, which often include socially-oriented themes ranging from cloning and youth drug abuse (*O clone, The Clone*, 2001–2), to race issues (*Duas caras, Two Faces*, 2007–8) to land reform (*O rei do gado, The Cattle King*, 1996–7) while the Mexican ones tend to go for more obvious melodramatic and sentimental effects (Lopez, 1995).

We have seen that the exploitation of comparative advantage within a geolinguistic region, and the cultural proximity which accompanies it, offers an adequate, though not comprehensive, explanation for the success of Televisa, Globo, Venevisión, and RCN in building their export markets within Latin America, Latin Europe, and the Spanish-speaking US. As we argue in this book, language is the vehicle of culture, so it is not similarities of language alone which give access to foreign markets, but 'cultural elements – dress, ethnic types, gestures, body language, definitions of humour, ideas about story pacing, music traditions, religious elements – that are often shared across national borders.' (Straubhaar, 2007, p. 237) These factors incline audiences to prefer programmes from their own culture or, when these are not available, from cultures similar to their own, and not necessarily with the same language. This would suggest that, in addition to language, there are 'pan-Latin' characteristics of successfully-exported programming from the major Latin American producers. Taken in conjunction with the economics of large markets, similarities of language and culture certainly seem to account for the success of Mexican and Brazilian programmes, particularly in the case of the *telenovela*, which still form the bulk of programme exports from these countries. However, the fact that such programmes have for some time also found eager audiences in linguistically and culturally remote territories such as Eastern Europe, Russia, China, and elsewhere far beyond the boundaries of the Latin world makes it clear that the geolinguistic regions and cultural proximity hypotheses only go so far in explaining the success of *telenovela* exports.

There are three quite different alternative explanations for this paradox: they are respectively anthropological, economic, and temporal. The anthropological one argues for a kind of cultural universality: that the *telenovela* as a genre is based on themes which are universal in their appeal, and that their simple melodramatic narrative mode can be understood and appreciated by audiences everywhere. This line of thought draws on traditional theories such as the archetypes theorised by Jung or the mythic structures of Lévi-Strauss, but there are less abstract approaches available. Notably, we can modify the cultural proximity concept to take account of 'genre proximity', where the programmes have resonance with traditional forms of story-telling in the receiving society; 'thematic proximity', where audiences are responding to stories built around the universal experience of urbanisation and modernisation in general (La Pastina and Straubhaar, 2005); and 'value proximity', which is where traditional values, including religion, triumph over their tension with modernity as a global phenomenon (Straubhaar, 2007). Thus, to take an example of value proximity, or the lack of it, programme exporters report that US series 'don't work' with Chinese audiences because they are more about individual than collective experience (Bielby & Harrington, 2002: p. 229n), whereas *telenovelas* have thematic proximity in that they reflect more of the realities of life in societies undergoing industrialisation (Madden, 2008).

The second kind of explanation comes from the 'dismal science' of economics, specifically that of the international programme trade. The annual value of *telenovelas* has been estimated at US$ 2 billion, but only around US$ 340 million of that value is in exports (TVMasNovelas, 2004). In other words, sales of advertising carried by the programmes in their home markets generates close to 80 per cent of revenue for the producers/distributors, as was seen explicitly in Chapter Two. This means that producers can sell *telenovelas* to foreign markets at much less than the cost of production. Furthermore, they can calibrate the price in accordance with the size and purchasing power of the particular market, and in any case costs of production are relatively low by international standards. Although there is a big variation between the higher production values of Brazilian *telenovelas* as against their Mexican counterparts, as of the mid-2000s, the cost range was put at between US$ 40,000 and 70,000 per hour (TVMasNovelas, 2004). This compares to US$ 2 million for an hour of drama in the US, where even reality shows were around US$ 700,000 per episode (Entertainment Industry Development Corporation, 2005). From the point of view of the importing countries, therefore, *telenovelas* are cheap programming in the first place, and come with the bonus of proven success in their home markets – however alien they might be. The spread of *telenovelas* out of their cultural-linguistic regions and into Eastern Europe and Asia in the 1980s and 1990s therefore has a plausible economic explanation in that these were then fairly underdeveloped markets with relatively little production capacity of their own, and *telenovelas* offered a very affordable option with which to fill expanding schedules.

Interestingly, as these markets have matured over the last decade, they have begun to produce their own serial fiction, and audiences have proved responsive to such domestic offerings. If television is a cultural industry, we can think of this development as a kind of import substitution process, as in manufacturing industry: reducing dependency on imports by making local adaptations of them. The Latin producers' ventures into co-production and format trading is significant in this regard. The receiving markets are now more sophisticated, at least in that audiences are demanding programmes that reflect their own culture and are in their own language, that there is now advertising better able to pay for domestic programming, and that local production capacity is increasing. In these circumstances, collaborative production, negotiation over formats, and remakes all flourish, as distinct from the sale of rights to programmes imported in cans. The paradigm case is the series English speakers know in its US version as *Ugly Betty* (2006–10), but which was originally a Colombian production, from RCN, and subsequently remade in China, India, Russia, Germany, Hungary, Greece and Belgium, and even in Mexico and Spain (Mikos & Perrotta, 2012).

Finally, there is the temporal explanation, which puts its emphasis on the intrinsic daily rhythm of the scheduling of *telenovelas*, and the habitual everyday shared ritual quality of watching and discussing them in specific social settings (González, 1994). The distinctive tradition in Latin America has been for *telenovelas* to be 'strip-programmed': that is, they occupy the same time-slot each day of the week, and one *telenovela* follows another throughout prime time. This is a practice which has been followed in many of the markets where they are shown, and anecdotes abound as to how the streets fall silent at the time when the latest *telenovela* is being shown. Whatever explanation one favours, there can be no dispute that the *telenovela* has been Latin America's most distinctive and influential contribution to global television culture.

This chapter has outlined the impact that Latin American television has had outside of its geographical region. We have seen that there was an initial exploitation of cultural-linguistic similarities. These enabled a regional exchange of programming to develop, particularly of *telenovelas*, the most characteristic, commonly popular, and exportable genre of Latin American television. Yet while cultural-linguistic commonalities helped Televisa of Mexico to create a market for such products amongst Spanish-speakers in the US, in Spain, the land of the mother tongue, Televisa found resistance against its ambitions, and deprecation of its programming. By contrast, Brazilian producers found an enthusiastic reception for their *telenovelas* in Portugal at a time when its television system was being opened to commercialisation. The fact that Portuguese *telenovelas* have ultimately become more popular than those from Brazil suggest that the importation of such content is a transitional phase in the maturing of television markets. The Lusophone markets of Africa, however, remain dependent on Brazilian product to fill their screens, lacking the critical mass to develop their own national markets: size still matters.

The surprising popularity of *telenovelas* in some territories of Eastern Europe and Asia, culturally as well as geographically remote from Latin America, bears out the import substitution explanation, however, to the extent that they too are now producing their own serial television fiction. This means in turn that the market opportunities for the *telenovela* trade have become more finite as the business has become both more competitive and transnationalised, seen in the increase in co-productions and remakes, and the trading of scripts and formats.

6

National Television Systems in the Global Era

In this chapter, we look at how new global forces are pressuring national television systems, a major issue since the 1990s. New technologies enabled new global penetration of outside channels and programmes, and new forms of television to compete with national networks. New institutions, models and ideas such as privatisation of government media, deregulation of government rules, and liberalisation of competition also came in. However, much of what was startlingly new in Africa, Asia, Europe, or the Middle East in the 1990s, such as privatisation, deregulation, and liberalisation, represented issues that Latin America had already dealt with in an earlier wave of US influence in the 1920s–50s, so we will review some of the patterns that were established then, both of global influence and of how it was dealt with throughout the region. We will emphasise the regional or transnational lens, as well as the national and global ones, arguing that regional processes of adaptation often mediate global influences on Latin American nations. For example, some regional patterns of adaptation from colonial days such as hybridisation still shape how national broadcasters and governments adapt new global influences.

Latin American nations often deal in very individual ways with new global patterns of television. Some nations, such as Bolivia or Venezuela, have taken left or populist stances of resistance to new global forces of commercialism. Venezuela's late President Chávez tried to re-appropriate satellite technology to create a television network for Latin America that gives new voice to government television networks, for example. In a less overtly confrontational way, Brazil's former President Lula used the transition to terrestrial digital television to strengthen government and public television in Brazil. He also used the digital transition to try to create a Latin America-wide digital television standard to reinforce regional hardware and content industries. However, most nations in Latin America have not tried to fight or shape the new changes in such clear, policy-driven ways, leaving it to national private networks to sort out how to adapt to the new competition from outside technologies and networks. Our argument is more that there are now regional patterns that partially mediate such forces between nations as well as within nations, as companies and regulators come to grips with them. Transnational patterns and influences, both colonial and regional, predated (and influenced) the nations and national forms of television in Latin America, and those transnational patterns continue to influence the interaction of the various national systems with global systems even now.

Now the forces bearing in on Latin America are transnational and global; economic, managerial, and technological. But if we see globalisation in one sense as the interaction of global, regional, national and local over time, then the outcome tends to be both an increased number of layers or spheres of possibility (global and regional television co-existing with national) and an evolving hybridisation of the local, national and regional as they absorb and adapt new global ideas, technologies, models and genres. First, we will start by reviewing the regional heritages of colonialism, post-colonialism and regional circulation before the creation of national television systems to examine the baseline they created, as well as the regional culture that in many ways mediates current global influences.

THE HERITAGE OF REGIONALISM

Latin America reflects just over five centuries of the interplay of national or local versus transnational forces and influences, in military force and conquest, in religion and culture, in economics, and now in television. It starts with the Spanish and Portuguese colonial empires, whose linguistic and cultural legacies still shape which audiences watch television in which language, and with whose flag in the background. Those empires themselves, and the nations that came out of them, were also shaped by decisions by the Catholic Church, which also determined national and linguistic boundaries with its decisions. Both empires and Church created the basis for post-national or transnational television and media spaces to emerge above the nation-state in the late twentieth century and early 2000s, the geocultural and geolinguistic regions, as described in Chapter One.

Nation-states rose above these colonial legacies, partly with the assistance of other emerging transnational powers, such as the British and United States' commercial and political interests that stepped in after independence in many Latin American nations to offer investment, advice, technology, and models for economic and cultural forms like commercial television broadcasting and networks. Much of this post-colonial experience for Latin America took shape in the nineteenth and early twentieth centuries, creating an interesting set of national forms of broadcasting, and the emergence of powerful hybrid television forms such as the *telenovela*. So Latin America is an excellent place to look at over a century and a half of the interplay of post-colonial processes, nation-states, national media, and the emergence of transnational and global forces that challenge those states and national television systems from above. So first we will look at the colonial, and transnational, post-colonial influences that shape Latin America as a geolinguistic and geocultural region. Then we will look at how national forms of television emerged out of those influences, and finally consider the interaction of both with new global and transnational influences from the US and elsewhere.

COLONIAL ORIGINS, LANGUAGE AND CULTURE

The Catholic Church created some of the crucial linguistic and cultural framing of modern Latin American media. The Church wished to minimise conflict between the growing Spanish and Portuguese empires, both Catholic, so very early in the colonisation process, in 1494, a Spanish-born Pope, Alexander VI, negotiated the Treaty of Tordesillas, which divided Latin America into Spanish and Portuguese zones of conquest. The dividing line was adjusted several times up through the 1700s to negotiate the lines of Portuguese occupation of Brazil, but the overall principle held up rather well, and the basic lines of Spanish-speaking Latin America versus Portuguese-speaking Brazil were established. Those linguistic lines became a major guiding principle for twentieth century television and telecommunications policy, particularly in Brazil, but also some of its neighbours, like Argentina and Uruguay.

For Brazilian military governments from 1964 until 1985, for example, it was a major national security issue to ensure that all Brazilians were primarily exposed to television in Portuguese. They spent billions of dollars on telecom infrastructure, first in microwave transmission towers between cities and regions, and then on four generations of BrasilSat satellites (see Chapter Three). These telecom investments had several purposes: to enable military communications; to enable a national voice and data network for economic development, and crucially for television; to assure an immersion in national Brazilian language and culture via television; and to promote economic development by creating a national consumer market via television advertising (Salles, 1975). While Brazil's plans and investments for building out telecom to spread television may have been the most ambitious in Latin America, Mexico carried out similar plans. So, curiously, colonial era interactions of Spanish empire, Portuguese empire, and a transnational Catholic Papacy created language lines prefiguring national boundaries that led modern nations to massively invest in expensive infrastructure to defend those linguistic boundaries in order to reinforce national identity. In the next section, we see how common patterns of cultural interaction led to common patterns of cultural hybridity that were able to cut across those linguistic and national borders to prefigure a modern transnational, regional market in television that rises to some degree above the national television markets protected and tended by the nation states of Latin America.

EUROPEAN COLONIALISM AND THE POST-COLONIAL HYBRIDITY OF POPULAR CULTURES

The colonial process brought in European conquerors, plantation owners, mining contractors and clerics, sometimes with families, sometimes not. At gun and swordpoint, they began the physical hybridisation of Latin America by creating children with indigenous people and by turning indigenous people into slaves and servants. When many of the indigenous simply died instead, the Spanish and Portuguese brought in African slaves to be their paramours, slaves and servants. This physical mixing of peoples, races and ethnicities created the process known today as *mestizaje* (literally, miscegenation) the prototype for the Latin American cultural studies paradigm of hybridity (García Canclini, 1990, 1995; Kraidy, 2002b, 2005).

This race mixing of peoples had correlates in the mixing of religion between varied European Catholic, indigenous, African, and, later, European and US Protestant traditions, saints, deities, rituals, and imagery. Anthropologists tended to refer to the religious mixing, per se, as syncretism (Bastide, 1978), but it became another layer in the evolving pattern of Latin American cultural hybridity (García Canclini, 1995), which included blends of European, indigenous and Afro-descendent elements in music, visual arts, design and decoration, dance, and festivals (Rowe and Schelling, 1991). The commonalities in these blends of culture created large regional patterns in popular culture, which ultimately make transnational Latin American television culturally proximate and attractive to many of its nations. Distinct national variations of that hybridity also make for national cultures that continue to frame television programming in distinct ways that both hold and reinforce national audiences.

Several current cultural globalisation theorists stress that over time, particularly over the long run, the result of cultural interaction, or cultural globalisation, is hybridity (Kraidy, 2002b; Nederveen Pieterse, 2004). However, we want to argue that, frequently in the short run, the experience of people that we have interviewed in Brazil, Mexico, and the Hispanic US is more often expressed in terms of multiplicity of experience and identity rather than hybridity per se. One starting point is Stuart Hall's example of how a young man might want to feel British, Caribbean and Black all at the same time, feeling a sense of multiplicity in identity (Hall, 1993). Multiple aspects of identity accumulate from individual and group or cultural experience, although a sense of position and situation is also important. A person might reflect one identity at church, another in school, and another in sports. People are born in one place, but migrate to another, maintaining aspects of identity tied to their original culture as well as acquiring aspects of the culture that they move to. A reflection of that

A ceremony of *candomblé*, as celebrated among Afro-Brazilian communities. The practices have helped preserve their cultural identities since slavery days

process is the code switching between Spanish and English very common among US Hispanics, many of whom feel comfortable in both languages and cultures, and who often switch from one to the other, depending on who they are talking to and what they are talking about (Poplack, 2000).

People may grow up in one religion, but are voluntarily, or forcibly (as in the conquest of Latin America) led to join another. In the short run, they are likely to continue aspects of both in their mind, in their practice and in their sociability with family and community. In the longer run, these elements of different religions may combine and blend, as in the theory of syncretism. There will also be real variation among people in these kinds of experiences. In the city of Salvador, or Bahia, in Brazil, many Afro-Brazilian religious communities (namely those that practice *candomblé*) genuinely mix Catholic saints with Yoruban deities known as *orixás* (Bastide, 1978*)*. However, some communities, like the well-known group Ilê Axê Opô Afonjá, have declared that they are putting away the Catholic saints, who were used as an outside protective layer to hide the African deities and practices within the community from outsiders who might disapprove (Afonjá, 1999). So multiple layers may simply accrue in a community, or they may sometimes be created strategically to enable the co-existence or protection of traditional layers of identity and practice that might be discouraged or even persecuted by outsiders if they were not protected by more visible layers of European or hybrid identity.

Attachments to nations were assumed to be exclusive, or at least primary under a modern logic of nationality. Waisbord takes the view, however, that there is no inherent contradiction for a Latin American teenager to wear a US baseball team cap, while still cheering for their national or local soccer team (1997). Like Hall's conception of multiple identities, cited above (1993), globalisation theorist Arjun Appadurai also sees a tendency toward multiplicity of identities in (post)modern times of large-scale movements of people, capital, technologies, media, and ideas (Appadurai, 1996).

Hybridity, a multiplicity of positions and actions, and a multiplicity of identities and cultural forms (linked to media choice and use) usually co-exist. People layer up experiences that form what seem to be multiple aspects or layers of identity. In the example above, people in Brazil may be actively involved with both Catholic and Afro-Brazilian forms of worship, performing different identities as they do so. Brazilian television viewers have identified themselves to Straubhaar in interviews over the years as combinations of city identity (such as *Carioca* from Rio), regional identity (*Bahiano* from Bahia), national (Brazilian), class (*pobre* or poor, working class, etc.), and racial identity. These have distinct implications for television viewing choices. Chapter Three noted the success that the SBT and TV Record television networks had in specifically targeting working class people in Brazil.

A great deal of this multiplicity has to do with long-running layers of cultural identity tied to geography. The larger Latin American nations like Mexico have major differences among their cities, states/provinces, and regions. Waisbord observes, for example, that 'Mexicanness has not trumped strong regional identities' (1997, p. 15). Nevertheless some Brazilian analysts of television do tend to think that national television itself has tended to reduce the previous major differences of sub-national regional identity in Brazil (Kottak, 1990; Porto, 2011), but it is also clear from ethnographic work in rural areas that Brazilian audiences also use regional identity as a filter for interpreting national television (La Pastina, 2003). Regional identities can be seen as a form of mediation, in Martín-Barbero's (1993) terms of examining what aspects of culture mediate the content of media for those who receive them, as applied to the mediation of largely national television content by various other levels of identity (Straubhaar, 2007).

People may watch television in different languages, as US Hispanics of the second or third generation of immigration tend to do (Straubhaar interviews in Texas 2005–9). As Chapter Five noted, new US Hispanic networks pursue viewers who prefer to watch television in English but still think of themselves as Hispanic (Piñón & Rojas, 2011). As a Pew Hispanic Center report found, young US Hispanics live in (at least) two worlds. Depending on how long they have lived in the US, they might present themselves as Mexican, Mexican-American, Hispanic/Latino, or just American, or combinations of the above (Taylor, Kochhar *et al.*, 2009). Some of those identities are presented as hybrid, such as Mexican-American or Latino, some are presented as potentially separate layers, Mexican, American, etc.

This section has discussed colonial and post-colonial approaches to cultural hybridity across Latin America that enabled a regional market characterised by some notable degree of cultural commonality or proximity to emerge. The next section examines more specifically political patterns of relationship between states and broadcasters that developed from southern European patterns of corporatism, clientalism and populism that were re-enacted in Latin America during the colonial and post-colonial eras. These patterns of ownership and of interaction between private media and the state created patterns that mediated the subsequent patterns of commercial network broadcasting that were brought to Latin America from the US, as described in Chapters One to Four, for various countries. The point here is not to downplay the extent of US influence on the commercial television of Latin America, but to nuance how it was shaped within forms that had developed earlier.

TRANSNATIONAL IBERIAN CORPORATIST AND CLIENTALIST TRADITION, AND THE MEDIA

Corporatism in Latin America is seen as an inheritor of Iberian, and also Italian, tendencies toward patrimonial, hierarchical economy and politics in which society is divided into major organisations by activity (Malloy, 1976). Those are frequently private, like regional groupings of corporations, or powerful individual corporations, like television networks.

Juan Perón and Getúlio Vargas saw the advantages of using radio, along with government-controlled labour unions, to mobilise the new working and middle classes to support their regimes. Similarly, Latin American states tended to develop chummy relations with one or two major television networks, raising them above possible competitors with favourable economic and regulatory treatment in return for favourable media treatment of government actions and policies. However, it is also possible to overestimate the power and durability of such alliances. Despite a fairly cosy relationship with the military from 1964 to 1984, TV Globo abandoned them when the relationship began to threaten their own core interests. (See Chapter Three).

TRANSNATIONAL LATIN AMERICAN POPULIST TRADITION

Another closely-related transnational Iberian and Latin tradition that has greatly affected Latin America is the populist form of rule or governance that involves strong-man rule (*caudillismo*) with the support of media mobilisation of working classes. Radio broadcasting was heavily used by populist leaders like Perón. Later populists, like Castro often made heavy use of national broadcast television news and talk programmes in their mobilisation of popular support (Rivero, 2010).

This tradition continues strongly in Latin America with a new wave of populist regimes in the 1990s and 2000s. Waisbord notes, '... the region has a tradition of populist administrations, which have historically sought to reform

The populist dynasty of Juan and Eva Perón was represented in 1950 as synonymous with a 'just, free and sovereign' Argentina

media systems. In the past, the goals of those policies were to curb the power of selected private companies, and enlarge the media power of governments. During the 2000s, populist administrations came to power in several countries. They include the governments of Néstor Kirchner (2003–7) and his spouse Cristina Fernández de Kirchner (2007–present) in Argentina, Evo Morales (2006–present) in Bolivia, Rafael Correa (2007–present) in Ecuador, Daniel Ortega (2007–present) in Nicaragua, and Hugo Chávez (1999–2013) in Venezuela' (Waisbord, 2011, pp. 98–99). Political leaders like Chávez, who died in 2013, used mass movements like his Bolivarianism to mobilise the poor and working class against elites and middle classes, relying heavily on television, both news and televised speeches.

These sections have shown how the political relations of state and broadcaster were shaped by colonial and post-colonial traditions of corporatism, clientalism, and populism. Those traditions mediated, or shaped, how US and global commercial forces on commercial television in Latin America created hybrid commercial forms that reflect both sets of influences. A closely related phenomenon was a distinctive Latin American approach to national identity formation that features the evolution of the imagined national community described by Anderson (1983) in the interactions of media capitalism, state and popular culture.

TRANSNATIONAL PATTERNS OF IMAGINING COMMUNITY IN LATIN AMERICAN NATIONS

The creation and diffusion of popular culture was part of the nation-building process in a number of Latin American countries. The Spanish and Portuguese empires broke up much earlier than most European counterparts, with Argentina independent in 1818 after eight years of war, Venezuela and Colombia becoming independent by insurrection by 1819, and Brazil becoming independent in

1832 when the son of the Portuguese king declared his own empire in Brazil. However, borders were initially very unsettled. Most post-independence political efforts in the early and mid-nineteenth century were devoted to settling national boundaries by war and negotiation, creating the basis for nation-formation.

It is, therefore, quite striking how quickly the newly organised countries were able to create and spread a sense of national identity within such recently set-tled boundaries. Benedict Anderson noted that newspapers and novels enabled people in the nineteenth century in Latin American countries to imagine them-selves as part of national communities (Anderson, 1983). He observed that 'print capitalism' effectively cooperated with national governments to create national frames for markets within which the newspaper and book publishing enterprises of print capitalism could prosper, simultaneously creating the national identities, and national languages, that states also desperately needed to consolidate their own legitimacy.

Print capitalism in Latin America was strongly coloured by that of southern Europe. French, as well as Portuguese and Spanish, narrative concepts migrated to Latin America, influencing both print media and television. For example, the French *feuilleton*, originally a literary and political supplement to newspapers, was transformed into the concept of the serialised story, then later the soap opera. Latin American analysts (Rêgo, 2003; Martin-Barbero, 1995) point to the *feuilleton* as a crucial source of influence on Latin American *telenovelas*, com-peting with the US soap opera. Latin American nations built on such common traditions from Europe, particularly Iberia, then also influenced each other, as different nations began to innovate with national versions of the newspaper, the novel, various music forms, dramatic traditions, dances, travelling circuses, musical and comedy variety, and, ultimately, the *telenovela*, and other television genres. Novelists, playwrights, musicians, composers, variety hosts, comedians, and scriptwriters very popular in one Latin American country were often popu-lar in others, especially within Spanish-speaking Latin America, but often enough hopping linguistic lines between Brazil and the Spanish-speaking coun-tries. As noted about the early development of the *telenovela* by Straubhaar (1982, 1991), there were often similarities of environment, scenery, racial make-up, religion, history and politics that made aesthetic traditions interesting, jokes funny and social commentary comprehensible across linguistic lines within Latin America. Print, theatrical or electronic capitalism in one country often influ-enced its neighbours, as regional genres in things like radio serial fiction, *radionovelas,* emerged.

If the effect of print media in creating national identity was powerful, in a time of limited literacy and economic affluence, when such media were only easily available to upper middle and upper classes, then such nationalising impacts of media were very likely magnified in the twentieth century by radio, film, and television. 'For some analysts, radio and film played a decisive role in the incorporation of popular classes into the nation-state after the 1930s' (Waisbord, 1998). Vargas in Brazil, for example, invented Brazilian national traditions via radio, building on the existing forms or genres of carnival, soccer, and samba music. None of them were seen as widely shared national cultural forms before the 1930s (Waisbord, 1998). After Vargas' purposeful diffusion of them across Brazil via radio (Morreira, 1991), all became seen as central elements of national identity (Ortiz, 1985; Waisbord, 1998). Speaking of samba, which in 1910 was stigmatised as 'black music', Hermano Vianna explains the 'mystery' by which it became the national music of Brazil in less than 25 years, taken up by Vargas for political purposes as a central symbol of national unification, and by commercial radio as a central genre for audience development (Vianna, 1999).

To point out that there were common regional, transnational patterns in the ways that states, media industries and popular cultures interacted over time is to not to deny the power of US influence, as noted by many analysts, including the time frames of US influence noted by Waisbord, summarised in Chapter One. Neither is it to deny the power of the state, which we examine briefly in the next section, to note that national state power can also sometimes mediate at least somewhat the US and other global powers that we examine later in this chapter.

NATION-STATES' POWER IN TELEVISION

Our emphasis so far on transnational influences on Latin American television should not be taken as diminishing the power that nation-states built up via television from the 1950s to now. Like radio, but unlike film, states had, and continue to have, a number of powerful levers of control over television stations and networks. Licensing frequencies gives almost all states in the world more power over television than over film, for example. States also controlled much of the infrastructure required for broadcasting, particularly for networks trying to cover large nations like Brazil or Mexico, although this power has diminished with privatisation since the 1990s.

States, particularly those powerful enough to operate in a state capitalist economic mode (Evans, 1979), also frequently have substantial advertising budgets that they can steer toward friendly television networks and away from less friendly ones (Mattos, 1984). States frequently make loans for capital investment. They can also subsidise credit to make the widespread acquisition of television sets easier for a potential mass audience (Straubhaar, 1984). They can also shape the national economy in major ways that benefit television networks and their advertisers, or not. States by and large wanted to see more creation of national content, so they could also offer incentives to create more national content. So it is not too surprising that despite the many transnational elements of television's origins in Latin America, and despite the many pressures on national broadcasters from above by globalisation with its new investors, technologies, competitors, paradigms, genres, and regulatory regimes, national television continues to be remarkably healthy in Latin America, as in most parts of the world (Morris & Waisbord, 2001; Straubhaar, 2007).

The licensing process for handing out permission for broadcasters to use the frequencies they need is a core element of the state's power. States can reward political allies with licences, as the hundreds of licences handed out to politicians in Brazil since the 1980s shows (Lima, 1988; Straubhaar, 2007). States, or more specifically their leaders, can also punish their enemies, as President Chávez of Venezuela demonstrated when he refused to renew the licence of RCTV, a television station that had frequently broadcast rallies and other news that seemed favourable to Chávez' political opponents, as noted in Chapter Four. The importance of having a broadcast licence, even in these days of satellite television and the internet is demonstrated by the difficulty RCTV is having as an online-only network after losing their licence. Until all television goes out over some sort of broadband network, which seems a distant prospect in a region where relatively few people have home access to broadband internet, the threat of pulling a licence is a very powerful means of keeping broadcast television stations in line.

All of these potential levers of power may give states some control, both in exercising domestic political power and in resisting forces of globalisation (Morris & Waisbord, 2001). However, that power varies considerably from state to state. Large emerging economies like Mexico and Brazil can exercise much more power over global actors than can smaller states with less developed power, such as Guatemala or Bolivia. With these considerations in mind, let us look at the influence of the US on Latin American television, historically and currently. We will look first at the impact of the US commercial model of television and then the impact of US programming.

US INFLUENCE ON LATIN AMERICAN TELEVISION, 1920s–70s

As US influence became quite important in the broadcasting structures of the twentieth century, as outlined in Chapter One, it encountered existing forms of nationalist capitalist media in Latin America, as described above. Chapter One noted the importance of US companies and national entrepreneurs. Here we want to add in the role of genres and programming models. The most visible twentieth century example was the development in Cuba, followed by rapid spread to other Latin American nations, of the *radionovela* in the 1930s and 1940s, and the *telenovela* in the 1950s and 1960s (Rivero, 2009). As was mentioned in Chapter One, it was a US corporation, Colgate-Palmolive, which wanted to build on its domestic success in selling soap via soap operas, and so turned to Cuba, a growing economy with strong ties to the US. First with radio in the 1930s, then television in the 1950s, Colgate-Palmolive paid Cuban producers to adapt the soap opera to Latin America (Rivero, 2007). They did so, but also included aspects of melodramatic tradition, such as the *feuilleton*, that came from Iberia via France and had developed further in Latin America already (Martín-Barbero, 1993), creating a hybrid genre. Other Latin American broadcasters observed the *telenovela*'s success in gaining audiences (and selling soap) so, spurred on by US and domestic advertisers, they imported Cuban scripts and professionals, as well as developing their own (Straubhaar, 2011). Time-Life's Joe Wallach, for instance, took recently hired colleagues at TV Globo to Argentina in 1966 to look at how Goar Mestre, who had started in Cuba, was adapting US commercial television and advertising models there, to see if there were ideas, particularly for selling advertising that they could borrow (Wallach, 2011).

Although there emerged transnational Latin American patterns of how to adapt US style capitalist, commercial television to the countries of the region, we should not understate the strong initial impact of the US commercial paradigm in the 1920s–60s, reinforced later in the neoliberal paradigm shift of the 1990s. Unlike other parts of the world, advertising became the dominant source of finance first for radio in the 1930s, then television in the 1950s through a combination of US government influence wanting to promote the US paradigm (as analysed in Chapter One), US corporate influence wanting to sell products and invest (as with the case of Time-Life analysed here), and national corporate influence of owners (like Roberto Marinho in Brazil and Emilio Azcárraga in Mexico) and advertisers. This commercial shift in Latin America anticipated the later global commercial media shift of the 1990s–2000s in the rest of the world, and its early patterns can help global scholars understand the subsequent shifts in other regions better.

The commercial tilt also accelerated an early embrace in Latin America of capitalist consumer economies. Commercial media opposed socialist revolutions in various countries: Cuba in 1959, Brazil in 1964, and Venezuela in the recent Chávez era. In Brazil, for example, there is good evidence that the military, commercial media, and the advertising industry shared a vision of capitalist development of a consumer economy that led to cooperation like that between TV Globo and the military (Hertz, 1987). Scholars of the consumer economy have noted the power of television as a medium of specific advertising and the larger creation of a desire to consume (Milanesi, 1978; Hamburger, 2007). Arguing from a political economy point of view, some scholars argued that it did not help countries like Brazil to develop national programming if those pro- grammes still sold soap and helped lock in a consumer identity (Oliveira, 1993).

INCREASED TELEVISION FLOWS AND FORMS CHALLENGE NATIONAL TELEVISION

Not only was there considerable influence of the US commercial model on Latin America, but the US and a few other dominant exporters of television pro- gramming also began to exercise considerable power via the heavy inflow of their television programs into the region. By the 1960s–70s, an increasingly heavy, seemingly one-way flow of television programmes from the US to the rest of the world seemed to signal a denationalisation of television (Nordenstreng & Varis, 1974; Beltran & Fox de Cardona, 1979). Similarly, foreign investment in Latin American television in the 1960s and 1970s by outside companies like Time-Life and ABC seemed to signal a loss of national control, as did the adop- tion of US commercial television network models and genres (Beltran & Fox de Cardona, 1979; Oliveira, 1993). However, others began to observe that national organisations were frequently transformed by such influences, while also main- taining a great deal of control and continuity, as noted in the example of TV Globo, above. 'If we look at television, frequently indicated as the best exam- ple of the process of de-nationalisation, it's not clear that the national has waned' (Waisbord, 1997). Waisbord notes that the challenges of globalisation tends to prod nation states to respond rather than automatically weakening them, or challenging national identities (1997).

Although quite a bit of US television programming flowed into Latin America in the 1960s and 1970s, both governments and national television networks had good reasons to decrease the inflow of canned, imported programmes and to promote national production. States such as Brazil wanted to see their own national identity promoted on television in both news and entertainment. There were specific things about US programming such as its depiction of race and its emphasis on violence that governments, such as Brazil in 1971, specifically objected to (Straubhaar, 1981). Commercial networks were beginning to dis- cover that they could make more money with local programming than with imported programmes, so commercial interest rather than national policy turned them towards creating their own productions.

Those national networks that could afford to create high quality national pro- gramming discovered that it was more attractive to both audiences and advertisers. Even if creating national programming costs more, it tends to be worth it, as it attracts larger and more enthusiastic audiences, which are more interesting to advertisers, even if they have to pay higher rates than they might on a lower-cost imported programme. Moran, for example, takes the example of a national network creating its own version of a programme like *Wheel of Fortune*, which costs more, versus simply importing the US version, which is usually (but not always) quite a bit cheaper. If the producer has the resources, it is nearly always worth the cost to produce their own version since it is so much more attractive to the audience when it features local faces, stars, jokes, etc. (Moran, 1998). This follows closely on the general precepts of cultural proximity, that those are precisely the advantages of local or national programming compared to imports (Straubhaar, 1981). For this reason, the large producers historically have aimed at satisfying their domestic audiences, not producing specifically with export in mind. Despite the success of some Latin American television networks in international exports, investments, and co-productions, all of them still depend primarily on their own national markets for the primary success. Even at the height of export success for TV Globo, for example, well over 90 per cent of its actual income came from its national market in Brazil. Similarly, as noted in Chapter Two, Televisa obtained only seven per cent of its 2011 income from exports (Televisa, 2011). Similar moves happened in other Latin American countries as the larger nations replaced imported US shows with national *telenovelas*, and smaller countries replaced the US imports with those from around the region, at least in prime time (Straubhaar, 2007).

To pick up a theme introduced in Chapter One and elaborated above, what came out of the interaction of US influence, pre-existing Latin American patterns and traditions and nation power and influence can be perhaps best understood in terms of hybridity. US organisational ideas combined with earlier Latin American ones to produce new hybrid television institutions. US and other global genre ideas combined with earlier patterns of Latin American and national popular cultures to produce hybrid genres.

THE FUNDAMENTAL PATTERN OF TELEVISION ORGANISATIONAL AND GENRE HYBRIDITY

By the 1960s and 1970s, Latin Americans began to think of the *telenovela* as a new cultural form of their own, as it dominated prime time and began to split into national versions in Brazil, Mexico and elsewhere. In this example, both global and national economic interests drove many decisions, but cultural innovation among producers and cultural response by audiences were also crucial to that decision-making. This corresponds to one common understanding of how genres like the *telenovela* evolve by the interaction of producers and publics over time.

We can illuminate these transnational economic processes using two key industry terms that have become theoretical concepts, localisation and glocalisation. In localisation, a transnational or global firm takes the initiative to take its product, process or capital into a new market, adapting it to local conditions to enable it to succeed. Colgate-Palmolive in Cuba is a good example of that, taking a known and successful commercial genre and adapting it to a new market. Glocalisation tends to refer to a process in which a local or national company takes the initiative to seek out a global partner to acquire things, such as capital, technology, production expertise, etc. The term derives from Japanese industry practice where industries (and government, too) would explicitly borrow and adapt international technologies and techniques (Robertson, 1995). The story of the interaction of The Globo Organization's glocalisation and Time-Life's localisation in the creation of TV Globo, between 1962 and 1971, is a good example, told in detail in Chapter Three. Briefly, Time-Life's Joe Wallach came to Brazil hoping to localise what Time-Life thought it knew how to do: use modern technology to create and run efficient national networks, and programme a successful schedule using imported US programmes. Roberto Marinho of TV Globo had in mind something more like the Japanese sense of glocalisation, selectively borrowing what he needed from an international partner. Wallach essentially moved from initially being the agent of localisation for Time-Life to rather quickly becoming an inside manager for TV Globo, figuring out how to selectively glocalise what TV Globo needed from Time-Life and other sources.

IF NATIONAL TELEVISION IS HYBRID, SO IS NATIONAL IDENTITY

Scholars in Brazil (Porto, 2008), Argentina (Mazziotti, 1993) and Colombia (Martín-Barbero, 1993) see television, and particularly the *telenovela*, as the mid- to late-twentieth century equivalent of earlier nationalising forms of content on radio and film. In Brazil, for example, the *telenovela* was initially seen as a transnationalised genre, based on imported scripts, international plots, or foreign-born scriptwriters, such as the Cuban writer Gloria Magadán. Plot ideas and scripts often came from international stories in the 1950s. Those were gradually regionalised and increasingly the most successful plots tended to tie into Latin American culture. For example, two plots tied broadly to Latin American culture were produced in a number of countries in the early growth of the *telenovela*. One of the classic plot devices is a search to find out what one's ancestry is, even who one's parents were. *El derecho de nacer* (*The Right to be Born*) was produced in a number of countries in the 1950s and 1960s. It was a huge hit in Brazil on TV Tupi, for example, introducing one of the first black television actresses, who played the nanny or nursemaid of a young man trying to figure out who his parents were (Araujo, 2000).

El derecho de nacer (*The Right to be Born*): originally a Cuban *radionovela* and then a Mexican film, has since been made as a *telenovela* in various countries

The plot device became a staple, particularly in Mexican *telenovelas,* where poor young women who marry a rich young man, in what seem like Cinderella stories, frequently discover late in the plot that they are really from a rich family, too. Another classic, foundational *telenovela,* particularly for those who began to examine the social impacts of *telenovela* content was *Simplemente Maria* (*Simply Maria*). That plot is concerned with another staple theme of the genre, social mobility. A young woman moves from the country to the city as a maid, then saves to buy a sewing machine and becomes a successful seamstress. That plot was one of several that began to get development planners trying to get pro-development themes into *telenovelas* and analogous melodramas elsewhere around the world (Singhal, Obregon *et al.*, 1994). Another example is the plain looking woman, who falls for a handsome man, and eventually discovers that she too is beautiful (Fernandes, 1987). The latest version of that theme is *Ugly Betty*, originally produced in Colombia as *Betty la fea*, sold in its original Colombia version to over 80 countries and since remade in over fifteen countries, including the US and Germany (Rivero, 2003).

By the late 1960s, however, *telenovelas* in some Latin American countries began to address more specifically national characters and issues, such as the typical Rio *malandro* (player) in *Beto Rockefeller* (1968) in Brazil. One study of the *telenovela* genre in Brazil asserted that while much of the audience there had enjoyed the more international *telenovelas* common to the 1950s and 1960s, the audiences grew much larger and more involved when the content became more nationally specific (Porto e Silva, 1979), which made them much more compelling to audiences. Brazil and Colombia, in particular, became known for very topical and socially-oriented *telenovelas*. For example, the first Brazilian *telenovela* exported to Portugal, *Gabriela,* was based on one of Brazil's better known novels, *Gabriela, cravo e canela* (*Gabriela, Clove and Cinnamon*) by the popular writer Jorge Amado, which concerns a beautiful mixed-race country girl who

Publicity for *Beto Rockefeller*, whose lead character, a charming, streetwise conman, was a familiar archetype from Brazilian popular culture

comes to a small town in Bahia and becomes involved with an Arab-Brazilian who runs a bar there. Like many of Amado's stories it involves elements of race, social mobility, city vs. country, regional folklore, and social change with economic development – elements that have adapted very well to *telenovela* form, and which help ground Brazilian *telenovelas* in the national culture, in part by making reference to the regional cultures of Brazil that help comprise the national culture. Several commentators on Brazilian television have noted that it had 'a nationalising vocation', that it has worked to draw the disparate parts of Brazil together (Straubhaar, 2001). Building on Anderson (1983), some authors (Ortiz, Simoes Borelli *et al.*, 1988) argue that narrative television fiction, particularly *telenovelas,* are as key as novels in their role in 'narrating the nation' (Bhabha, 1990), particularly in carrying that narration to the mass audience.

Although *telenovelas* developed national specificity, many retained regional appeal. The growth after decades of interaction with television among Latin Americans, from the early *telenovela* scripts that flowed outward from Cuba to a variety of other contacts, led to a certain form of regional cultural capital, in the sense of a familiarity with variations on common Latin American genres. For example, while most Brazilian audiences are quite loyal to the specific Brazilian form of *telenovela* developed by TV Tupi and Excelsior in the 1960s, and TV Globo since then, some Brazilian audiences (typically more rural, youth and older viewers) prefer the simpler, more romantic *telenovelas* typical of Mexico (La Pastina, 1999). SBT in Brazil found that it obtained a certain level of audience success with dubbed Mexican *telenovelas* and an even greater level of success when it began to adapt those Mexican scripts with their own productions.

OTHER REGIONALISED AND NATIONALISED TELEVISION GENRES

While *telenovelas* are the best known and most widely watched prime time genre in Latin America and widely cited as an example of hybridity, they are not the only popular television genre in the region, nor the only one to display extensive hybridity between global, regional and national forms. A number of television genres have developed as virtually universal across Latin American broadcast television. Many of them are in some form hybrid combinations of national traditions, global genres, and regional adaptations of those genres. Some are expensive enough, like the fiction genres of drama, *telenovela*, series and miniseries, that they are primarily produced by the first and second tier producers noted above. However, many of the genres common to Latin America are sufficiently low cost that they have been produced nationally in almost all countries, including the smallest and poorest. Those include live talk, live music, debate and discussion, local/national news, sports, live variety, live comedy, game shows, talent competition, and, increasingly, reality shows.

Waisbord notes that although *telenovelas* have received most of the attention, sports and news on television also have a great deal to do with 'the construction and renovation of national identities' (1998, p. 393). Sports can be 'nation-making' media events. One of the most hard-line military presidents of Brazil, Medici, was known for having effectively used a Brazilian victory in the World Cup, to draw attention away from controversies over military rule by creating an upsurge of patriotism and national pride. Waisbord notes, '[sports] suspend, at least momentarily, internal dissent and forcefully peg personal and collective histories to particular instances and places where the national is lived and played out' (1998, p. 393).

Waisbord also argues that 'Plenty of anecdotal evidence suggests that broadcast news also construct and renovate sentiments of national belonging by highlighting moments, issues and values that identify and separate political communities' (1998, p. 393). One extensive national ethnographic study of the impact of television in Brazil in the 1980s noted that national news helped to standardise a certain set of references to national holidays, national sports, main national events. The ethnographers found, for example, that with exposure over time to national news, local saints' days and other local holidays began to take a back seat to national holidays that were covered on television (Kottak, 1990, 1994).

The main national evening news programmes on networks like Televisa or TV Globo became quasi-official platforms for communicating the goals of national governments to national audiences, especially in the years of their hegemony and their close relations with governments in the 1960s–90s (Lima, 1988; Lima, 1993; Fernández & Paxman, 2001). These news programmes were popular and perceived as powerful (Lima, 1993), but increased competition, starting in the 1990s, began to challenge them. Mayer documents from interviews in Rio that populist, tabloid reality programmes like *Aqui Agora* (*Here, Now*), began to seriously challenge the news hegemony and popularity of networks like TV Globo (Mayer, 2006).

Game shows and talent competitions were often copied directly from US or other international models. Straubhaar found in interviews in São Paulo in 1989 that at least one lower ranked network hired people in the US to send tapes of game shows to provide models to 'borrow' and adapt. However, in several genres, notably music, talk, news, comedy, debate and discussion, and variety, interesting Latin American variations developed that created programming differentiated from US and other global models. Perhaps the most important of these genres, based on their placement in prime time, as an indicator of programmers' perception of audience interest in the genre (Straubhaar, 2007), were the variety show, news, music and comedy.

Variety shows are perhaps the most prevalent national or regional genre, aside from *telenovelas*. Variety shows from the 1970s–90s occupied most of Sunday afternoon and evening on many networks, as well as often prominent prime time spots. In the 1970s, even in major countries like Brazil, the live variety show (*show de auditório*) competed favourably with *telenovelas* in prime time (Straubhaar, 1983). Some prominent variety shows, like *Siempre en Domingo* (*Always on Sunday*), from Mexico, were widely exported throughout the region and their hosts became regional celebrities (Paxman, 2003). Live variety shows frequently had the highest budgets and best production values in a number of the smaller markets like the Dominican Republic. Live variety was curtailed in the 1970s by the military in Brazil for being too unpredictable, but returned in the 1980s as the main genre on the number two network, SBT, whose owner, Silvio Santos, had long hosted the most popular live variety show in Brazil. Critics, like Sodré, noted that variety shows drew from deep popular cultural sources, like traveling circuses, and that they tended toward a kind of cultural populism (*o popularesco*), based in rural, slum and working class cultures (Sodré, 1972). One widely cited example was an SBT programme hosted by '*Ratinho*' (*Little Rat*), whose show had everything from music to comedy to political commentary. In 1998, it was one of the first shows to threaten the long ratings domination of TV Globo (Bentes, 2003; Goulart, 2011).

Live music and comedy were often key elements in variety shows, but were increasingly spun off into their own genres as well. Live music shows were a focus of political protest and counter-culture in the 1960s in countries like Brazil and Chile (Dunn, 2001). Live music festivals were very effective counter-programming, giving a new station, like TV Globo in the 1960s, a way to break into greater popularity (Wallach, 2011), or for an existing station like TV Rio to draw audiences away from competitors' *telenovelas* (Straubhaar, 1981). Live comedy tended to be similar in its roots and functions, a low-cost, very effective way to counter imported US programmes, or, to much more limited degree, *telenovelas*. They also tended to be a good way for lower income networks in smaller countries, like the Dominican Republic to substitute for imported US programmes, since the costs were low and the programmes frequently more popular (Straubhaar, interviews in Dominican Republic, 1986–8). Like variety, music and comedy tended to draw from earlier popular culture roots.

Another distinct Latin American form of a basic global television genre has been the talk show. Political talk on television has been popular in many countries, depending on the openness of the political climate (Alisky, 1981). Some populist politicians, like the late Hugo Chávez, essentially create their own political talk shows, sometimes enforced on all channels, to bolster their own popularity. One of the crucial elements of Fidel Castro's rise to power in Cuba in 1959–61 was his effective use of the existing television talk shows to promote himself and his party. Even today, shows like *Mesa redonda* (*Round Table*) are still very important in party communication with the Cuban public (Rivero, 2010). Another populist use of television talk has been at a much lower level of politics, the city. Shows in Bolivia, Brazil and elsewhere have featured hosts who decried the poor state of city services, letting people call in to complain about roads, uncollected garbage, etc. SBT and TV Record in Brazil both used similar shows at a national level to gain increased popularity at the national level, finding them one effective counter to TV Globo's popular *telenovelas*, as noted above.

Since the earliest days of television, low cost genres in Latin America have been performed live in front of a simple studio set up. For example, Straubhaar visited several studio sets at two networks in the Dominican Republic in 1986–8. Most of the studios had two or three old studio cameras, minimum lighting, minimal microphones, all leading into modest switchers and mixers, costing perhaps US$ 60–80,000 at the time. (Needless to say a comparable set-up would be much cheaper now, which has enabled the multiplication of Latin American channels and producers since then.) All three of the major Dominican networks were, in the mid-late 1980s, producing 6–10 hours of low-cost live programming a day, filling a surprisingly large amount of the broadcast day with their own production, despite the low budgets available in a small, low-income nation (Straubhaar, 1990). The Dominican channels emphasised live music, talk and comedy during the day, live comedy and variety in prime time, supplementing imported *telenovelas* and comedy series from elsewhere in Latin America. A few imported US series and films would be visible in prime time, but the tendency was to fill prime time with national and geocultural regional programming (Straubhaar, 1991), reflecting the overall regional push toward programming on the basis of cultural proximity, even in the smallest, poorest nations. In richer nations, like Brazil, variety, talk and proto-reality shows like *Aqui Agora* (see above), were increasingly better produced, incorporating location shooting, more complex sets and editing, etc.

By the 1970s–80s, many of these genres were extensively produced and adapted to the interests of national audiences across Latin America. The regional genres had a strong element of shared cultural proximity. Many of them had developed into national versions that had even stronger, specific cultural proximity for national audiences. That created a challenging situation in many ways for global satellite and cable operations that showed up in the 1980s–90s to try to break into Latin America. Their initial offering of imported programme channels was not always appealing outside globalised elites, forcing them into more extensive localisation than they had initially planned (Duarte & Straubhaar, 2004).

THE CHALLENGE TO NATIONAL NETWORKS FROM CABLE AND SATELLITE TELEVISION

For many national television systems around the world, the advent of satellite and cable television in the 1980s–90s disrupted the monopoly of public or state television, as in India, South Korea, Taiwan and much of first Western and then Eastern Europe. In those countries, cable and satellite technology coincided with a new global regulatory regime of neoliberalism that promoted increased competition, privatisation of state media, and deregulation (Harvey, 2005). Cable and satellite television had dramatic impact in a few parts of Latin America in the 1980s and 1990s. Some Caribbean nations, like the Dominican Republic (Straubhaar, 1991) and some Central American nations, like Belize (Oliveira, 1986), were directly under the footprint of the satellites that served the US and Mexico, so they received their satellite television channels early on in the 1980s as spillover. Cable television did flourish in Argentina, as noted in Chapter Four. However, that was largely because broadcast television had been weakened. The main stations had been seized and badly run by the military.

However, in most parts of Latin America, several cycles of alternative television technologies, including the videocassette recorder (VCR) in the early-mid 1980s (Boyd, Straubhaar *et al.*, 1989), cable television (Reis, 1999), and satellite television (Duarte, 2001; Straubhaar & Duarte, 2005), had achieved relatively little penetration, especially when compared to affluent countries in other parts of the world (Straubhaar, 1988; Boyd, Straubhaar *et al.*, 1989). The authors noted above tended to conclude that this was because potential audiences for such new television media in Latin America were sufficiently satisfied with the entertainment and information available on to them on national broadcast television that it was not worth it to them to invest much of their often low incomes in them.

Satellite dishes did gradually spread in much of the region but, more often than not, their initial use, particularly in poorer rural and urban areas was to pull down national television channels off satellites when local broadcast service at a reasonable quality did not reach households in those areas (Straubhaar, 2007). International channels required subscription to a pay television package and pay television spread very slowly. Boyd and Straubhaar (1985) observed that VCRs spread more slowly in most of Latin America than in the Middle East and other regions because Latin American consumers seemed to be reasonably content with what was already on broadcast television, which unlike many other regions, already had a great deal of well-produced national or regional entertainment content. Audiences often did not see the value in spending money on less culturally proximate programming from outside. A survey conducted by Straubhaar in Venezuela in 1984 as part of that research noted that social class and VCR ownership were highly correlated, and that those for whom VCR purchase would have required much financial sacrifice were not buying them, since the marginal value of the extra programming choices made available to them was not worth the cost. Reis made similar observations about the reasons for the slow growth of pay television in Brazil, for example, noting that the extra cost was not worth it to consumers who were relatively satisfied with broadcast television entertainment (Reis, 1999).

Originally, most pay channels were limited to small elite groups who had a specific interest in a particular kind of imported content. One of the first pay systems in Brazil, owned by Editora Abril, had foreign language channels aimed at Italian, German, Japanese and a few other specific diasporic immigrant groups, who retained language ability and an interest in their home countries. They also carried MTV Brasil, which was aimed at the relatively small group of Brazilian youth interested in heavy metal music (one of the original emphases of MTV in the USA), who were generally affluent enough to be interesting to a specific group of advertisers and who might lobby parents to subscribe to a system which got them access to MTV (Straubhaar interviews with MTV media research staff, 1987–94).

As the overall market for US satellite and cable pay TV packages improved slowly in Latin America, global programmers began to package together certain channels, based on popular US programming not widely available on the largely nationalised and regionalised television systems of Latin America (Duarte, 2001). The packages carried many channels and networks familiar to US or European viewers. The two main systems, Sky Latin America and Galaxy, initially did as little adaptation as possible, carrying existing channels like HBO, MTV, CNN, Discovery, Cartoon Channel and Nickelodeon. Some channels were created to carry the best of a certain genre, like the Sony Channel, which packaged US sitcoms for Latin America or AXN for US action shows. After a while, the pay-TV programmers for Latin America began to discover that more localisation of things like sports and music might be required (Duarte & Straubhaar, 2004). Some channels like Discovery began to go further by adding local segments and regionally produced shows. Some more extensively localised channels were adaptions of US channel formats, like Fox Sports for Latin America, which emphasised regionally popular sports, like soccer. Different MTV operations began to spring up, which featured varying degrees of localisation depending on how elite or mass an audience they were pursuing.

The audiences for pay-TV, which emphasised imported programmes with little adaptation, also had somewhat limited appeal to Latin American mass audiences. One explanation is the role of audience economic class or cultural capital. The Sony channel, which broadcast *Friends* to Latin America, found that it had an audience of perhaps 500,000 across the 190 million people of Brazil (Duarte, personal communication, 1998). Some of those were so enthusiastic that they called themselves the 'Sony-maniacs'. They were able to enjoy *Friends* because they had the education, travel, and knowledge of US popular culture to understand it. They were a group large enough and wealthy enough when cobbled together from countries across Latin America, but not large enough for broadcast television in any single country.

Straubhaar's interviewing in the Dominican Republic 1986–8 found that non-elite audiences were most likely to tune into US film, documentary, and music channels, which required less language ability and cultural capital to enjoy. A survey of slum dwellers who had access to cable TV and pay TV channels in the late 1990s in Rocinha, in Rio, tended to prefer cartoons and documentaries, especially for their children. They particularly like channels like Discovery because they were both educational and entertaining (Letalien, 2009). However, pay-TV penetration in Brazil, overall, remained under 10 per cent of households until 2001 (Multichannel News 10 August 2001).

Foreign cable and satellite pay-TV channels have begun to make greater inroads into Latin America in the 2000s. At the end of the 2000s, pay-TV was in a third of TV homes in Mexico ('Web reach rises in Latin America', 2010). Audiences for pay-TV grew in Brazil past the 20 per cent mark (Redação, 2012). As noted in Chapter Three on Brazil, that had to do in some large degree with the increasing affluence of the Brazilian popular classes, particularly the lower middle class, who began to see pay-TV as affordable and desirable. It may also have had to do with a background process of cultural globalisation that slowly made national audiences more familiar with the globalised cultural capital required to enjoy the international channels. However, that growth in audience for pay-TV was also correlated with a growth in nationally produced pay-TV channels, as noted in Chapters Two and Three. TV Globo, for example, was reluctant to invest in pay-TV channels, and risk cannibalising its large broadcast audience, until audience growth made pay-TV a more attractive proposition. However, it has recently created a number of channels in national film, news, *telenovelas*, documentaries, etc. that make the service attractive to non-globalised national audiences as well.

So there seems to be a dual process of influence at work. As audiences become more affluent, better educated, and more widely travelled with economic growth, there tends to be an increase in interest in pay-TV channels, including foreign ones. However, part of the appeal of cable, satellite and pay-TV also appears to be an increase in national viewing options, which major networks like Globo are moving increasingly quickly to supply. So global influence probably increases, but is somewhat tempered by habits, tastes and senses of proximity shaped by decades of exposure to national and regional entertainment on television. Now we will look at a different, perhaps substantially deeper form of global influence, that of regulatory and institutional models and ideologies, that work more at the level of structure than culture, although the two clearly interact.

CHALLENGES FROM THE NEW ECONOMIC AND REGULATORY MODELS OF GLOBALISATION

Although privatisation of television ownership and operation largely happened well before the 1990s in Latin America, the neoliberal push by the US government, World Bank and others, starting in the 1980s for greater privatisation, deregulation, and liberalisation of competition across the economy, including media, manufacturing and telecommunications (Harvey, 2005), still had considerable impact on television. Perhaps most significantly, the privatisation and deregulation of telecommunications companies created new private entities that began to enter cable television and eventually compete with television networks in cable per se and in triple-play packages of television/pay television, internet access and telephone connection, as described in the chapter on Mexico. In some cases, the push towards increased liberalisation of competition in the 1980s–2000s also pushed several states to offer new television licences to increase the number of competing networks, sometimes beginning to break down the cosy relations that had existed between governments and dominant private networks like Televisa, TV Globo and Venevisión.

State control over infrastructure was crucial in the build-up of national television in most Latin American countries, particularly before the 1990s, when the state still owned the microwave towers and satellite systems that television networks depended on to reach their affiliated stations. Such power over infrastructure may be diminishing substantially since the 1990s, an era of privatisation of telecommunications. Most Latin American countries have now privatised all telecommunications companies or at least liberalised their rules to allow in private competitors, who could now provide the interconnections that television networks need.

Those private telecom competitors also now compete directly with established television companies to offer cable television services and related services in internet access. Televisa now faces direct competition in cable television, internet and triple-play services from Telmex, which emerged from the privatisation process as a very rich private monopoly, which makes it a formidable competitor. Telmex has also gone on to become a powerful transnational force in the Latin American region. It bought former state companies in Central America and former AT&T companies in Argentina, Brazil, Chile, Colombia, Peru, Uruguay and the USA. Its cellular company, América Móvil, now owns companies in most of the same countries. It is investing in cable television systems, starting in Colombia and aiming at others.

Telefónica of Spain entered a number of Latin American countries by buying Bell South's Latin American investments in Venezuela, Colombia, Ecuador and Uruguay (Wharton, 6 October 2004). It has moved to compete across the board with Telmex, tending to have somewhat greater penetration of more markets. It bought most of TV Globo's cable assets in NET, after the Globo Organization had become over-extended in its hardware investment (See Chapter Three) and now offers triple-play options to consumers in Brazil.

NEOLIBERALISM, THE STATE AND LATIN AMERICAN TELEVISION
States tended to withdraw from the economy in most but not all of Latin America during the neoliberal movement of the 1990s. When commercial television first boomed in the 1960s and 1970s, many Latin American states controlled huge sectors of the economy, in what were usually considered to be

capitalist economies. For many of the years of key growth for TV Globo or Televisa, for example, their partnership with the governments of the day, well up through the late 1980s, could be guided and rewarded with advertising from state-owned enterprises, banks, holding companies, etc. (Mattos, 1984). Most countries, notably including Brazil and Mexico, have gone through major waves of privatisation since the 1990s that have reduced this economic power that the state used to have. Not all powerful national firms were privatised, however. Brazil's giant oil company Petrobras is only partially privatised and still serves the role as a crucial advertiser and investor in all kinds of cultural production, from theatre to film to television (Castro, Marques de Melo *et al.*, 2010). A quick look at the opening credits of almost any Brazilian film will show the logo of Petrobras as an investor. Furthermore, new waves of economic populism have brought regimes back into power in Argentina, Bolivia, Ecuador, and Venezuela, where national economic power is being reasserted and some firms that had been previously privatised, such as the massive oil companies of Argentina and Venezuela, are being renationalised, as recently as 2012 in the case of Argentina.

One place where states' and national television networks' interest continued to combine was in increasing the amount of national production on television. Unlike countries in East Asia and Europe, the national governments of most Latin American countries did not create explicit quotas for national production. They were more likely to simply suggest to national broadcasters that they would like to see fewer imported programmes and more national programming. For example, in 1971 the Communications Minister of Brazil suggested in a couple of speeches that the government was concerned about violence and other foreign values in imported US programming, and would like to see more programming that reflected national values and ideas (Straubhaar, 1981). As mentioned in Chapter Two, President Echeverría of Mexico took a similar but more confrontational stance later in that decade.

For governments, the logic of import substitution applied as much to television as to steel or automobiles, in economic terms. National programme production and equipment manufacturing created jobs and economic activity. In order to make sure that television sets were manufactured in Brazil, for example, the government has consistently manipulated television standards to create unique standards for Brazil that had to be made in Brazil. While Brazil initially accepted the US NTSC black and white television standard, leading to set imports, the government created its own colour television standard by keeping the line system of NTSC but adding the European PAL colour system, resulting in the unique system PAL-M, which was manufactured in Brazil by both Brazilian and global companies. The Brazilian government recently made a very similar policy move by adapting the Japanese, rather than US or European, standard for broadcast digital television, but modifying it with local standards designed to enhance interactivity, and minimise the ease with which hardware, programmes or software could simply be imported from elsewhere (Soares & de Souza Filho, 2007). After aggressive diplomacy by Brazil, its standard has now been adopted by most Latin American countries. That creates the possibility of greater interchange among Latin American television stations, especially public or government channels, which have been the first to take up the interactive parts of the new standard.

TELEVISION IN LATIN AMERICA AND ITS REGIONAL AND NATIONAL CHALLENGES

In this chapter, we have argued that despite transnational regional transformation and global challenges, the television medium in Latin America remains fundamentally national. The question is complex, however, since national television institutions and genres are built on a regionalised base of influences. National institutions were influenced by post-colonial, regional patterns of family control (as noted in Chapter One), corporatist and clientalist relations between media and the national state, and regional patterns of hybridity in both organisational structure and cultural influences. Those institutions have created a series of culturally hybrid genres with both regional and national characteristics. For example, the cultural DNA of the *telenovela* is first European, then US, then Cuban, then differentiated in national versions and variations, then re-regionalised by players such as the Colombian networks, Telemundo, and others in the media capital of Miami (Sinclair, 2003; Piñon, 2011).

These regional roots and influences have been glocalised by increasingly strong national television institutions in most Latin American countries. After 60 or more years of commercial broadcasting in much of Latin America, television has become thoroughly imbricated in the development of national markets and national consumer cultures, although regional and global television is now beginning to rise in popularity and importance.

Both early and current forms of globalisation have profoundly changed the political economy of Latin American media by using commercial television as a means for incorporation of Latin American populations in consumer economies at both national and global levels. One early sign was the desire for television itself. Television sets were the most avidly desired consumer durable for decades and still are, in the few places such as remote parts of the Amazon where television signals and sets are not easily available. Television to some degree became synonymous with consumer culture and the promotion of both ideas and goods.

In this degree, early critics of commercial television development (Schiller, 1969; Beltran & Fox de Cardona, 1979) were probably correct in some of their anticipations of the impact of commercial television. It probably did help consolidate capitalism, advertising-based media and consumer culture as dominant paradigms in Latin America (Oliveira, 1993; Bolaño, 1999; Mastrini, 2009; Sinclair, 2012b). This impact on the underlying political economy of the region is the most pervasive and profound, as noted in Chapter One. Moreover, it has increased recently, as formerly nationally-owned telecoms have been privatised since the 1990s and are now becoming multichannel and broadband competitors to national broadcast television.

However, the economics of national broadcast television continue to give it a strong competitive base. Broadcast television is still the advertising medium of choice, even when audiences decline relative to other new media that chip away at the audience's time and attention. In the latter 2000s, free-to-air television was still attracting around 60 per cent of advertising expenditure in Brazil and Mexico, ranging down to 32 per cent in Argentina, with the average for the region being 52.7 per cent (ACHAP, 2007). This is because free-to-air television continues to be a true mass medium, while pay-TV is an elite, or upper middle class one: that is, access to television in Latin America corresponds to the sharp social stratification which still typifies the region. Moreover, key genres on broadcast television, such as the prime-time *telenovela*, music and late prime time mini-series, still engage truly massive audiences, including middle classes and elites, more than in many other countries, such as the US. So one complexity of globalisation in Latin America is that the growth of consumer capitalism also enables national cultural industries to produce key genres that have largely maintained their strength over against regional and global competitors. However, it is also true that the rapidly growing lower middle classes of Latin America, particularly in Brazil, are also expressing their interest in key media, such as pay-TV and broadband internet, that will gradually expose them to many other choices, so the relative primacy of national television in places like Brazil may yet decline against global and regional competition.

Decades of exposure to and cultivation by the national television genres described above have created audiences that tend to be quite loyal to national broadcast television. Even globalised members of the Brazilian elite, interviewed by Straubhaar over the years since 1979, have nearly always been quite attentive to a few key national television genres: the main 8 pm evening *telenovela* (since they know everyone will be talking about it), one or another national news programme, late night talk, late evening miniseries, major musical events, etc. Lower middle class audiences are slowly becoming more interested in global programming via pay-TV, but at least in interviews by Straubhaar since 1979 remain very attentive to the main prime time national programmes. However, global technological infrastructure, global and regional channels, are steadily expanding the range of television viewing options. So it will be interesting to see if audience loyalty to national genres holds up as choices increase.

Conclusion: Latin American Television – Summary and Prospect

This book has traced the development of the television industry in Latin America from its roots in the days of radio, through its entrepreneurial beginnings, into a long settled period of consolidation, characterised by the oligopoly of a few large family-owned private networks. This was eventually challenged by privatisation and deregulation, which allowed in new technologies, notably cable, satellite and internet-based television, as well as a liberalisation of competition, which allowed in new broadcast television competitors, from government or private industry, ultimately arriving at a complex and uncertain new era.

Latin American television enjoyed a golden age in the 1970s and 1980s, dominated by a generation of media entrepreneurs in the major countries of the region who were able to tap foreign investment, particularly from the United States; successfully manage their relationships with successive governments; create popular programming genres; attract both international and national advertisers; and keep their competition at bay. The organisations which they built have exhibited some common 'Latin' characteristics, above all a patriarchal and autocratic mode of leadership, passed on from one generation to the next, lending a dynastic character to the industry. Furthermore, in different national settings and at various historical stages, they readily adapted to traditional political cultures of corporatism, patronage, and populism. Yet above all, the undoubted commercial acumen of the networks' entrepreneurial leaders and the sense of audiences' tastes institutionalised by these leading producers/distributors enabled each of them to come to dominate their respective national markets. They developed distinct national versions of variety shows, comedies, and music programmes that captivated loyal national audiences, as well as the key television genre of the *telenovela*. This national market dominance and genre development in turn opened up possibilities for the export of their programming. Initially, this was to neighbouring countries which had remarkable similarities in their historical formation, and more importantly, in culture and language. The same comparative advantage of cultural-linguistic commonalities was later employed in entering the television markets of the former colonial powers in Iberian Europe and the Spanish-speaking networks in the US, as well as the Lusophone countries of Africa in the case of Portuguese-speaking Brazil. On the other hand, the cultural-linguistic similarities of the region were no barrier to exporting programming into totally alien markets in Eastern Europe and Asia, where audiences proved most receptive to the characteristically Latin genre of the *telenovela*. As we have explained in this book, while the initial export markets were established on the basis of cultural proximity, the latter-day foreign markets have been a matter of genre proximity, demonstrating the broad appeal of Latin American-style melodrama, which includes a dash of social issues along with its family drama and romance.

The rise of the *telenovela* to regional dominance as a genre of both national production and intra-regional export is another crucial piece of the story of Latin American television. It shows how strong cultural influence from outside powers like the US can be adapted and hybridised to the point of substantial transformation (Straubhaar, 1981). As we have pointed out in this book, the *telenovela* was adapted from the US soap opera in Cuba by Colgate-Palmolive to more effectively sell soap to Latin Americans, effectively drawing them further into a consumer role in the global economy. However, in cultural terms the *telenovela*, as adapted first by professionals versed in a cultural imagination and modes of narrative common to Latin Americans (Martín-Barbero, 1987), and subsequently given a more specific national shape in Argentina, Brazil, Colombia, Mexico, Peru and Venezuela, demonstrates something quite different: that the economic forms of global capitalism can support cultural production that has a very strong connection to both national and regional culture, and that adaptiveness became almost synonymous with the distinctiveness of those cultures.

In the golden age of the 1970s and 1980s, producers in Mexico (Televisa) and Brazil (TV Globo) were consistently large exporters, the first tier of Latin American production and export (Roncagliolo, 1995), while the next tier, from Argentina (Artear, Telefé) and Venezuela (RCTV, Venevisión), were also active exporters. The third tier were from Colombia, Chile, and Peru, beyond which other Latin American countries were classified as being 'net importers', although it is worth noting that even the poorest of them, such as the Dominican Republic, were producing much of their own programming by the 1990s (Straubhaar, 1991, 2007). However, increasingly in the 1990s and 2000s, a number of countries and transnational markets, including the special case of the Hispanic market in the US, were getting more involved in television format trade and transnational co-productions, beyond the classic pattern of national production and export. We have noted in particular how Colombia has risen into the second tier of producers, with shows widely exported both as programmes and formats.

As in the other major producing nations of Europe and the US, Latin American producers have increasingly been using imported formats to produce national television programmes. A recent almanac of reality shows from 2000 to 2010 in Brazil, for example, listed the following kinds of reality formats that have been imported: survival, talent shows, disputes, confinement (like *Big Brother*), professional help, and real life/'life as it is' shows (Trevisan, 2011). Importation or copying of formats is one strategy for facilitating local-looking production without having to go to the cost of creating an entirely new reality format or scripted programme (Moran, 1998). Most of the imported formats, like *Big Brother,* come from major global format exporters like Endemol, but the national networks are adept at tweaking them to have a culturally proximate look and feel. The truly global character of such arrangements in the future may be well exemplified by a 2012 deal between Sony Pictures Television (SPT) and Televisa, under which Sony has a first option on all Televisa's formats for prospective worldwide co-production, outside of Televisa's home territories of Latin America and the US. Conversely, Televisa has first-look rights at Sony's formats for possible production in Spain. Another example again of such format globalisation is the series, *Los Simuladores* (*The Pretenders*). Originally from Telefé in Argentina in 2002, it was produced by Sony for Televisa in 2008 (Hecht, 2012).

Within the region, trading in scripts and ideas goes back to the days of radio and television's earliest years. The *telenovela* itself started with the export of scripts and production expertise from Cuba in the 1950s to the rest of Latin America. Now Latin American countries are selling scripts to each other again, and on an increasing scale. The Brazilian SBT network had a substantial hit with *Carrossel* (*Carousel*) a dubbed version of *Carrusel*, a Mexican children's *telenovela*, in 1991. SBT subsequently made another success out of their own adaptation of the original script in 2012 (Roxo, 2012). In 1997, SBT had had another hit with an adaptation of the Argentine children's musical *telenovela, Chiquititas* (*Little Girls*), which had first run on Telefé in 1995, and continued until 2001. Mexican network TV Azteca also remade the show. Both adaptations were done in Argentina, so as to use the sets, etc. from the original, but with new casts representing Brazil and Mexico.

These examples are emblematic of what we may think of as the transnationalisation of television production and distribution, as a distinct dimension of the overall pattern of global expansion. Jean Chalaby identifies three paradigms in the development of global communication (2005). The first is internationalisation, or nation-to-nation communication, as with the international telegraph or, as we have outlined in this book, the influence of the US on the development of broadcasting in Latin America. The second paradigm is globalisation, which arises with the advent of communication satellites and other technologies able to distribute the same content to many nations, and more or less at the same time. In practice, however, such global content is usually received in forms modified to suit the conditions of each particular nation. This is where a greater or lesser degree of glocalisation occurs: the selective local borrowing and adaptation of global ideas and forms. This includes the commercial exchange of scripts and the rights to produce certain formats. It is as if, from the consumption side, viewers see programming which is familiar and seemingly expressive of their national culture, but the reality behind the screen is that there is a thriving trade, not only in finished programmes, as in the past, but in formats and scripts as the more abstract components from which culturally proximate programmes can be made for different national markets. In line with Chalaby's third paradigm, transnationalisation, we believe there is a distinction to be drawn between the kinds of local adaptations of globally-available cultural forms such as Endemol's *Big Brother* on the one hand, and the kind of Mexican-Brazilian-Argentine adaptations mentioned, which take place on a more lateral, regional axis. This is a new stage in which greater interpenetration of markets within the geocultural region is facilitating ever more refined and specific tailoring of programmes to national audiences, building on the logic of geographic, cultural and linguistic proximity. In the Latin American case, this is particularly significant for national audiences in those countries that traditionally have had little productive capacity of their own, the 'net importers', yet it also implies that the differences between national cultures in the region have hitherto been downplayed in the interests of exploiting linguistic similarities. A classic example which we have referred to more than once in this book is *Yo soy Betty la fea* (*Ugly Betty*), which, although originally made in Spanish by RCN in Colombia, was remade for Mexico and Spain, suggesting that a common language was not enough to cross the national cultural barriers (Mikos & Perrotta, 2012).

The US Hispanic market is of particular interest in this regard. In spite of its size and wealth, Spanish-language television has not until recently produced much of its own material, at least of exportable fiction genres. Instead, as was shown in Chapter Five, the main US Hispanic networks have traditionally imported programming from the major producing countries in Latin America, driven by an economics of supply rather than demand. Just like audiences in the Latin American nations, US Latinos like to see television programming which expresses their culture and language, and to see people like themselves on TV. However, Univisión and its predecessor, SIN, principally imported from Televisa for decades, locked in to the power of its ownership. In later years, programming has been dominated by output deals with Televisa and also, to a lesser extent, Venevisión of Venezuela. Azteca America almost exclusively shows productions from its parent, TV Azteca in Mexico. However, Telemundo, having no such pipeline of low-cost, ready-made programming, has experimented with a variety of regional imports and co-production strategies, involving producers from Brazil, Colombia, Miami, and others.

As noted in Chapter Four, Telemundo is a part-owner of RTI in Colombia, and produces *telenovelas* in Bogota and Miami as well as Mexico City. The NBC-owned company has business ventures with other major regional programming providers such as Televisa, Globo, Caracol, RCN, and TVE of Spain. As Piñon and Rojas see it, 'Telemundo's production strategies are having a hemispheric impact through the multinational character of their casting and the exportation of its *telenovelas* to Latin America and worldwide.' (2011, p. 139) The pivotal role of Miami more generally as a 'media capital' in this regard for all of the Americas was discussed in Chapter Five. Deterritorialised production in Miami by companies based in Colombia or Venezuela puts it into a new category of its own as at least a second tier exporter for Latin America, despite its location in the US. So, if it is not too fine a distinction, we can say that the television programme trade in the region has become 'transnational', or even 'post-national', in the way that it now criss-crosses national borders, such as in how it reaches a dispersed minority audience as it does in the US, rather than 'international' in the old sense of an exchange between one nation and another. This capacity to cross borders has become even more enhanced with the digitisation of programming and its transmission.

Globally, the television industry is in a state of transition. Ever since the advent of international satellite delivery and the growth of pay-TV, television as a medium has been moving towards a 'post-broadcast' (Sinclair, 1999, p.162; Turner & Tay, 2009), or 'post-network' era (Lotz, 2009). We have noted how, in cable content and services, Televisa and Globo in particular reinforced their free-to-air, broadcast market dominance with strategic stakes in satellite and cable television in their respective markets. The natural monopolies in programming which they enjoyed behind the cultural protective barrier of language came to be challenged in the early 1990s with the advent of Spanish-language and, later, Portuguese-language satellite-to-cable channels from US companies such as HBO, CNN, CBS, and MTV. Their respective prime positions were recognised in the strategic alliances formed by the US-based companies that introduced DTH to the region in the mid-1990s, so that today, Liberty Media and News Corporation operate DTH services Sky Mexico in conjunction with Televisa, and Sky Brazil with Globo.

Television delivery options have proliferated well beyond these satellite-to-cable subscription services, given the convergence of broadcasting as we knew it not only with telecommunications but also the internet, so that television can now be watched, for example, on computers, mobile phones or via an Xbox console. Although pay-TV has begun to take off in Latin America, as was noted in the Introduction, for decades free-to-air broadcast television has been the major medium of information and entertainment for the mass of people in the region and, accordingly, the preferred medium for advertisers (Sinclair, 2012b). This corresponded to the sharp social stratification of most societies in Latin America, so that the elites integrated into the global system had both the cultural and economic capital to enjoy pay-TV (Straubhaar, 2007), while the bulk of the population, *la gente corriente*, contented themselves with national and regional popular programming on broadcast television, typically their beloved *telenovelas*. This was the relatively settled and stable mediascape in which Televisa in Mexico and TV Globo in Brazil rose to dominance. Now, as multichannel television seems to be rising in the region, Globo and Televisa are also beginning to produce more of their own channels for cable and satellite, and generally becoming more involved with the trend.

Looking towards the future of television in Latin America, new convergent forms of distribution are already making television more diverse and accessible to wider audiences, but not via broadcasting as we have known it. One of the commonplaces about globalisation is that it is driven in large part by technological change which disrupts existing powers, and that includes national television broadcasters. Yet in Latin America since the 1990s, this truism has come to apply even more to telecommunications as to broadcasting. Former government-owned telecom monopolies in almost all countries have been strongly pushed by both technological and economic or regulatory paradigm changes toward deregulation, privatisation, and/or liberalisation to allow competition with incumbents. While privatised telecommunication companies have in several cases been purchased, at least in part, by foreign interests, a pattern has developed in which those outside companies that have persisted in the market over time and that emerged dominant by the late 2000s tended to be from within the Iberoamerican world itself, including Telefónica of Spain and Telmex of Mexico. So global forces of change in telecoms have tended to create new power arrangements that fall within Iberoamerican institutions rather than global actors from without the region.

As discussed in Chapter Two, a privatised Telmex has been dominated by one investor, Carlos Slim, who became the world's richest man through his private monopoly on both wire line and cellular telecoms, as well as the internet services which have tended to build on them. However, the game-changer has been the advent of triple-play: the bundling of cable, telephone, and internet connection, giving access to pay-TV at more affordable prices. Televisa and Azteca have positioned themselves strongly in the new converged market, and enjoy regulatory protection against Telmex entering the television business, per se, as opposed to the cable television business.

It has been a different story in Brazil, where, as mentioned in Chapter Three, the Globo Group invested heavily and badly in cable TV infrastructure, incurring so much debt that the group as a whole almost went under. This came at much the same time as TV Globo was losing its dominance in the free-to-air arena, although it should be made clear that Globo's apparent decline is relative: it remains the major player in Brazil and its region, still outdrawing its nearest competitor by over two to one.

So, overall, while the advent of cable, satellite and telecom technology has allowed new television entrants from within the larger Iberoamerican cultural and media space, which has created new competition for the dominant powers of Latin American television, those powers have also adapted to the new technologies themselves. The new television in Latin America is thus not exactly 'post-network', but does create new spaces of competition against the traditional incumbents. There is somewhat more space for a truly global inflow of US, European and even Asian television, but the popular networks remain national and regional.

So, as in the rest of the world, the television industry in Latin America is in a state of flux, both technologically, as new modes of delivery come on to the market, and commercially, as broadcasters seek to reinvent themselves and devise new business models able to exploit those technologies financially. At the same time, in programming, there is ever greater exchange not only within the Iberoamerican cultural-linguistic space, but also with producers and distributors from outside the virtual geolinguistic and geocultural regions within which Televisa and TV Globo in particular built their export empires. Although Latin American markets have thus been opened up to the world, the process is one of heterogenisation rather than homogenisation, so that Latin American television remains a distinctive and resilient zone within the global mediascape.

Bibliography

¿Quién es el empresario Ángel González, *el fantasma*? (2007, January 17). *El Universal (Mexico)*. Retrieved from http://www.eluniversal.com.mx/notas/400749.html

Afonjá, I. A. O. (1999). Iansã is not Saint Barbara. In R. M. Levine & J.J. Crocitti (eds), *The Brazil Reader: History, Culture, Politics* (pp. 408–10). Durham: Duke University Press.

Akyuz, G. (1997, January). Heart of the community. *TV World*, pp. 49–52.

Albavisión. (2012). Retrieved 18 January 2012, from http://www.albavision.tv/

Alisky, M. (1981). *Latin American Media: Guidance and Censorship*. Ames, IA: Iowa State University Press.

Alsema, A. (2009). NBC's Telemundo buys 40% stake in Colombia TV producer RTI. *Colombia Report*s. Retrieved 18 January 2012, from http://colombiareports.com/ colombia-news/economy/6157-nbcs-telemundo-buys-40-stake-in-colombia-tv-producer-rti.html

Alvarado Miquilena, M., & Torrealba Mesa, L. E. (2011). Venezuela: New rules, old prohibitions. In G. Orozco Gómez & M.I. Vassallo de Lopes (eds), *Obitel Yearbook 2011: The quality of fiction and the audience's transmedia interactions*. Available from http://obitel.net

Amaral, R. & Guimaraes, C. (1994). Media monopoly in Brazil. *Journal of Communication*, 44(4), pp. 26–38.

Anderson, B. (1983). *Imagined Communities: Reflections on the Origin and Spread of Nationalism*. New York: Verso.

Andreeva, N. (2011, May 26). Final network rankings for 2010–11 season: English-language nets down, Univision up. *Deadline Hollywood*. Retrieved 21 December 2011, from http://www.deadline.com/2011/05/final-network-rankings-for-2010-11-season/

Anguloa, J., Calzadab, J. & Estruch, A. (2011). Selection of standards for digital television: The battle for Latin America. *Telecommunications Policy*, 35(8), pp. 773–87.

Antola, A. & Rogers, E. M. (1984). Television flows in Latin America. *Comm Res*, 11(2), pp. 183–202.

Appadurai, A. (1996). *Modernity at Large: Cultural Dimensions of Globalization*. Minneapolis: University of Minnesota Press.

Aprea, G. & Kirchheimer, M. (2011). Argentina: Fiction backs out, and a style prevails. In G. Orozco Gómez & M.I. Vassallo de Lopes (eds), *Obitel Yearbook*

2011: The quality of fiction and the audience's transmedia interactions. Available from http://obitel.net

Aquino, M. (2012). Anatel quer TV Globo fora do controle da Net Serviços até junho deste ano. *Tele Síntese*. Retrieved 15 October 2012 from http://www.telesintese. com.br/index.php/plantao/18269-anatel-quer-tv-globo-fora-do-controle-da-net-servicos-ate-junho-deste-ano

Araujo, J. Z. (2000). *A negacao do Brasil: o negro na telenovela brasileira*. Sao Paulo, SP: Editora SENAC Sao Paulo.

Aranguren, F., Bustamante, B., Gutiérrez, O., Mendoza, D., Rusinque, A., Sánchez, H., & Sánchez, M. (2011). Colombia: television and the sense of the public sphere. In G. Orozco Gómez & M.I. Vassallo de Lopes (eds), *Obitel Yearbook 2011: The quality of fiction and the audience's transmedia interactions*. Available from http://obitel.net

Argentina Broadband Overview. (2011). *Point topic operator profiles*. Retrieved 16 January 2012, from http://point-topic.com/content/operatorSource/profiles2/argentina-broadband-overview.htm

Arriaga, P. (1980). *Publicidad, Economía y Comunicación Masiva*. Mexico: Nueva Imagen.

Astroff, R. (1997). Capital's Cultural Study: Marketing Popular Ethnography of US Latino Culture. In M. Nava, A. Blake, I. MacRury, & B. Richards (eds), *Buy This Book: Studies in Advertising and Consumption* (pp. 120–36). London and New York: Routledge.

Athayde, A. (1991). O carrosel atolado no Pantanal. *Imprensa*, *4*, p. 68.

Aufderheide, P. (1993). Latin American grassroots video: Beyond television. *Public Culture*, *5*, pp. 579–92.

Avanza TV Azteca. (1997, May 16). *La Jornada*, p. 16.

Avila, A. (1997, January–February). Trading punches. *Hispanic*, pp. 39–44.

Azteca into El Salvador. (1997, June). *Broadcasting & Cable International*, p. 8.

Bagamery, A. (1982, November 22). SIN, the original. *Forbes*, *p.* 97.

Baldwin, K. (1995). Montezuma's Revenge: Reading Los Ricos Tambien Lloran in Russia. In R. C. Allen (ed.), *To Be Continued … Soap Operas Around the World* (pp. 256–75). London: Routledge.

Barnouw, E. (1979). *The Sponsor: Notes on a Modern Potentate*. Oxford: Oxford University Press.

Barrera Diaz, C. (2011, February 22). *UPDATE 2-Mexico's DISH sees tripling subscribers by 2014*. Retrieved 15 October 2011, from http://www.reuters.com/article/2011/02/22/dishmexico-idUSN2229149520110222

Barros, R., de Carvalho, M., Franco, S., & Mendonça, R. (2010). Determinantes da queda na desigualdade de renda no Brasil. Rio de Janeiro: Instituto de Pesquisa Econômica Aplicada. Retrieved from http://www.ipea.gov.br/sites/000/2/publicacoes/tds/td_1460.pdf

Bastide, R. (1978). *The African Religions of Brazil: Toward a Sociology of the Interpenetration of Civilizations*. Baltimore: Johns Hopkins University Press.

Beltran, L. R. S., & Fox de Cardona, E. (1979). Latin America and the United States: Flaws in the free flow of information. In K. Nordenstreng & H. I. Schiller (eds), *National Sovereignty and International Communications* (pp. 33–64). Norwood, NJ: Ablex Publishing Corp.

Bentes, I. (2003). *Guerrilha de Sofá ou A Imagem é o Novo Capital*. Rio de Janeiro: Federal University of Rio de Janeiro.

Bernal Sahagún, V. (1978). *México: la publicidad*. In Centro de Estudios de la Comunicación (ed.), *Televisión, Cine, Historietas y Publicidad en México* (pp. 49–66). Mexico: Universidad Nacionál Autónoma de México.

Besas, P. (1990, April 11). Mexicans ride again in Hispano TV sweeps. *Variety*, pp. 41 & 58.

Bhabha, H. K. (1990). Introduction: Narrating the nation. In H. K. Bhabha (ed.), *Nation and Narration*. New York City: Routledge.

Bielby, D., & Harrington, C. (2002). Markets and meanings: the global syndication of television programming. In D. Crane, N. Kawashima & K. Kawasaki (eds), *Global Culture: Media, Arts, Policy, and Globalization* (pp. 215–32). London: Routledge.

Big shuffle in Mexican TV ownership. (1991, March 25). *Variety*, p. 66.

Billionaires vie for Mexico's telecoms market. (2011, May 27). *Los Angeles Times*. Retrieved from http://phys.org/news/2011-05-billionaires-vie-mexico-telecom. html

Biltereyst, D. & Meers, P. (2000). The international telenovela debate and the contra-flow argument. *Media, Culture and Society*, 22(4), pp. 393–413.

Birman, P. & Lehmann, D. (1999). Religion and the media in a battle for ideological hegemony: The Universal Church of the Kingdom of God and TV Globo in Brazil. *Bulletin of Latin American Research*, 18(9), pp. 145–64.

Bolaño, C. (1988). *Mercado Brasileiro de Televisão*. Aracaju: Universidade Federal de Sergipe.

———. (1999). A economia política da televisão brasileira. *Revista Latina de comunicación social*, p. 17.

Borelli, S. H. S., & Priolli, G. (2000). *A deusa ferida : por que a Rede Globo nao e mais a campea absoluta de audiencia*. Sao Paulo: Summus Editorial.

Borges, J. (2007). Das novelas brasileiras aos mercados populares da África. *ReporterBrasil*. Retrieved 17 May 2012 from: http://www.reporterbrasil.com.br/exibe.php?id=983

Boyd, D. A. & Straubhaar, J. D. (1985). The developmental impact of the home videocassette recorder in the third world. *Journal of Broadcasting and Electronic Media* 29(1), pp. 5–21.

Boyd, D. A., Straubhaar, J. D., & Lent, J. (1989). *Videocassette Recorders in the Third World*. New York: Longman.

Brittos, V. C., & C. Bolaño, eds. (2005). *Rede Globo: 40 anos de poder e hegemonia*. São Paulo: Paulus.

Brittos, V. C., & Kalikoske, A. (2009). História, modelos e economia da telenovela em mercados globais. In C. Bolaño, C. Golin & V. Brittos (eds), *Economia da arte e da cultura*. Porto Alegre: Unisinos.

Budde, P. (2006). *Mexico – Convergence, broadband and internet market*. Retrieved 16 November 2011, from http://advertising.microsoft.com/mexico/WWDocs/User/es-mx//ResearchLibrary//ResearchReport/Mexico%20-%20Convergence,%20Broadband%20and%20Internet%20market.pdf

Bunce, R. (1976). *Television in the Corporate Interest*. New York: Praeger.

Buonanno, M. (2004). Foreign fiction: From threat to resource. Toward a new critical theory of international television flows. *Studies in Communication Sciences*, 4(1), pp. 31–47.

Calmon, J. (1966). *Duas invasões: O Livro Negro da Invasão Branca*. Rio de Janeiro: Edições O Cruzeiro.

Camargo, J. C. (1990). Lista dos mais consumidos só revela quantidade. *Folha de São Paulo*, p. E-5.

Canal Caracol una década al aire. (2008). *Farandula.com*. Retrieved from http://www.farandula.co/2008/07/canal-caracol-una-decada-al-aire-2/

Cantu, H. (1991, February). The gathering storm in broadcasting. *Hispanic Business*, pp. 14–64.

Cardoso, V. (1997, May 17). Pagan 650 mdd a Televisa por su parte de la empresa PanAmSat. *La Jornada*, p. 16.

Carroll, R. (2012, June 27). Mexican media scandal: Televisa condemns Guardian reports. *The Guardian*. Retrieved from http://www.guardian.co.uk/media/2012/jun/27/mexico-media-scandal-televisa-condemns-guardian-report-intimidating

Castano, I. (2011). *Mexico: Azcarraga's Televisa gains muscle in TV war vs. Carlos Slim*. Retrieved 15 November 2011, from http://www.forbes.com/sites/ivancastano/2011/10/25/mexico-azcarragas-televisa-gains-in-tv-war-vs-carlos-slim

Castro, D., Marques de Melo, J., & Castro, C. (2010). *Panorama da comunicação e das telecomunicações no Brasil: Colaborações par a o debate sobre telecomunicações e comunicação*. Brasília: Ipea.

Chalaby, J. K. (2005). From internationalization to transnationalization. *Global Media and Communication* 1(1), pp. 30–33.

Chávez changes channels. (2007, May 29). *The Economist*. Retrieved 12 January 2012, from: http://www.theeconomist.com.node/9248319/print

Chestnut, R. A. (1997). *Born Again in Brazil: The Pentecostal Boom and the Pathogens of Poverty*. New Brunswick, NJ: Rutgers University Press.

Chozik, A. & Vranica, S. (2010, May 20). Univision focuses on original shows. *The Wall Street Journal*. Retrieved from http://online.wsj.com/article/ SB10001424052748704691304575254740924757542.html

Cisneros Group of Companies. (2012). Retrieved 12 January 2012, from http://www.cisneros.com/(en)Home.aspx

Classe C troca geladeira por TV a cabo e poupança. (2012). *Folha de S. Paulo*. Retrieved from http://www1.folha.uol.com.br/mercado/1086267-classe-c-troca-geladeira-por-tv-a-cabo-e-poupanca.shtml

Company profile for Grupo Televisa SAB. (n.d.) Retrieved 22 October 2011, from http://www.reuters.com/finance/stocks/companyProfile?symbol=TV.N

Conaculta. (n.d.) *Corporativo: Cobertura*. Retrieved 22 October 2011, from http://www.canal22.org.mx/cobertura.html

Country Profile: Mexico. (1996, May 6). *TV International*, pp. 5–8.

Critser, G. (1987, January). The feud that toppled a TV empire. *Channels*, pp. 24–31.

Curtin, M. (2007). *Playing to the World's Biggest Audience: The Globalization of Chinese Film and TV*. Berkeley, CA: University of California Press.

———. (2009). Thinking globally: From media imperialism to media capital. In J. Holt & A. Perren (eds), *Media Industries: History, Theory, and Method* (pp. 108–19). Malden, MA: Wiley-Blackwell.

da Costa, A. H. (1986). Rio e Excelsior: projetos fracassados? In, *Um país no ar*. São Paulo: Editora Brasiliense.

D'amorim, S., & Foresque, F. (2012, May 6). Classe C troca geladeira por TV a cabo e poupança. *Folha de S. Paulo*. Retrieved from http://www1.folha.uol. com.br/mercado/1086267-classe-c-troca-geladeira-por-tv-a-cabo-e-poupanca.shtml

Dávila, A. (2001). *Latinos Inc.: The Marketing and Making of a People*. Berkeley, CA: University of California Press.

De Cordoba, J. (2010, October 6). Mexican media stand-off ends. *The Australian*. Available from http://theaustralian.newspaperdirect.com/epaper/viewer.aspx

De Cordoba, J., & Harrup, A. (2011, April 8). Mexico's Televisa buys Iusacall stake. *The Australian*, p. 25.

De la Fuente, A. M. (2005, August 25). Televisa tube tussle. *Variety*. Available from http://www.variety.com/article/VR1117928096?refCatId=14

De Noriega, L. A., & Leach, F. (1979). *Broadcasting in Mexico*. London: Routledge and Kegan Paul.

de Sola Pool, I. (1977). The changing flow of television. *Journal of Communication*, 27(2), pp. 139–79.

Dickerson, M. (2005, January 17). Battle intensifies over control of Mexican TV. *Los Angeles Times*, p. 2.

Digital TV homes to triple in Latin America. (2011, June 2). *Broadband TV News*. Retrieved from http://www.broadbandtvnews.com/2011/06/02/digital-tv-homes-to-triple-in-latin-america/

Dorfman, A., & Mattelart, A. (1975). *How to Read Donald Duck: Imperialist Ideology in the Disney Comic*. New York: International General.

Duarte, L. G. (2001). *Due South: American Television Ventures into Latin America*. (Doctoral dissertation, Michigan State University, 2001).

Duarte, L. G., & Straubhaar, J. (2004). Adapting U.S. transnational television channels to a complex world: from cultural imperialism to localization to hybridization. In J. Chalaby (ed.), *Transnational Television Worldwide* (pp. 216–53). New York: I.B. Tauris.

Dunn, C. (2001). *Brutality Garden: Tropicalia and the Emergence of a Brazilian Counterculture*. Chapel Hill: The University of North Carolina Press.

Durand, J.C. (1993). The field of advertising in Brazil, 1930–1991. In J. Marques de Melo (ed.), *Communications for a New World, Brazilian Perspectives* (pp. 253–62). São Paulo: Escola de Comunicação e Artes/USP.

EchoStar. (2008). *MVS Multivisión and EchoStar launch satellite TV service in Mexico*. Retrieved 22 October 2011, from http://sats.client.shareholder.com/releasedetail.cfm?releaseid=350489

Eilemberg, D. (2008). *The TV wars*. Retrieved 16 December 2011 from http://www.podermagazine.com/article_detail.php?id_article=289

Entertainment Industry Development Corporation. (2005, August 19). *Television sustains Los Angeles entertainment production*. Retrieved 5 August 2008, from http://www.eidc.com/EIDC_-_Production_Trends_Release_081905.pdf

Esparza, E. (1997, July–August). Life after *El Tigre*. *Hispanic*, pp. 48–52.

Evans, P. (1979). *Dependent Development: The Alliance of Multinational, State and Local Capital in Brazil*. Princeton: Princeton Press.

Felinto, M. (2002). Moçambique/Mozambique. *Trópico, UOL*. Retrieved from http://pphp.uol.com.br/tropico/html/textos/2366,1.shl

Ferin Cunha, I. (2011). *Memórias da Telenovela: Programas e recepção*. Lisbon: Livros Horizonte.

Ferin Cunha, I., Duff Burnay, C., & Castilho, F. (2011). Portugal: New challenges. In G. Orozco Gómez & M.I. Vassallo de Lopes (eds), *Obitel Yearbook 2011: The quality of fiction and the audience's transmedia interactions*. Available from http://obitel.net

———. (2011). The quality of fiction and the audience's transmedia interactions. In G. Orozco Gómez & M.I. Vassallo de Lopes (eds), *Obitel Yearbook 2011: The quality of fiction and the audience's transmedia interactions*. Retrieved 5 May 2012, from http://obitel.net

Fernandes, I. (1987). *Memoria da telenovela brasileira*. Sao Paulo: Brasiliense.

Fernández Christlieb, F. (1975). *Información colectiva y poder en México*. (Unpublished professional dissertation, Universidad Iberoamericana, Mexico DF, 1975).

———. (1976). La industria de radio y television. *Nueva Politica*, 1(3), pp. 237–48.

———. (1985, March 2). Canal 7 ¿Para que? (11). *La Jornada*.

———. (1987). Algo más sobre los origenes de la televisión latinoamericana. *DIA. Logos de la Comunicación*, 18, pp. 32–45.

Fernández, C. & Paxman, A. (2000). *El Tigre: Emilio Azcárraga y su Imperio Televisa*. Mexico DF: Grijalbo.

Ferraz Sampaio, M. (1984). *História do Radió e da Televisão no Brasil e no Mundo*. Rio de Janeiro: Achiamé.

Festa, R. & Santoro, L. (1991). Os novos rumos do espaço audiovisual latino-americano. *Comunicação e Sociedade* 10(18), pp. 9–18.

Fisher, C. (1992, February 3). Azcarraga looms as return player. *Advertising Age*, p. 25.

Fox, E. (1995). Latin American broadcasting. In L. Bethell (ed.), *Latin America since 1930: Ideas, Culture, and Society* (pp. 519–68). Cambridge: Cambridge University Press.

———. (1997). *Latin American Broadcasting: From Tango to Telenovela*. Luton: John Libbey Media.

Francis, G., & Fernandez, R. (1997, February). Satellites south of the border. *Via Satellite*, pp. 28–42.

Frappier, J. (1968). US media empire/Latin America. *NACLA Newsletter*, II(9), pp. 1–11.

Fraser, M. (2005). *Weapons of Mass Distraction: Soft Power and American Empire*. New York: St Martin's Press.

FT: la batalla por el control en Televisa parece "una telenovela". (1997, June 18). *La Jornada*, p. 24.

Fuenzalida, V., & Julio, P. (2011). Chile: 2010 the end of university television? In G. Orozco Gómez & M.I. Vassallo de Lopes (eds), *Obitel Yearbook 2011: The quality of fiction and the audience's transmedia interactions*. Available from http://obitel.net

García Canclini, N. (1990). *Culturas hibridas: estregias para entrar y salir de la modernidad*. Grijalbo: Comsejo Nacional para la Cultura y las Artes.

García Canclini, N. (1995). *Hybrid Cultures: Strategies for Entering and Leaving Modernity*. Minneapolis: University of Minnesota Press.

Giménez Saldivia, L., & Hernández Algara, A. (1988). *Estructura de los Medios de Difusión en Venezuela*. Caracas: Universidad Católica Andres Bello.

Godard, F. (1997, October). TV Azteca is building an empire. *Broadcasting & Cable International*, p. 48.

Gonzalez Amador, R. (2006, December 13). Televisa y TV Azteca, aliadas para bloquear a nuevos competidores. *La Jornada*. Retrieved from http://www.jornada. unam.mx/2006/12/13/index.php?section=economia&article=028n1eco

González, J. (1994). *Más (+) Cultura(s)*. Mexico DF: Consejo Nacional para la Cultura y los Artes.

Gott, R. (2006, May–June). Venezuela's Murdoch. *New Left Review*, 39. Retrieved from http://www.newleftreview.org/A2622

Goulart, A. (2011). Da rede manchete à rede tv! *Tv em questão: Contextos e programação dos últimos 30 anos de TV no Brasil*, Parte 7, Observatório da Imprensa. Retrieved 15 October 2012, from http://www.observatoriodaimprensa. com.br/news/view/_contextos_e_programacao_dos_ultimos_30_anos_de_tv_no_ brasil__parte_7

Granados Chapa, M. (1976). La televisión de estado: en busca del tiempo perdido. *Nueva Politica*, pp. 223–36.

Grupo Clarín. (2012). Retrieved 16 January 2012, from http://www.grupoclarin. com/

Grupo de Mídia. (2009). *Mídia Dados Brasil 2009*. São Paulo: Grupo de Mídia.

———. (2011). *Mídia Dados Brasil 2011*. São Paulo: Grupo de Mídia.

Grupo Televisa. (1997). *Annual Report 1996*. Mexico DF: Televisa.

Gutiérrez, F. (1979). Mexico's television network in the United States: the case of Spanish International Network. In H. Dordick (ed.), *Proceedings of the Sixth Annual Telecommunications Policy Research Conference* (pp. 135–59). Lexington, MA: Lexington Books.

Hall, S. (1993). Culture, Community, Nation. *Cultural Studies* 7(3), pp. 349–363.

Hamburger, E. I. (2007). "A expansão do "feminino" no espaço público brasileiro: novelas de televisão nas décadas de 1970 e 80. *Rev. Estud. Fem.* 15(1), pp. 153–175.

Harrison, C. (2011). *Slim's move into web TV draws protests of piracy from rivals*. Retrieved 15 November 2011, from http://www.bloomberg.com/news/print/2011-11-08/slim-s-move-into-web-tv-draws-protests-of-piracy-from-rivals.html

Harvey, D. (2005). *A Brief History of Neoliberalism*. Oxford: Oxford University Press.

Havens, T. (2006). *Global Television Marketplace*. London: British Film Institute.

Hay 20 millones de usarios hispanos de internet en Estados Unidos. (2009, April 20). *Adlatina*. Available from http://www.adlatina.com/node/108514

Hecht, J. (2011, August 8). Sony Pictures Television in co-production deal with Colombia's Caracol. *Hollywood Reporter*. Retrieved from http://www.hollywood reporter.com/news/sony-pictures-television-production-deal-220391

———. (2012, January 23). Mexico's Televisa and Sony Ink co-production deal. Retrieved 20 June 2012, from http://www.hollywoodreporter.com/news/mexico-televisa-sony-ink-production-283982

Hernández Lomeli, F. (1992–93). Televisa en España. *Comunicación y Sociedad*, 16–17, pp. 74–105.

Hernández Lomeli, F., & Orozco Gómez, G. (2007). *Televisiones en México: Un Recuento Histórico*. Guadalajara: Universidad de Guadalaraja.

Hernandez, O. D. (2001). *A Case of Global Love: Telenovelas in Transnational Times*. (Doctoral disertation, University of Texas-Austin, 2001). Retrieved from http://www.lib.utexas.edu:2048/login?url=http://wwwlib.umi.com/cr/utexas/ fullcit?p3037498

Hertz, D. (1987). *A Historia Secreta da Rede Globo*. Porto Alegre, Brazil: Tche.

Hoag, C. (2000, September 4). Empire building: The slow track. *Businessweek Online*. Retrieved from http://www.businessweek.com:/2000/00_36/b3697159. htm?scriptFramed

Hoskins, C., McFayden, S., & Finn, A. (1997). *Global Television and Film: An Introduction to the Economics of the Business*. Oxford: Clarendon Press.

Hyun, K. (2007). *New Asian Cultural Proximity, Korean Modernity In Between, and Reception of Korean TV Drama in the East Asia*. Paper presented at the Intercultural/Developmental Communication division, International Communication Association, San Francisco.

IBOPE. (1989). *Consumer report*. Rio de Janeiro: Instituto Brasileiro de Opinião Pública e Estatística.

Informe Anual TV Azteca 2010. (2011). Retrieved 22 October 2011, from https://www.irtvazteca.com/downloads/anuales.aspx

Iwabuchi, K. (2002). *Recentering Globalization: Popular Culture and Japanese Transnationalism*. Durham: Duke University Press.

Jake Adams Editorial Services and Research Consultancy, Miami Beach. (2010). *Hispanic Markets Overview 2010*. Retrieved 19 December 2011, from http://www. hispanicad.com/banners2/HMO10/HMO2010.pdf

Janus, N., & Roncaglio, R. (1990). *A survey of the transnational structure of the mass media and advertising, report prepared for the Center of Transnationals of the United Nations*. Mexico DF: Instituto Latinoamericano de Estudios Transnacionales.

Kottak, C. P. (1990). *Prime-Time Society — An Anthropological Analysis of Television and Culture*. Belmont, CA: Wadsworth.

———. (1994). *Assault on Paradise*. New York: McGraw-Hill.

Kozlov, N. (2007, March 18). Telesur Director: "We're not Anti U.S." *Venezuel analysis*. Retrieved from http://venezuelanalysis.com/print/2283

Kraidy, M. M. (2002a). Arab satellite television between regionalization and globalization. *Global Media Journal*, *1*(1).

———. (2002b). Hybridity in Cultural Globalization. *Communication Theory*, *12*(3), pp. 316–339.

———. (2005). *Hybridity, or the Cultural Logic of Globalization*. Philadelphia: Temple University Press.

La Pastina, A. (1999). *The Telenovela Way of Knowledge: An Ethnographic Reception Study Among Rural Viewers in Brazil*. (Doctoral dissertation). University of Texas.

———. (2003). *Viewing Brazil: Local Audiences and the Interpretation of the Nation*. Presented at the conference Media in transition 3, Massachusetts Institute of Technology, Cambridge, MA.

La Pastina, A. & J. Straubhaar. (2005). Multiple proximities between television genres and audiences: the schism between telenovelas' global distribution and local consumption. *Gazette* 67(3), pp. 271–288.

LAMAC. (2011). *Pay-TV charms Latin Americans*. Retrieved from http://www. lamac.org/america-latina-ingles/releases#

Lent, J. (1990). *Mass Communications in the Caribbean*. Ames, Iowa: Iowa State University Press.

Lesser, J. (2005, April). Brazil Week invited talk at the University of Texas, Austin, TX.

Letalien, B. (2009). Pay television among low-income populations: Reflections on research performed in the Rio de Janeiro Favela of Rocinha. *Contemporânea: Jornal de Comunicação e Cultura*, 1(1), pp. 105–127.

Lettieri, M., & Garcia, G. (2006). *The tail wags the dog*. Retrieved 26 October 2011, from http://www.coha.org/the-tail-wags-the-dog-mexico%E2%80%99s-%E2%80%9Ctelevisa-law%E2%80%9D-another-nail-in-the-coffin-of-fox%E2%80%99s-legacy

Lima, V. A. d. (1988). The state, television and political power in Brazil. *Critical Studies in Mass Communication*, 5, pp. 108–128.

———. (1993). Brazilian television in the 1989 presidential elections. In T. Skidmore (ed.), *Television, Politics and the Transition to Democracy in Latin America* (pp. 97–117). Washington, DC: Woodrow Wilson Center.

Lobo, T. (1991, August 22). MTV inova e fatura US$ 10 milhões em 91. *Jornal do Brasil*.

Lopez, A. (1995). Our welcomed guests: Telenovelas in Latin America. In Robert Allen (ed.), *To Be Continued ... Soap Operas Around the World* (pp. 256–75). London and New York: Routledge.

Lopez, H. (2011, March 13). U.S. Hispanic population is growing, but this isn't your abuela's Latin community. *Advertising Age*. Available from http://adage.com/article/guest-columnists/u-s-hispanic-population-growing-abuela-s-latino-community/149331/

Lotz, A. (2009). *Beyond Prime Time: Television Programming in the Post-Network Era*. Routledge: London and New York.

Luis López, O. (1998). *La Radio en Cuba* (2nd corrected edn). La Habana, Cuba: Editorial Letras Cubanas.

Madden, N. (2008, April 16). *Ugly Betty* looks very attractive to Unilever in China. *AdAgeChina*. Retrieved 4 January 2012, from http://adage.com/china/article.php?article_id=126395

Mahan, E. (1985). Mexican broadcasting: Assessing the industry-state relationship. *Journal of Communication*, 35(1), pp. 60–75.

Maiello, C. (1990). Setor de vídeo está de olho no grande público. *Folha de São Paulo*, p. F-4.

Maio, M. (2009, November 19). Globo e Record se destacam com canais internacionais. *Terra TV*. Retrieved from http://diversao.terra.com.br/tv/noticias/ 0,,OI4107486-EI12993,00-Globo+e+Record+se+destacam+com+canais+ internacionais.html

Malkin, E. (2006, December 6). Mexico's newest TV drama is a bid to block a third broadcaster. *New York Times*, p. C3.

Malloy, J. M. (1977). *Authoritarianism and Corporatism in Latin America*. Pittsburgh: University of Pittsburgh Press.

Marques de Melo, J. (1988). *As telenovelas da Globo*. Sao Paulo: Summus.

———. (1991, May 22). Lecture on Brazilian television presented at Michigan State University, East Lansing, M.I.

———. (1992, May). *Brazil's role as a Television Exporter Within the Latin American Regional Market*. Paper presented at the 42nd Conference of the International Communication Association, Miami.

Martín-Barbero, J. (1987). *De los medios a las mediaciones: Comunicacion, cultura y hegemonia*. Barcelona: G. Gili.

———. (1993). *Communication, Culture and Hegemony: From the Media to the Mediations*. Newbury Park, CA: Sage.

———. (1995). Memory and form in the Latin American soap opera. In R.C. Allen (ed.), *To Be Continued ... Soap Operas Around the World* (pp. 279–280). London: Routledge.

Martínez, S. (1996, September 8). Televisa se asocia a Radio Televisión Española, con la bendición de Aznar. *Proceso*, pp. 48–50.

Mastrini, G. (2009). Developing countries and the challenges facing commercial culture. *Television and New Media*, 10(1), pp. 96–99.

Matos, C. (2011). Media and democracy in Brazil. *Westminster Papers in Communication and Culture 8*, pp. 178–196

Mattelart, A. (1991). *Advertising International. The Privatisation of Public Space*. London: Routlege.

Mattelart, M., & Mattelart, A. (1990). *The Carnival of Images: Brazilian Television Fiction*. New York: Bergin & Garvey.

Mattos, S. (1984). Advertising and Government Influences on Brazilian Television. *Communication Research*, 11(2), pp. 203–220.

———. (1984). Efeitos da publicidade, uma introdução ao debate. *Televisão educativa*. (46), pp. 9–10.

———. (1990). *Um perfil da TV Brasileira (40 anos de história: 1950–1990)*. Salvador: Associação Brasileira de Agências de Propaganda.

———. (1992, August). *A Profile of Brazilian television*. Paper presented to the 18th Conference of the International Association for Mass Communication Research, Guarujá.

————. (2000). *A televisão no Brasil: 50 anos de história (1950–2000)*. Salvador: Ianamá.

Mavise. (2010). Database on television channels and TV companies in the European Union. Retrieved 4 January 2012, from http://mavise.obs.coe.int/country?id= 12#section-10

Mayer, V. (2006). A vida como ela é/pode ser/deve ser? O programa Aqui Agora e cidadania no Brasil. *Intercom – Revista Brasileira de Ciências da Comunicação*, 29(1), pp. 15–37.

Maza, E. (1986, July 14). A la vista, la telaraña del poder de Azcárraga en Estados Unidos. *Proceso*, pp. 20–25.

Mazziotti, N. (1993). Acercamientos a las telenovelas latinoamericanas. In A. Fadul (ed.), *Serial Fiction in TV: the Latin American Telenovelas*. Sao Paulo, Brazil: Robert M. Videira.

McAnany, E. (1984). The logic of the cultural industries in Latin America: the television industry in Brazil. In V. Mosco & J. Wasko (eds), *The Critical Communications Review Volume II: Changing Patterns of Communications Control* (pp. 185–208). Norwood, New Jersey: Praeger.

Media Research and Consultancy Spain. (1997, July). *La industria audiovisual iberoamericana: datos de sus principales mercados 1997*. Report prepared for the Federación de Asociaciones de Productores Audiovisuales Españoles and Agencia Española de Cooperación Internacional, Madrid.

Megacable. (2010). *Investor Relations*. Retrieved 22 October 2011, from http://inversionistas.megacable.com.mx/en/

Mejía Barquera, F. (1989). *La Industria de la Radio y de la Televisión y la Política del Estado Mexicano (1920–1960)*. Mexico DF: Fundación Manuel Buendía.

————. (1995). Echoes of Mexican media in 1993. *Mexican Journal of Communication*, 2, pp. 71–91.

Mejía Prieto, J. (1972). *Historia de la Radio y la TV en México*. Mexico DF: Editores Asociados.

Messmer, J. (2012, July 25). MundoFox is aiming young and bilingual. *TVNewsCheck*. Retrieved from http://www.tvnewscheck.com/article/60996/mundofox-is-aiming-young-and-bilingual

Mexico media regulator gets tough on Televisa deal. (2007, July 17). Retrieved 22 October 2011, from http://www.warc.com/LatestNews/News/Mexico%20 Media%20Regulator%20Gets%20Tough%20on%20Televisa%20Deal.news?ID= 21954

Mexico's satellite TV subscribers reach 5 million in 2Q 2011. (2011, October 10). Retrieved 24 October 2011, from http://www.digitaltvnews.net/content/?p=20357

Mikos, L. & Perrotta, M. (2012). Traveling style: Aesthetic differences and similarities in national adaptations of *Yo soy Betty, la fea*. *International Journal of Cultural Studies* 15(1), pp. 81–97.

Milanesi, L. A. (1978). *O Paraiso via EMBRATEL*. Rio de Janeiro: Editora Paz e Terra.

Moffett, M., & Roberts, J. (1992, July 30). Mexican media empire, Grupo Televisa, casts its eye on US market. *Wall Street Journal*, pp. A1, A6.

Molinski, D. (2011, December 7). Colombia's Grupo Santo Domingo buying stake in Chile's CorpBanca. *WSJ*. Retrieved from http://online.wsj.com/article/BT-CO-20111207-707303.html

Moran, A. (1998). *Copycat Television : Globalisation, Program Formats and Cultural Identity*. Luton: University of Luton Press.

Moreno Esparza, G. A. (2011). Televisa and Univision, 50 years of post-nationalism. *Global Media and Communication 7*(1), pp. 62–68.

Morgan Stanley and Company. (1992). *Grupo Televisa: company report*. Mexico DF: Thompson Financial Networks.

Morreira, S. V. (1991). *Radio no Brasil*. Rio de Janeiro: Rio Funda Editora.

Morris, N., & Waisbord, S. (2001). *Media and Globalization: Why the State Matters*. Lanham, MD: Rowman & Littlefield.

Moura, F. R. d. & C. R. S. Bolaño. (2007). A internacionalização da TV brasileira nos anos 1990 e 2000: Globo e Record. Paper presented at Intercom – Sociedade Brasileira de Estudos Interdisciplinares daComunicação, IX Congresso Brasileiro de Ciências da Comunicação da Região Nordeste Salvador – BA.

Mozzo, J. (2008). Prisa, Planeta,Cisneros bid for Colombia TV channel. *Reuters*. Retrieved from http://www.reuters.com/article/2008/07/30/colombia-television-idUSN3042637220080730

Multichannel News. (2001, August 10). Brazil's pay TV downturn. *Multichannel News International*, p. 1.

Muraro, H. (1985). El "modelo" Latinoamericano. *Telos, 3*, pp. 78–82.

Nederveen Pieterse, J. (2004). *Globalization and Culture: Global Mélange*. New York: Rowan and Littlefield.

Netto, A. (1987). Exclusivo: o homem da Telemontecarlo. *Imprensa*, pp. 16–22.

News Corp sells Sky Latin America stakes. (2004, October 12). *Sydney Morning Herald*. Retrieved from http://www.smh.com.au/articles/2004/10/12/1097406560171.html

Nordenstreng, K., & Varis. T. (1974). *Television Traffic—A One-Way Street*. Paris: UNESCO.

Obitel. (2011). Qualidade na ficção televisiva e participação transmidiática das audiências. Rio de Janeiro: GloboUniversidade. Retrieved 1 March 2012 from http://obitel.net/

Obregon, R. (1995). *Telenovelas: An Exploration of Genre Proximity in International Television*. Unpublished paper, State College, PA.

Oliveira, O. S. d. (1986). Satellite TV and dependency: An empirical approach. *International Communication Gazette, 38*(1), pp. 127–145.

———. (1993). Brazilian soaps outshine Hollywood: Is cultural imperialism fading out? In K. Nordenstreng & H. Schiller (eds), *Beyond National Sovereignty: International Communication in the 1990s* (pp. 116–131). Norwood, NJ: Ablex Pub. Co.

Olsen, S.R. (1999). *Hollywood Planet: Global Media and the Competitive Advantage of Narrative Transparency*. Mahwah, NJ: Lawrence Erlbaum.

Organizações Globo. (1992). *Organizações Globo*. Rio de Janeiro: Organizações Globo.

Orozco Gómez, G., & Vassallo de Lopes, M. I. (2011). Quantitative comparison of television fiction in Iberoamerican countries. In G. Orozco Gómez & M.I. Vassallo de Lopes (eds), *Obitel Yearbook 2011: The quality of fiction and the audience's transmedia interactions*. Available from http://obitel.net

Ortiz, R. (1985). *Cultura brasileira e identidade nacional*. São Paulo: Brasiliense.

Ortiz, R., Simoes Borelli, S. H., & Ortiz Ramos, J.M. (1988). *Telenovela: historia e producao*. Sao Paulo: Brasiliense.

Pasquali, A. (1967). *El Aparato Singular: Un Día de Televisión en Caracas*. Caracas: Universidad Central de Venezuela.

Paxman, A. (1998). Disputes stall cable in Brazil, Colombia. *Variety*, pp. 80–82.

———. (2003). Hybridized, glocalized and hecho en México: Foreign influences on Mexican TV programming since the 1950s. *Global Media Journal*, 2(2).

Paxman, A., & Saragoza, A. (2001). Globalization and Latin media powers: The case of Mexico's Televisa. In V. Mosco & D. Schiller (eds), *Continental Order? Integrating North America for Cybercapitalism*, (pp. 64–85). Lanham, MD: Rowman and Littlefield.

Pérez Espino, E. (1979). El monopolio de la televisión comercial en México. *Revista Mexicana de Sociología*, 4, pp. 1435–68.

Pew Research Center. (2009). *Between Two Worlds: How Young Latinos Come of Age in America. Pew Hispanic Center Report*. Washington, D.C: Pew Research Center.

Piñón López, J. d. D. (2007). *The Incursion of Azteca America into the U.S. Latin Media*. (Doctoral disertation, University of Texas, Austin. 2007).

Piñón, J. & Rojas, V. (2011). Language and cultural identity in the new configuration of the US Latino TV industry. *Global Media and Communication*, 7(2), pp. 129–147.

Piñon, J. (2011). *Crafting the Post-National: The Rising Transnational Industrial Model in the Ibero-American Audiovisual Space*. Paper presented at the Global Fusion conference, Temple University, Philadelphia.

Poplack, S. (2000). Sometimes I'll start a sentence in Spanish y termino en Español: toward a typology of code-switching. In W. Li (ed.), *The Bilingualism Reader* (pp. 221–56). London: Routledge.

Population Division of the Department of Economic and Social Affairs of the United Nations Secretariat. (2011). *World Population Prospects: The 2010 Revision, Volume 1, Comprehensive Tables*. Retrieved from http://esa.un.org/unpd/wpp/Documentation/pdf/WPP2010_Volume-I_Comprehensive-Tables.pdf

Porto e Silva, F. (1979). Interview with author Straubhaar. São Paulo.

Porto, M. P. (2008). *Telenovelas and National Identity in Brazil*. Paper presented at the Ninth International Congress of the Brazilian Studies Organization (BRASA), New Orleans, March 27–29, 2008.

———. (2011). Telenovelas and representations of national identity in Brazil. *Media Culture and Society*, 33(1), pp. 53–69.

Prieto Bayona, M.D.S. (2011, July 4). *TV Azteca: the end of Televisa's monopoly of the Mexican television market*. Retrieved 21 October 2011 from http://www.inaglobal.fr/en/television/article/tv-azteca-end-televisa-s-monopoly-mexican-television-market

Priolli, G. (1988). Imagens que custam os tubos. *Imprensa*, p. 70.

Puig, C. (1997a, March 30). Alemán, de regreso a Televisa, al frente de un compacto grupo de jóvenes priístas. *Proceso*, p. 33.

———. (1997b, March 30). Azcárraga Jean. *Proceso*, pp. 30–4.

———. (1997c, April 20). El emperio construido por Emilio Azcárraga en México sí tuvo reveses ... en el extranjero. *Proceso*, pp. 12–16.

Ramón Huerta, J. (1997, June 4). Noticias del otro imperio. *Expansión*, pp. 19–35.

Randewich, N. (2007, June 8). *Shake-up of Mexico TV law seen good for competition*. Retrieved 23 October 2011 from http://www.reuters.com/article/2007/06/08/idUSN0838026520070608

Raoul Silveira, J. (1975, October 4). O desenvolvimento da televisão no Brasil. *O Estado de São Paulo*.

Rattner, J. (1992). Globo e Opus Dei ganham canais de televisão privada em Portugal. *Folha de São Paulo*, p. C-1.

RCN. (2012). Retrieved 25 January 2012, from http://www.canalrcnmsn.com/quienessomos

RCTV International. (2012). Retrieved 16 January 2012, from http://www.rctvintl.com/eng/index_about.php#

Read, W. (1976). *America's Mass Media Merchants*. Baltimore: Johns Hopkins University Press.

Record. (2012). *Programação de qualidade em mais de 150 países*. Retrieved 17 May 2012, from http://www.recordeuropa.com/?q=C/-/763.

Redação, S. (2012, June 20). TV por assinatura teve 1,5 milhão de novos clientes no ano. *Correio da Bahia*. Salvador, Bahia, Brazil.

Rêgo, C. M. (2003). Novelas, novelinhas, novelões: The evolution of the (tele)novela in Brazil. *Global Media Journal*, 2(2). Retrieved from http://lass.purduecal.edu/cca/gmj/sp03/gmj-sp03-rego.htm

Reis, R. (1999). What prevents cable TV from taking off in Brazil? *Journal of Broadcasting & Electronic Media* 43(3), pp. 339–415.

———. (2006). Media and religion in Brazil. *Brazilian Journalism Research*, 2(2), pp. 167–82.

Reveron, D. (2001, January–February). South Florida's cyber-success. *Hispanic Business*, pp. 28–30.

Riding, A. (1984, December 1). On a booming television network, Brazil gets a clearer view of itself. *New York Times*.

Rivero, Y. M. (2007). Broadcasting modernity: Cuban television, 1950–1953. *Cinema Journal*, 46(3), pp. 3–25.

———. (2009). Havana as a 1940s–1950s Latin American media capital. *Critical Studies in Media Communication*, 26(3), pp. 275–293.

———. (2010). Watching TV in Havana: Revisiting the past through the lens of the present. Paper presented at conference, New Agendas in Global Communication. Austin, Texas.

Robertson, R. (1995). Glocalization: Time-space and homogeneity-heterogeneity. In M. Featherstone, S. Lash & R. Robertson (eds), *Global Modernities* (pp. 25–44). Thousand Oaks, CA: Sage Publications.

Rockwell, R., & Janus, N. (2003). *Media Power in Central America*. Champage-Urbana, IL: University of Illinois Press.

Rodrigues, A. (2012, April 17). Bienal de Brasília — Novelas brasileiras passam imagem de país branco, critica escritora moçambicana. *Agencia Brazil (Empresa Brasil de Comunicação*. Retrieved 15 October 2012 from http://agenciabrasil. ebc.com.br/noticia/2012-04-17/novelas-brasileiras-passam-imagem-de-pais-branco-critica-escritora-mocambicana

Rodrigues, A. I. (2002). *MPM Propaganda : a história da agência dos anos de ouro da publicidade brasileira* (Unpublished master's thesis). Universidade Federal do Rio Grande do Sul.

Rodríguez, A. (1996). Objectivity and ethnicity in the production of the *Noticiero Univisión*. *Critical Studies in Mass Communication*, 13, pp. 59–81.

———. (1997). Creating an audience and remapping a nation: a brief history of US Spanish Language Broadcasting 1930–1980. *Quarterly Review of Film and Video* 16(3–4), pp. 357–374.

———. (1999). *Making Latino News: Race, Language, Class*. Thousand Oaks, CA: Sage Publications.

Rogers, E. & Antola, L. (1985). *Telenovelas*: a Latin American success story. *Journal of Communication*, 35(4), pp. 24–35.

Rogers, E. & Schement, J. (1984). Media flows in Latin America. *Communication Research*, 11(2), pp. 305–19.

Rohter, L. (1978). The noble hours of Brazilian television, *American Film Institute Bulletin* no. 4 (February), pp. 56–9.

Roncagliolo, R. (1995). Trade integration and communication networks in Latin America. *Canadian Journal of Communication*, 20(3), pp. 335–42.

Rønning, H. (1997). Language, cultural myths, media and *Realpolitik*: The Case of Mozambique. *Media Development, XLIV*(1), pp. 50–4.

Rowe, W., & Schelling, V. (1991). *Memory and Modernity: Popular Culture in Latin America*. London: Verso.

Roxo, E. (2012, June 3). "Carrossel" leva SBT á vice-liderança com viagem no tempo. *Folha de São Paulo*. Retrieved from http://www1.folha.uol.com.br/ilustrada/ 1099036-carrossel-leva-sbt-a-vice-lideranca-com-viagem-no-tempo.shtml

Rucker, P., & Comlay, E. (2011, November 15). *Special report: New Mexican TV probe hits embattled Slim*. Retrieved November 15, 2011, from http://www.reuters.com/ article/2011/07/12/us-slim-television-idUSTRE76B5UB20110712

Salles, M. (1975, September 10). *Opinião Publica, Marketing e Publicidade no Processo Brasileiro de Desenvolvimento*. Paper presented to the Escola Superior de Guerra, Rio de Janeiro.

Salwen, M. (1994). *Radio and Television in Cuba: The Pre-Castro Era*. Ames, Iowa: Iowa State University Press.

Sánchez Ruiz, E. (1991). Historia mínima de la televisión Mexicana. *Revista Mexicana de Comunicación, 18*, pp. 29–36.

Santos, W. R. (1989). A guerra surda pela expansão de território. *O Estado de São Paulo*, p. B-4.

Schiller, H. (1969). *Mass Communications and American Empire*. New York: A.M. Kelley.

Schwartsman, A. (1991, September 15). TVA entra no ar ao meio-dia de hoje. *Folha de S. Paulo*, p. 6-3.

Schwoch, J. (1990). *The American Radio Industry and its Latin American Activities, 1900–1939*. Urbana: University of Illinois Press.

Silva, L. (1971). *Teoría y Práctica de la Ideología*. Mexico DF: Editorial Nuestro Tiempo.

Sinclair, J. (1986). Dependent development and broadcasting: the "Mexican Formula". *Media, Culture and Society, 8*(1), pp. 81–101.

———. (1990). Spanish-language television in the United States: Televisa surrenders its domain. *Studies in Latin American Popular Culture 9*, pp. 39–63.

———. (1997). The business of international broadcasting: Cultural bridges and barriers. *Asian Journal of Communication, 7*(1), pp. 137–55.

———. (1999). *Latin American Television: A Global View*. Oxford: Oxford University Press.

———. (2003). "The Hollywood of Latin America": Miami as regional center in television trade. *Television & New Media, 4*(3), pp. 211–229.

———. (2005). Globalization and grass roots: Local cable television operators and their household subscribers in India. *Media Asia: An Asian Communication Quarterly, 32*(2), pp. 69–77.

———. (2006). From Latin Americans to Latinos: Spanish-language television and its audiences in the United States. In S. Harvey (ed.), *Trading Culture: Global Traffic and Local Cultures in film and Television* (pp. 119–32). Eastleigh, UK: John Libbey Publishing.

———. (2012a). *Advertising, the Media and Globalization*. London and New York: Routlege.

———. (2012b). The advertising industry in Latin America: A contemporary overview. In J. G. Sinclair & A.C. Pertierra (eds), *Consumer Culture in Latin America*, (pp. 35–50). New York: Palgrave Macmillan.

Sinclair, J. S., Jacka, E., & Cunningham, S. (1996). Peripheral vision. In J. Sinclair, E. Jacka & S. Cunningham (eds), *New Patterns in Global Television* (pp. 1–15). New York: Oxford University Press.

Singhal, A., Obregon, R., & Rogers, E.M. (1994). Reconstructing the story of *Simplemente María*, the most popular *telenovela* in Latin America of all time. *Gazette 54*(1), pp. 1–15.

Smirnoff, M. (1994a, February). Argentina. *Television Business International*, 23.

———. (1994b, February). Chile. *Television Business International*, pp. 24–25.

Soares, L. F. G., & de Souza Filho, G. L. (2007). *Interactive Television in Brazil: System Software and the Digital Divide*. Paper presented at the EUROiTV conference, Amsterdam.

Sodre, M. (1972). *A comunicação do grotesco*. Rio de Janeiro: Editora Vozes.

Sogecable. (2008). *Annual Report*. Retrieved January 4, 2012, from http://www.prisatv.es/media/576958.pdf

Sorkin, A. R. (2006, June 28). Univision jilts Televisa for rival bid. *The New York Times*. Available from http://www.nytimes.com/2006/06/28/business/media/28univision.html

Sousa, H. (1996, August). *Portuguese Television Policy in the International Context: An Analysis of the Links with the EU, Brazil and the US*. Paper presented to the conference of the International Association for Mass Communication Research, Sydney.

———. (1997, July). *Crossing the Atlantic: Globo's Wager in Portugal*. Paper presented to the conference of the International Association for Mass Communication Research, Oaxaca.

———. (2002). The liberalisation of media and communications in Portugal. In S. Syrett (ed.), *Contemporary Portugal, Dimensions of Economic and Political Change*. Hampshire, UK: Ashgate.

Straubhaar, J. D. (1981). *The Transformation of Cultural Dependency: The Decline of American Influence on the Brazilian Television Industry*. (Doctoral dissertation, Fletcher School of Law and Diplomacy, Tufts University, 1981).

———. (1982). The development of the telenovela as the pre-eminent form of popular culture in Brazil. *Studies in Latin American Popular Culture*, 1, pp. 138–50.

————. (1983). Brazilian variety television programs: Popular culture, industry and censorship. *Studies in Latin American Popular Culture*, pp. 71–78.

————. (1984). The decline of American influence on Brazilian television. *Communication Research*, 11(2), pp. 221–40.

————. (1988). A Comparison of Cable TV Systems. In T. Baldwin & S. McEvoy (eds), *Cable Communication* Englewood Cliffs, NJ: Prentice Hall.

————. (1990). The effects of cable TV in the Dominican Republic. In S. Surlin & W. Soderlund (eds), *Mass Media and the Caribbean.*(pp. 273–86). New York: Gordon and Breach.

————. (1991a). Beyond media imperialism: Asymmetrical interdependence and cultural proximity. *Critical Studies in Mass Communication, 8*, pp. 39–59.

————. (1991b). Class, genre and the regionalization of the television market in Latin America. *Journal of Communication 41*(1), pp. 53–69.

————. (1992, August). *Asymetrical Interdependence and Cultural Proximity: A Critical Review of the International Flow of Television Programs*. Paper presented at the conference of the Asociación Latinoamericana de Investigadores de la Comunicación, São Paulo.

————. (1996). The electronic media in Brazil. In R. Cole (ed.), *Communication in Latin America: Journalism, Mass Media, and Society* (pp. 217–43). Wilmington, Delaware: Scholarly Resources.

————. (2001). Brazil: The role of the state in world television. In N. Morris & S. Waisbord (eds), *Media and Globalization: Why the State Matters*. Lanham, Maryland: Rowman & Littlefield.

————. (2007). *World Television: From Global to Local*. Los Angeles: Sage Publications.

————. (2011). Telenovelas in Brazil: From traveling scripts to a genre and proto-format both national and transnational. In T. Oren & S. Shahaf (eds), *Global Television Formats: Understanding Television Across Borders* (pp. 148–77). New York: Routledge.

Straubhaar, J., & Duarte, L. G. (2005). Adapting U.S. transnational television to a complex world: From cultural imperialism to localization to hybridization. In J. Chalaby (ed.), *Transnational Television Worldwide: Towards a New Media Order* (pp. 216–53). London: I.B. Taurus.

Subervi-Vélez, F., Ramírez Berg, C., Constantakis-Valdés, P., Noriega, C., & Wilkinson, K. (1994). Mass communication and Hispanics. In F. Padilla (ed.), *Handbook of Hispanic Cultures in the United States: Sociology* (pp. 304–57). Houston, TX: Arte Público Press & Instituto de Cooperación Iberoamericana.

Sutter, M. (1996, August). Home-grown programming takes off. *Business Mexico*, pp. 12–14.

————. (2003, January 19). A savvy grab for auds. *Variety*. Available from http://www.variety.com/article/VR1117879103?refCatId=1427

Telefe. (2012). Retrieved 18 January 2012, from http://www.telefe.com/institucional/

Telemundo hires Cristina, adds bilingual telenovela app. (2011, May 17). *Advertising Age*. Retrieved from http://adage.com/article/special-report-tv-upfront/telemundo-hires-cristina-adds-bilingual-telenovela-app/227613/

Telesur. (2012). Retrieved 1 March 2012, from http://www.telesurtv.net/

Televisa acquires piece of Spain's "La Sexta" production company. (2011, December 14). *Hispanically Speaking News*. Retrieved 4 January 2012, from http://www.hispanicallyspeakingnews.com

Televisa anunció oficialmente la compra de canal peruano. (1992, July 11). *La Época*, p. S33.

Televisa compro 49 por ciento de Megavisión. (1991, December 22). *El Mercurio*.

Televisa to sell stake in Univision. (2006, October 6). *HispanicBusiness.com*. Retrieved from http://www.hispanicbusiness.com/2006/10/11/televisa_to_sell_stake_in_univision.htm

Televisa. (2011, July 14). *Investor presentation*. Retrieved 16 December 2011, from http://i2.esmas.com/documents/2011/07/14/1825/investor-presentation-website.pdf

Thomas, E. (2010). Organizações Globo. *INA Global: the Review of Creative Industries and Media*. Retrieved from http://www.inaglobal.fr/en/television/article/organizacoes-globo

Thussu, D. K. (2006). *International Communication: Continuity and Change*, 2nd edition. London: Hodder Education.

Tomlinson, J. (1991). *Cultural Imperialism*. Baltimore: Johns Hopkins University Press.

Tomlinson, J. (1999). *Globalization and Culture*. Cambridge: Polity Press.

Toussaint, F. (1996, December 22). Entre Sky y Galaxy Latin America. *Proceso*, p. 61.

Trevisan, K. (2011). *Almanaque dos Reality Shows no Brasil*. São Paulo: Panda Books.

Tunstall, J. (1977). *The Media are American: Anglo-American Media in the World*. London: Constable.

Turner, G., & Tay, J. (2009). *Television Studies after TV: Understanding Television in the Post-Broadcast Era*. London and New York: Routledge.

Turner, N. (2012, May 7). ABC News teams with Univision to target Hispanic viewers. *Bloomberg Businessweek*. Retrieved 4 June 2012 from http://www.businessweek.com/news/2012-05- 07/abc-news-teams-up-with-univision-news-to-target-hispanic-viewers

TV in Mexico. (1951, December 17). *Newsweek*.

TVMasNovelas. (2004). Second world summit of the telenovelas industry. Retrieved 18 August 2008, from http://www.onlytelenovelas.com/Only_2/5_2_EEUU.php

UOL. (2011). Telefônica compra parte da TVA recuperado Universo Online. Retrieved 19 May 2012, from Universo Online, São Paulo.

U.S. Census Bureau, Population Division. (2011, September). *Intercensal Estimates of the Resident Population by Sex, Race, and Hispanic Origin for the United States: April*

1, 2000 to July 1, 2010. Retrieved from http://www.census.gov/popest/intercensal/national/US-EST00INT-02.xls

United Nations. (2011). Population division of the Department of Economic and Social Affairs of the United Nations Secretariat, *World Population Prospects: The 2010 Revision*, volume 1, comprehensive tables. Retrieved 4 June 2012, from http://esa.un.org/unpd/wpp/Documentation/pdf/WPP2010_Volume-I_Comprehensive-Tables.pdf

Valenzuela, N. (1986). Spanish language TV in the Americas: From SIN to PanAmSat. In J. Miller (ed.), *Telecommunications and Equity: Policy Research Issues* (pp. 329–38). North Holland: Elsevier Science Publishers.

Varis, T. (1978). *The Mass Media TNCs: An Overall View of their Operations and Control Options*. Paper prepared for a meeting of the Asian and Pacific Development Administration Centre, Kuala Lumpur.

———. (1984). The international flow of television programmes. *Journal of Communication*, *34*(1), pp. 143–52.

Vasallo de Lopes, M. I. (2004). *Telenovela – Internacionalização e interculturalidade*. São Paulo: Edições Loyola.

Vianna, H. (1999). *The Mystery of Samba*. Chapel Hill, NC: University of North Carolina Press.

Waisbord, S. (1997). *Cultural Boundaries and Identity in Latin America*. Paper presented at the International Communication Association, Montreal.

———. (1998). Latin America. In A. Smith (ed.), *Television: An International History*.

———. (1998). The ties that still bind: Media and national cultures in Latin America. *Canadian Journal of Communication*, *23*, pp. 381–401.

———. (2011). Between Support and Confrontation: Civic Society, Media Reform, and Populism in Latin America. *Communication, Culture & Critique*, *4*(1), pp. 97–117.

Waisbord, S., & Jalfin, S. (2009). Imagining the national: Gatekeepers and the adaptation of global franchises in Argentina. In A. Moran (ed.), *TV Formats Worldwide* (pp. 55–74). Bristol & Chicago: Intellect.

Wallach, J. (2011). *Meu capítulo na TV Globo*. Rio de Janeiro: Editora Topbooks.

Wells, A. (1972). *Picture Tube Imperialism? The Impact of US Television in Latin America*. New York: Orbis Books.

Wentz, L. (2007, May 16). Telemundo, like NBC, embraces digital platform. *Advertising Age*. Retrieved from http://adage.com/article/special-report-upfront07/telemundo-nbc-embraces-digital-platform/116710/

———. (2009, January 22). Univision, Televisa settle TV-programming dispute. *Advertising Age*. Retrieved from http://adage.com/article/hispanic-marketing/univision-televisa-settle-tv-programming-dispute/134031/

————. (2010, October 5). Mexico's Grupo Televisa invests $1.2 billion in Univision. *Advertising Age*. Retrieved from http://adage.com/article/hispanic-marketing/mexico-s-grupo-televisa-invests-1-2-billion-univision/146304/

Wharton. (2004, October 6). Telmex and Telefónica step on the gas pedal in Latin America. Retrieved from http://www.wharton.universia.net/index.cfm?fa=viewfeature&id=845&language=english

Wilkinson, K. (1995). *Where Culture, Language and Communication Converge: The Latin-American Cultural Linguistic Market*. (Doctoral dissertation, University of Texas-Austin, 1995).

Woodard, J. P. (2002). Marketing Modernity: The J. Walter Thompson Company and North American Advertising in Brazil, 1929–1939. *Hispanic American Historical Review, 82*(2): pp. 257–90.

Young, J. (2011, July 18). Mexico juices pubcasters to jolt TV biz. *Variety*, p. 12.

Zellner, M. (1989, March 20). Televisa as target: The media empire's credibility is on the line. *Mexico Journal*, pp. 16–21.

Zepeda Patterson, J. (1997, April 20). Neotelevisa. *Siglo 21*, p. 3.

Index

LIST OF ILLUSTRATIONS

While considerable effort has been made to correctly identify the copyright holders, this has not been possible in all cases. We apologise for any apparent negligence and any omissions or corrections brought to our attention will be remedied in any future editions.

Sortilego, Televisa; *I Love Lucy,* Desilu Productions; *Los ricos también lloran,* Televisa; *El Chapulín Colorado,* Televisa S.A. de C.V.; *Carrossel,* Sistema Brasiliero de Televisão; *Avenida Brasil,* Rede Globo de Televisão/Central Globo de Produção; *Yo soy Betty, la fea,* RCN Televisión; *Cristal,* Radio Caracas Televisión; *A corazón abierto,* RCN; *Sábado gigante,* Univisión Network; *Gabriela* magazine, issue 3, RTP/TV Globo; *El derecho de nacer,* Producciones Galindo Hermanos; *Beto Rockefeller,* TV Tupi.